The European Convention on Human Rights

"It seems a very difficult sort of easiness"
Flann O'Brien, *The Third Policeman*

THE EUROPEAN CONVENTION ON HUMAN RIGHTS: COMPLIANCE WITHOUT INCORPORATION

DAVID KINLEY

Dartmouth

Aldershot · Brookfield USA · Hong Kong · Singapore · Sydney

Published by
Dartmouth Publishing Company Limited
Gower House
Croft Road
Aldershot
Hants GU11 3HR
England

Dartmouth Publishing Company
Old Post Road
Brookfield
Vermont 05036
USA

British Library Cataloguing in Publication Data

Kinley, David
   European Convention on Human Rights:
   Compliance without Incorporation
   I. Title
   341.481

ISBN 1 85521 298 6

Reprinted 1996

Printed and bound in Great Britain by
Biddles Limited, Guildford and King's Lynn

CONTENTS

PREFACE

This book (like most) has been written out of curiosity, that is despite the fact that its basis lies in a doctoral thesis. The thesis was written 1986–9 at Cambridge University, and its metamorphosis into the book between 1991–2 at the Australian National University. The germ of the idea that pre-legislative scrutiny might effectively detect and deflect potential legislative infringements of the Convention came from a single-line reference to the Council of Europe's 1977 *Czernetz Report*, part of which touches on this issue, in the voluminous *Minutes of Evidence* of the 1977–8 House of Lords Select Committee on a Bill of Rights. As I followed up this reference it became clear not only that this was a matter of considerable significance to the protection and advancement of the human rights enshrined in the Convention (especially in respect of the United Kingdom), but that it was also an almost wholly neglected area of study and comment.

My endeavours to bring this subject to life have been greatly aided by a number of people who have been especially generous with their time and efforts: Colin Turpin of Clare College, Cambridge, for his encouragement and suggestions; Michael Ryle (the former Clerk of Committees in the Commons), Henry Knorpel (Speaker's Counsel) and Derek Rippengal (Counsel to Lord Chairman of Committees in the Lords) for their invaluable insights into the vagaries of Westminster; the staff of the Squire Law Library in Cambridge, Bill Noblett and the staff of the Official Publications section of the Cambridge University Library and the staff of the Law Library of the Australian National University for their unfailing courtesy and efficiency; the staff of the Information Office of the House of Commons for their fittingly informative and immediate responses to my enquires; Andrew Drzemczewski of the Council of Europe's Directorate of Human Rights for his enthusiastic expertise; Glenda Waddell and Peggy Dwyer of the Law School of the Australian National University for their editorial acumen and patience, and

John Irwin and Sonia Hubbard of Dartmouth for their empathy and expedition. Without the benefit of the skills of these people, the faults of this book would be even more substantial than at present. For this, and to them, I am most grateful.

David Kinley
January 1993

1 COMPLIANCE WITH THE EUROPEAN CONVENTION: BILLS OF RIGHTS AND PRE-LEGISLATIVE SCRUTINY

Since the United Kingdom's ratification of the European Convention for the Protection of Human Rights and Fundamental Freedoms on 8 March 1951, the question of the compliance of its law (whether statutory or common law) with the Convention has been dominated by the subject of the Convention's incorporation into the legal system as a Bill of Rights. Presently the constitutional status of the Convention is that of a treaty; its provisions, therefore, are not justiciable in the courts of the United Kingdom. Nevertheless, its value to the judiciary as a source of guidance as to the interpretation of both common law principles and statutory provisions[1] is now firmly established.[2]

The debate over the various suggestions that the European Convention should be fully incorporated has been lengthy and complex, with strong arguments being offered by those in favour and in opposition to the proposal. Numerous books, articles, pamphlets, debates and reports devoted to the examination of the issues involved have been produced,[3] and no fewer

---

1   For an example of the former, see *Blathwayte v Baron Cawley* [1976] AC 397, 426; and for examples of the latter, see *Pan American World Airways Inc. v Dept of Trade* [1976] 1 Lloyd's Rep. 257, 261, and *Waddington v Miah* [1974] 1 WLR 683, 694.

2   In particular, see *Garland v British Rail* [1983] 2 AC 751, 771 (*per* Lord Diplock), and most recently, *R v Secretary of State for the Home Dept, ex parte Brind and Others* [1990] 1 All ER 469, 477–8 (CA), (*per* Lord Donaldson MR), and [1991] 1 All ER 720, 722–3 (HL) (*per* Lord Bridge). In addition, see *R v Secretary of State for the Home Dept, ex parte Phansopkar* [1976] 1 QB 606, 627, and *R v Secretary of State for the Home Dept, ex parte Bhajan Singh* [1976] QB 198, 207.

3   The literature is voluminous; the following, however, represent some of the most influential works: Sir Leslie Scarman, *English Law – The New Dimension* (1974), *Report*

than 12 bills have been introduced into one or the other House of Parliament since 1971 seeking, in varying degrees, to incorporate the Convention into the law of the United Kingdom.

In spite of the continuance of some enthusiastic support for incorporation of the European Convention on Human Rights as a Bill of Rights[4] it can be legitimately argued that the debate has reached something of a stalemate – certainly, that is the case within the party political arena of Parliament.[5] This fact is perhaps best illustrated by recent attempts to initiate a legislative change (four of the bills indicated above were introduced between December 1983 and January 1990), only one of which (the third of the quartet of bills mentioned) reached debate at the Common's second reading stage.[6] Even this bill, however, fell on account of its failure to obtain the requisite minimum support of 100 votes upon a division of the House at the conclusion of the second reading debate.[7] Neither the Labour nor Conservative parties have demonstrated much enthusiasm for any of the proposals.[8] Indeed, the Labour party, in its most recent pronouncement on the issue, whilst indicating its concern for "the protection and extension of individual rights", did not even refer to the European Convention in its suggested *Charter of Rights*, still less advocate incorporation of the Convention.[9] The Conservative party unequivocally rejects any suggestion that the Convention ought to be incorporated, considering such a move as serving "no useful purpose".[10] The Liberal Democrats and their predecessors

---

of the House of Lords Select Committee on a Bill of Rights, HL 176 (1977–8), P Wallington & J McBride, *Civil Liberties and a Bill of Rights* (1976), J Jaconelli, *Enacting a Bill of Rights* (1980), M Zander, *A Bill of Rights?* (1985), Lord McCluskey, *Law, Justice and Democracy* (1987), and "Charter 88" (Nov. 1988).

4   See "Charter 88" (Nov. 1988); R Blackburn, "Legal and Political Arguments for a United Kingdom Bill of Rights" in R Blackburn and J Taylor (eds), *Human Rights For The 1990s* (1990), and a discussion document published by the Institute for Public Policy Research (IPPR) entitled *A British Bill of Rights* (1990).

5   See, for example, the comments of S de Smith & R Brazier, *Constitutional and Administrative Law* (1989, 6th edn), p.431.

6   The four are: European Human Rights Convention Bill (Mr R Maclennan), HC Bill No.73 (1983–4) – lapsed after introduction, HC Deb. Vol.50, cols 852–854 (13 Dec. 1983); Human Rights and Fundamental Freedoms Bill (Lord Broxbourne), HL Bill No.21 (1985–6) – having successfully completed its passage through the Lords the Bill lapsed at second reading in the Commons at the close of a parliamentary session, HC Deb. Vol.100, col.1367 (4 July 1986); Human Rights Bill (Sir E Gardner), HC Bill No.19 (1986–7) – failed at second reading, HC Deb. Vol.109, cols 1223–1289 (6 Feb. 1987); and Human Rights Bill (Mr Graham Allen) HC Bill No.50 (1989–90) – the Bill's second reading was nominally deferred till another day, but the Bill effectively lapsed as it never received another debate, HC Deb. Vol.165, col.1241 (26 Jan. 1990).

7   *Supra*, n.6. The minimum is set by HC S.O. No.36, HC 1 (1988–9).

8   See generally, M Zander, *supra*, n.3, pp 1–26 & 90–1; C Graham & A Prosser, "Conclusion" in Graham & Prosser (eds), *Waiving The Rules* (1988), pp 176–7 & 184–185, and J Jaconelli, *Lord Broxbourne's Human Rights and Fundamental Freedoms Bill*, a paper prepared for the Standing Advisory Commission on Human Rights, *Annual Report 1985–6*, HC 151 (1986–7), p.42. "Charter 88" found no support from the Conservative party, see HC Deb. Vol.143, cols 505–6 (w) (13 Dec. 1988); and, it was received frostily by the Labour party, *The New Statesman and Society*, Editorial (16 Dec. 1988), p.4.

9   The Labour Party, *The Charter of Rights: Guaranteeing Individual liberty in a free society* (1990), p.3.

10   Rt Hon. John Patten, *Political Culture, Conservatism and Rolling Constitutional Change* (The 1991 Swinton Lecture, published by the Conservative Political Centre, 1991), p.8; see also similar sentiments voiced by members of the party in parliamentary debate on the subject of incorporation of the Convention, HL Deb. Vol.524, cols 209–13 (5 December 1990).

have traditionally shown far greater support for the idea.[11] Presently, however, the number of Liberal Democrat MPs – together with those like-minded members of the two main parties – is not sufficient to ensure that any human rights bill would receive the support necessary to proceed beyond its second reading.

At the heart of the problematic question of incorporation of the European Convention there lies principally two contentious and closely related issues: how, and indeed whether, the Convention might be entrenched in the United Kingdom's legal system; and the effect of incorporation on the constitutional status and operation of the judiciary. The first of these is no longer viewed to be an insurmountable problem.[12] This is due largely to the widespread acceptance that incorporation of the European Convention as a Bill of Rights would not be by way of *full* but rather *partial* entrenchment. That is, the relevant statute would not be beyond derogation or repeal either by an ordinary Act, provided the appropriate amending provisions were sufficiently unambiguous, or by a statute enacted in accordance with extraordinary procedures (for example, by a two-thirds majority or subject to a referendum) expressly provided for the purpose. In respect of the first mentioned option – the approach thus far favoured by those introducing Bill of Rights legislation – there are at least two means by which it may be implemented. For precedence to be granted to a later Act it might be required that the repealing or derogating provision expressly stipulate that it is to operate notwithstanding the provisions of a Bill of Rights,[13] or it might be required only that where it is unavoidable that the construction of a later Act is inconsistent with the Bill of Rights then precedence is to be given to the later Act.[14] It has always been presumed, however, that in either event such action would seldom be undertaken as the infringement or suspension, no matter how limited in extent, of statutorily protected rights would likely attract intense public and parliamentary scrutiny.[15]

Though difficulties may persist in respect of the degree of entrenchment with which the European Convention might be incorporated as a Bill of Rights, at least it may now be said that the largely doctrinal concerns over whether in fact *any* form of entrenchment is possible in the face of the

---

11   See, for example, The Liberal Democrats, Federal Green Paper No.13, *"We the People ..."* – *Towards a Written Constitution*, pp 24–26.

12   See CR Munro, *Studies in Constitutional Law* (1987), pp 105–8 (esp. p.106); AT Bradley, "The Sovereignty of Parliament" in J Jowell & D Oliver (eds), *The Changing Constitution* (1989, 2nd edn), pp 46–52, and N Lacey, "A Bill of Rights for the United Kingdom" in R Hoggart (ed), *Liberty and Legislation* (1989), pp 149–58. For a concise survey of the views of a range of constitutional commentators on this matter see CC Turpin, *British Government and the Constitution* (1990, 2nd edn), pp 127–133; and for an analysis of case law relevant to the question of entrenchment and parliamentary sovereignty see JB Elkind, "A New Look at Entrenchment" (1987) 50 MLR 158–175.

13   This was the form adopted in clause 3 of Lords Wade's 1976 Bill of Rights Bill, which read "[I]n case of conflict between any enactment subsequent to the passing of this [Bill of Rights] Act ... [the provisions of this Act] shall prevail unless subsequent enactment shall expressly state otherwise."

14   This was the form adopted in clause 4(2) of Lord Broxbourne's 1986 Human Rights and Fundamental Freedoms Bill, and (in identical terms) clause 4(2) of Mr Graham Allen's 1990 Human Rights Bill, *supra*, n.6, which proclaimed that " [n]o provision of an Act passed after the passing of this Act shall be construed as authorising ... [an infringement of this Act] unless such a construction is unavoidable if effect is to be given to that provision and to the other provisions of the Act."

15   See Zander, *supra*, n.3, p.73.

United Kingdom's continuing parliamentary sovereignty are no longer
critical. The long-standing Diceyan notion of impregnable parliamentary
supremacy, whilst never having been without its critics, has been especially
conspicuously challenged by recent developments before the European
Communities' European Court of Justice concerning the registration
requirements for fishing vessels under the United Kingdom's Merchant
Shipping Act 1988. Part II of the Act provided for the establishment of a new
system of registration of all British fishing vessels in order to determine their
eligibility to fish in British waters. The conditions for registration under the
new scheme had the effect of excluding some vessels which had previously
been registered as British fishing vessels. One group of companies, headed
by Factortame Ltd, whose vessels fell into this disadvantaged category,
challenged the new legislation on the grounds that it operated contrary to
Articles 7, 52 and 221 of the Treaty of Rome which together prohibit Member
States from discriminating in trade and commerce on the grounds of
nationality. Though s.13 of the 1988 Act, together with regulations made
pursuant to the same section,[16] effectively established the new register, it
was s.14 that stipulated the eligibility criteria for registration, and it was the
suspension of this latter section that the applicants sought. Unsurprisingly,
the question of the 1988 Act's compliance with European Community law
was referred by the High Court to the European Court of Justice under
Article 177 for a definitive ruling. Subsequently, the Court concluded that
the 1988 Act was incompatible with European Community law.[17] In the
meantime, however, the High Court granted interim relief to the applicants,
directing that the impugned provisions of the Act be disapplied in respect of
the applicants.[18] Upon the immediate appeal of the Secretary of State for
Transport, the Court of Appeal reversed the decision of the Divisional Court
and the case proceeded to the House of Lords.[19] Their Lordships, in turn,
referred the question of whether interim relief ought to be granted in such
circumstances to the Court of Justice and withheld their decision pending a
ruling from the latter.[20] In due course the Court of Justice replied indicating
that the national law must be set aside if it stands in the way of relief which
is otherwise provided for under Community law.[21] Shortly afterwards the
House of Lords restored the applicants' now modified grant of interim
relief.[22] In respect of the present context, however, the most significant
development occurred some nine months earlier when the European
Commission sought and obtained from the President of the Court of Justice
an Interim Order stating categorically that the nationality requirements of
s.14 of the Merchant Shipping Act 1988 were to be suspended pending the
conclusion of the main proceedings.[23] As a consequence, the Government

16 Merchant Shipping (Registration of Fishing Vessels) Regulations 1988, SI 1988 No.1926.
17 [1991] 3 CMLR 589.
18 *R v Secretary of State for Transport, ex parte Factortame & others* [1989] 2 CMLR 353.
19 *Ibid.*
20 *R v Secretary of State for Transport, ex parte Factortame & others* [1990] 2 AC 85. For an
    account of the significance of proceedings up to this point see NP Gravells, "Disapplying
    an Act of Parliament Pending a Preliminary Ruling: Constitutional Enormity or
    Community Law Right", [1989] PL 568.
21 See *R v Secretary of State for Transport, ex parte Factortame & others (no 2)* [1990] 3 WLR
    818, 861
22 *Ibid,* 818.
23 Case 246/89R, *Commission v United Kingdom* [1989] CMLR 601. The Order was made on

had immediately issued regulations giving effect to that Order.[24] The importance of this event lies in its manifest illustration of what already lay implicit in the United Kingdom's membership of the European Community. If not since the enactment of the European Communities Act 1972,[25] then at least since *McCarthys Ltd v Smith*,[26] it has been recognized that Parliament's legislative authority in matters covered by European Community law is subject to compliance with the latter. Whilst it must be said that the constitutional balance enshrined in this tenet has proved difficult for the judiciary to determine accurately and consistently,[27] never before has its potential been so clearly illustrated as in *Factortame*. The suspension of a provision of an Act of Parliament on the ground that it contravened Community law enlightens us as to the true nature of the constitutional relations between the Parliament and courts of the United Kingdom and the legislative and judicial organs of the European Community. There indeed exist prior examples of the introduction of legislation in response to adverse rulings of the Court of Justice,[28] but never were they predicated on the revocation of domestic legislation.[29]

It is submitted that by analogy, therefore, there is now little reason not to assume that an Act incorporating the European Convention on Human Rights might not also obtain the same degree of entrenchment and limitation on the legislative sovereignty of Parliament.[30] Indeed, it has been argued in

---

[24]   10 October 1989.
       The Merchant Shipping Act 1988 (Amendment) Order 1989, S.I. 1989 No.2006. Part 3 of the Order replaced the impugned nationality provisions under s.14 of the 1988 Act. Upon the European Court of Justice's ruling as to the granting of interim relief (*R v Secretary of State for Transport, ex parte Factortame & others* [1990] 3 CMLR 867) the House of Lords duly granted interim injunctions against the Secretary of State from effecting the new registration scheme: [1990] 3 WLR 818.
[25]   Principally under ss 2(1) & (4) and 3(1).
[26]   [1979] 3 AER 325. Lord Denning MR pronounced that "[i]f on close investigation it should appear that our legislation is deficient or inconsistent with Community law by some oversight of our draftsmen then it is our bounden duty to give priority to Community law. Such is the result of sub-ss 2(1) and (4) of the European Communities Act 1972;" at 329. He adds (in the following paragraph) the only qualification to this "duty" – namely, where Parliament has passed an Act that stipulates in express terms that it is to operate notwithstanding any inconsistency with Community law.
[27]   See for example, *Duke v GEC Reliance Ltd* [1988] AC 618, and *Pickstone v Freemans Plc* [1989] AC 66.
[28]   See, for instance, the examples listed in S de Smith & R Brazier, *Constitutional and Administrative Law* (1989, 6th edn), p.82, n.80.
[29]   For a hostile analysis of this innovation see the speeches of Dr NA Godman and Mr J Aitken during the Commons debate on the amending Order (*supra*, n.24), see HC Deb. Vol.158, cols 1000–2 (25 Oct. 1989).
[30]   It was once argued by Mr D Rippengal, in his submission as Specialist Adviser to the House of Lords Select Committee on a Bill of Rights in 1977, that "the European Communities Act provides no precedent for suggesting that Parliament could effectively entrench a Bill of Rights", *Minutes of Evidence*, HL 81 (1977–8), p.9; the Select Committee agreed with this conclusion, see *supra*, n.3, para.13. Mr Rippengal's reasoning was based on the contention that s.2(4) of the European Communities Act 1972 – which provides that all present and future Acts of Parliament are to be read subject to European Community law – did *not* involve "a transfer of Parliament's sovereign power, as respects legislation on Community matters, from Parliament to the Communities", *Minutes of Evidence*, ibid, p.9. The consequences of the *Factortame* litigation, however, provide an irrefutable illustration of such a transfer of power. A sound basis is thereby provided for the argument that an analogous transfer of sovereign legislative power in respect of the European Convention on Human Rights might be established by similar means.

respect of this very point that "it is hardly defensible for Parliament to qualify
its own sovereignty in commercial and employment matters [principally
under the European Communities Act 1972] while refusing to do so in
matters of human rights."[31]

The second-mentioned obstacle to the legislative incorporation of the
European Convention is an issue of much greater complexity and
significance. It concerns the assertion that to incorporate the Convention
and thereby enable the enforcement of its provisions in the domestic courts
is necessarily to require the judiciary to make political decisions. The
"politicization" of the judiciary, it is claimed, not only offends the prevailing
constitutional divisions of governmental authority, but it also involves the
judiciary in decision-making processes with which they are both unfamiliar
and manifestly ill-suited to perform.[32] Despite the gravity of such charges it
is by no means a simple task to understand precisely what is meant by the
term "politicization" or the prefix "political" when added to the words "judge",
"case", "judgment" or "decision".[33] It is perhaps fair to say, however, that in
nearly all cases where such terminology is employed the intention is to
connote a degree of judicial involvement in determining "policy" – that is, the
process of deciding between competing interpretations as to how best to
apply available resources in a given set of circumstances. It is considered
that such value-laden activity is properly the concern exclusively of the
legislative and executive organs of government.

The arguments to this end – that it would be unwise, if not illegitimate, to
invest in the judiciary adjudicative power in respect of a Bill of Rights –
obtain especial significance when it is recognized that amongst the most
vociferous critics of incorporation are many prominent members of the
judiciary.[34] For some, like Lords Diplock and Devlin, any pressure on the
judiciary to adjudicate between policy options that might be the consequence
of the introduction of a Bill of Rights would compromise the fundamental
principle of the independence of the judiciary;[35] for others, like Lord

---

31   IPPR, *supra*, n.4, p.6.
32   See generally, JAG Griffith, "The Political Constitution" (1979) 42 MLR 1, and also,
     KD Ewing & CA Gearty, *Freedom Under Thatcher, Civil Liberties in Modern Britain* (1990),
     pp 267-8.
33   On the definitional difficulties raised by these notions, see generally, J Jaconelli,
     "Incorporation of the European Human Rights Convention: Arguments and
     Misconceptions" (1988) 58 Political Quarterly, 352-6; and also, J Bell, *Policy Arguments
     in Judicial Decisions* (1983), pp 6-7.
34   This is, of course, not to deny that one of the most vociferous proponents of the
     introduction of a Bill of Rights is a former senior judge – namely, Lord Scarman (see in
     particular *supra*, n.3), but his fellow judges have offered him little support. Though, for
     example, Lord Hailsham appears also to support a Bill of Rights (*viz: The Dilemma of
     Democracy* (1978), pp 173-4 and in his evidence to the House of Lords Select Committee
     on a Bill of Rights, *supra*, n.30, pp 10-26), it is clear that this was not always his
     opinion: *A Sparrow's Flight: Memoirs of Lord Hailsham of St Marylebone* (1990), p.198.
35   Lord Devlin, "Judges as Lawmakers" (1976) 39 MLR 1, and Lord Diplock, *The Courts as
     Legislators* (1965); (whilst neither judge referred directly to a Bill of Rights, it is beyond
     question that the type of judicial activism which they denounced is of precisely the sort
     that would be required in the event of such a bill being introduced). Lord Diplock made
     the point explicitly some years later, first in the *Minutes of Evidence*, House of Lords
     Select Committee on a Bill of Rights, *supra*, n.30, p.92, and once again in HL Deb.
     Vol.396, col.1367 (29 Nov. 1978). See also similar sentiments expressed by Lord
     Denning, HL Deb. Vol.369, col.797 (25 March 1976); and, more lately, Sir Patrick
     Mayhew (when Solicitor-General), HC Deb. Vol.109, col.1267 (6 Feb. 1985) JAG Griffith

Denning, the concern centres on the effective usurpation of Parliament's legislative authority by the courts and the concomitant transfer of power to determine policy, that may be the result of a Bill of Rights.[36] Lord McCluskey's objections draw upon similar lines of argument. He maintains that in an effort to overcome the interpretational difficulties associated with any "vaguely worded Charter of Human Rights" the judiciary would be inevitably propelled into "the political arena",[37] and in consequence of which there would be a corresponding shift in the balance of governmental powers.[38]

Despite the emphasis in all of the above accounts of the heightened (and undesirable) significance of policy arguments in the adjudicative process that would be the result of the incorporation of the European Convention, it remains a widely accepted view that consideration of such matters already constitutes part of the adjudicative process. There can be little doubt that this is the case when it is recalled that the House of Lords has proved itself not averse to the task of determining the most sweeping of policy issues. The questions, for instance, of how best and to whom the allocation of financial resources ought to be made are perhaps the quintessence of governmental policy-making, yet during the final years of the Greater London Council their Lordships were to entertain these very questions on a number of occasions.[39]

There exists a substantial body of reasoning and evidence attesting to the judiciary's use of policy arguments in deciding the issues before it. A particularly strong case has been established by John Bell through his development of a structural model that accurately reflects the adjudicative process operating in United Kingdom courts. The "interstitial legislator model" is premised on the understanding that there do *not* exist sharp lines of demarcation between the adjudicative function of the judiciary and the other (legislative and executive) functions of government. At the fundamental level, therefore, the judiciary is obliged to make certain basic value-judgments or assumptions over policy goals:

> Whether in making a rule or standards for the future, or basing a decision on an open-ended standard, the judge has to balance a variety of social interests and come to a decision which, within the limits of the discretion available, he considers to be best. It is this activity, an adjunct to the predominant role of judges, though the staple diet of appellate court work, which is politically important, much as the value-judgments in executive decisions are of more political concern than the routine administration of matters such as social security payments. To the extent that these value-judgments are integral to the

---

expands on what such a compromise might entail – namely, that the prevailing conservative (if not right-wing) political sympathies of the judiciary would necessarily play a critical role in the adjudication of disputes concerning any entrenched human rights provisions, *The Politics of the Judiciary* (1991, 4th edn), p.235.

36   HL Deb. Vol.469, col.171 (10 Dec. 1985).

37   *Law, Justice and Democracy* (The Reith Lectures 1986) (1987), p.54.

38   *Ibid*, p.45. For further commentary on possible judicial concern over such constitutional changes, see C Palley, *The United Kingdom and Human Rights*, The Hamlyn Lectures, 42nd series (1991), pp 120–1.

39   See, principally, *R v Greater London Council, ex parte Bromley LBC* [1983] 1 AC 768, and *In Re Westminster City Council and Others* [1986] 2 WLR 807. It is difficult to distinguish the "legal" pretext upon which their Lordships based the justification for their actions in the latter case from ("non-legal") principles of financial management; see DW Kinley, "The House of Lords' Farewell to the Greater London Council: A Comment on the Post-

current operation of the judicial function, and, indeed, would seem to some extent inescapable in any legal system, it is in vital respects qualitatively similar to other governmental functions. Especially in the view of the parallel with delegated legislation and the discretionary decisions of the executive branch of government, judges have a politically creative and important role to play. Indeed, it may be best to understand governmental activity as a continuum of politically creative functions exercised by legislators, administrators, and judges in the formulation and elaboration of policy goals and the means of achieving them. While much of general outline may be settled by a democratically elected body, important interrelations between goals and adjustments to changed circumstances may well be made by others, whether in the executive or the judiciary, in implementing such policies.[40]

JAG Griffith expresses a similar view in respect of that (expanding) band of cases in which there arise questions concerning the "administrative authorities of within the State". He remarks that "[j]udicial decisions in such cases are intimately connected with policy, and raise problems which ... affect the nature of judicial decision-making."[41]

Further support for the notion is to be obtained from the judiciary itself. Lords Reid,[42] Diplock,[43] Denning,[44] and Hailsham[45] on separate occasions have expressly alluded to their consideration of policy issues in determining cases before them. Lord McCluskey, in the 1986 Reith Lectures, was loathe to recognize such a use of policy by the judiciary, preferring instead an attempt to distinguish the use of "principle" from "policy"; however, as I have argued elsewhere,[46] this attempt was ill-fated and he too cannot avoid concluding that when faced with deciding matters not adequately covered by legislation or common law the judiciary's "formulation of the law is in truth a policy choice".[47]

If it is accepted, therefore, that matters of policy play a part in existing adjudicative practices, why is it that one of the most forceful criticisms of a Bill of Rights (provided often by the very commentators who have highlighted the current use of policy arguments by the judiciary) is based on the fact that its introduction would result in the adjudication of policy issues? This apparent oxymoron, despite being seldom recognized and still less often addressed, must be explained. There are a number of interrelated aspects to the explanation.

At the outset it can be confidently stated that the objections in respect of the judiciary's involvement with policy are generally misplaced; the concern is not, as, perplexingly, some commentators have sought to argue,[48] that the enactment of a Bill of Rights would mark the *introduction* of policy issues

---

Abolition Grants Case" (1987) 38 NILQ 67.

40   *Supra*, n.33, p.245.

41   "Judicial Decision-making in Public Law" [1985] PL, 565; thorough analyses of a number of illustrative cases are provided in the article.

42   "Judge as Lawmaker" (1972) JSPLT, 22, 27.

43   See *O'Reilly v Mackman* [1983] 2 AC 237, 285.

44   See *Magor and St Mellons RDC v Newport Corp* [1950] 2 AER 1226, and *Spartan Steel and Alloys Ltd v Martin & Co.* [1973] 1 QB 27, 36.

45   HL Deb. Vol.396, col.1384 (29 Nov. 1978), and in his submission of evidence to the Select Committee on a Bill of Rights, *supra*, n.30 (*Minutes of Evidence*), pp 10–26.

46   (1988) 51 MLR 804–8.

47   *Supra*, n.37, p.32; see also his likening of the adjudicative and legislative functions, *ibid*, p.16.

48   See for example Lord McCluskey, *supra*, n.3, pp 46–50 & 54.

into the processes of adjudication, but rather would enhance their *existing* role. "The difference", it has been observed, would "be one of degree and not kind. Admittedly the imperspicuity of broad statements of human rights might prove more difficult to unravel, but that is merely an accentuation of a problem already in existence."[49]

The mooted explanation, therefore, is more complex than merely pointing to concerns aired over the anticipated expansion of policy arguments in judicial decisions. It is suggested that the more likely reasons are of a subtler character; being both less often and less clearly articulated by the contributors to the Bill of Rights debate. It has been observed by a number of writers that an inevitable consequence of a Bill of Rights enforceable in the courts would be a telling exposure of the judiciary's law-making potential; or, to put it another way, there would be an illumination of the use made by judges of social, economic, political and philosophical values in reaching their decisions. Though observations of this sort have almost invariably been made by those who embrace the prospect of such an outcome,[50] the point is of great significance in effecting an understanding of the nature of the "politicization" arguments raised against a Bill of Rights. In this respect the issue is not so much one of concern over the judiciary having more often to employ such value-judgements, but rather that they would be *manifestly seen* to do so. It is surely this point that more precisely identifies the basis for, in particular, the judiciary's objections to its perceived "politicization" and the illegitimate redistribution of constitutional power that would follow the incorporation of the European Convention.

In seeking to understand the true nature of the "politicization" arguments, one is best served by an analysis of the *manner* in which the judicial enforcement of a Bill of Rights would be effected. For the judiciary would be at liberty to implement, where relevant, an incorporated European Convention largely as it saw fit; it would in this respect have effective authority to set its own agenda of interpretive activism or passivity.[51] A combination of the peculiarities of an unelected body, having necessarily to employ policy arguments in order to interpret and apply both the broadly drafted rights and their broadly drafted qualifications in the Convention, would bestow this power on the judiciary.

So long as the European Convention remains unincorporated, any attempt to predict the likely bearing of the judiciary in applying its provisions should it be incorporated is largely a matter of conjecture. What little evidence there is, however, points to an attitude of conservatism; and in particular a readiness to rely on the substantial qualifications to many of the most

---

49 Kinley, *supra*, n.46, p.807. See also Jaconelli, *supra*, n.3, p.352.
    It might be suggested, in addition, that the senior members of the UK's judiciary are already part way attuned to the consideration of broadly drafted human rights provisions through the Privy Council's consideration of appeals on constitutional matters from Commonwealth countries (today an almost otiose function); and through the higher courts' interpretive experiences with certain aspects of European Community law (on which see, for instance, A Lester, "Fundamental Rights: The UK Isolated?" [1984] PL 70), and, to a lesser degree, the European Convention on Human Rights itself.
50 See, for example, A Lester, *Minutes of Evidence*, House of Lords Select Committee on a Bill of Rights, *supra*, n.30, p.138; Zander, *supra*, n.3, p.65; Jaconelli, *supra*, n.3, p.354, and Lacey, *supra*, n.12, p.156.
51 See Ewing & Gearty, *supra*, n.32, p.268.

important rights enshrined in the Convention.[52] For example, in the two most recent cases in which the House of Lords has seen fit to comment on the compatibility of separate Government restrictions on the media with Article 10 of the Convention (which guarantees freedom of expression), their Lordships showed no willingness to read this guarantee in any way other than its most restricted form. In both the 1987 *Spycatcher* case (in which certain newspapers were restrained from publishing extracts from Peter Wright's book of that name) and, most recently, *ex parte Brind* (which concerned the restraint placed on the IBA and the BBC from televising unedited recordings of members of certain terrorist organizations) their Lordships were of the opinion that in any case the actions of the Government fell within the qualifications to Article 10 as stipulated in sub-paragraph (2) – that is where the restriction is "necessary in a democratic society".[53] Furthermore, in *Brind* the House of Lords was prepared apparently to treat the conformity of the impugned actions of the Government to the Convention as axiomatic upon establishing that the Government claimed to have addressed this issue prior to its taking action.[54] It is perhaps easy to understand this reluctance on the part of judges to be more enterprising in this regard in the light of their declared unease over taking on the additional interpretive responsibilities that would be the likely consequence of the incorporation of the Convention. Admittedly, there have appeared occasional indications of judicial activism in respect of the Convention, exhibited, principally, by Lord Scarman.[55] However, whether the judiciary would be likely to adopt a restrictive or activist attitude in its interpretation of Bill of Rights provisions is not really the issue; rather, the crucial point is whether it ought to be entrusted with this discretion in the first place.[56] As with the previous point, it is surely this conclusion that more accurately represents the principal concern of those who oppose the establishment of a Bill of Rights.

The foregoing analysis leads one to consider that it is questionable to conclude that rights would be better protected and promoted by the incorporation of the European Convention. In addition to the substantial questions over the legitimacy of any shift in the balance of constitutional

---

52 Articles 2, 5, 6, 7, 8, 9, 10, and 11 are all qualified with exceptions to the generally stated protection of the individual right; those relating to Articles 6, 8, 9, 10 and 11 are couched in the imprecise form of being "necessary in a democratic society". See further, Appendix 2, *infra*.

53 Respectively, *Attorney-General v Guardian Newspapers Ltd* [1987] 1 WLR 1248, 1297–9 (*per* Lord Templeman); and *R v Secretary of State for the Home Dept, ex parte Brind* (1989) 139 NLJ 1229, 1230 (*per* Watkins LJ), and later endorsed by the House of Lords in [1990] 2 WLR 588, 592–5.

54 [1990] 2 WLR 588, 594–5 (*per* Lord Templeman). A craven acceptance of the Government's assurances of "necessity" in respect of its actions in matters of national security appears to have become firmly established since the GCHQ case: *Council for Civil Service Unions v Minister for the Civil Service* [1985] AC 374

55 See, for example, *Ahmad v ILED* [1978] QB 36, 48–50, where his Lordship stood alone amongst his Court of Appeal colleagues in his preparedness to apply the freedom of religion guarantees of Article 9 of the Convention to domestic legislation.

56 The IPPR has suggested that a stipulation be made in any Bill of Rights that the exceptions and qualifications to certain provisions be granted only where they are demonstrated to be *strictly* necessary. It is difficult to see how this would alter the presently required standard of proof; in any case it is surely unrealistic to suppose that this minor drafting change would "ensure ... that the exception clauses are interpreted strictly in favour of individuals and minorities ...", *supra*, n.4 pp 13–4.

power, and the ability of judges (steeped as they are in the tradition of English common law)[57] to comprehend and satisfactorily apply the widely drafted provisions of the Convention drawn from the civil code jurisprudence of continental Europe, there exist more pragmatic reasons for opposition to the idea both from within the domains of party politics and the judiciary. Even if one is unwilling or unable to support unequivocally either side in the Bill of Rights debate, it must be conceded by all that the debate itself has reached a position of stultifying intransigence.

Yet, surprisingly perhaps, beyond this embargoed Bill of Rights debate, there has been little serious investigation of alternative means by which the United Kingdom might better comply with the demands of the European Convention. Still less effort has been directed towards the establishment of explicitly *preventive* measures, that would require neither the Convention to be entrenched nor its provisions to be justiciable in United Kingdom courts. There have been occasional references throughout the last 30-year history of the modern Bill of Rights debate to the possibility of instituting a Human Rights Commission or a parliamentary scrutiny committee that might advise the legislature or executive on the compatibility of legislative proposals with human rights provisions (either international or domestic). Invariably, however, they have been barely properly aired let alone analysed. Anthony Lester, for instance, both in one of the earliest and one of the most recent contributions to the debate, has made suggestions for the creation of such organs,[58] but upon neither does he dwell for more than a sentence or two. For Lester – in common with the authors of almost all other examples (as the assessment in Chapter Six of all such suggestions illustrates) – this brevity is due largely to the fact that the question of establishing such a commission or committee is viewed to be *tangental* to the principle concern of the implementation of a Bill of Rights. The principal purpose of this book is not simply to reverse this emphasis, but rather to suggest a scheme that might adequately *replace* the Bill of Rights proposals. A scheme, namely, by which all legislation might be scrutinized, *prior to enactment*, for potential inconsistencies with rights guaranteed by the European Convention, *as it presently stands*, and not as an incorporated Bill of Rights.

The rationale of focusing on legislation (both primary and secondary) is twofold. First, no fewer than 22 of the 28 European Court of Human Rights cases decided against the United Kingdom have involved direct violations of Convention-protected rights by domestic legislation.[59] What is more, the impact of the Convention extends well beyond those adverse judgments of the European Court; applications to the European Commission and hearings before the Committee of Ministers have also precipitated alterations in

---

57   See Zander, *supra*, n.3, 59–64; and Lord McCluskey, *supra*, n.3, pp 45–50. Lord Denning MR summed up the judicial attitude towards the terms of the Convention as "not the sort of thing that we can easily digest", *R v Chief Immigration Officer, Heathrow Airport, ex parte Salamat Bibi* [1976] 1 WLR 979, 985.

58   First in *Democracy, and Individual Rights*, Fabian Tract 390 (1968), p.15, and then as co-author of the IPPR's, *A British Bill of Rights* (1990), p.23.

59   See Appendix 1 *infra*, for details of these statistics. The total figure for adverse judgments against the UK of 28 *excludes* the *Soering* case (ECHR Series 'A', No. 161 (7 July 1989)) as the Court there found only a *potential* violation, which never finally occurred. The most prominent of those cases involving legislative breaches of the Convention are considered in Chapters 3 and 4, *infra*.

legislation.[60] It has been estimated that "[i]n total some 80 United Kingdom laws or regulations have been repealed or amended as a result of proceedings under the European Convention".[61] The significance of this impact is unlikely to diminish in the light of the escalation of Convention-based litigation. Not only has it been calculated by the current President of the European Court of Human Rights that the number of cases referred to the Court in 1990 was approximately equal to the total number for the first 24 years of its existence,[62] but in respect specifically of the United Kingdom, the number of adverse judgments between 1960 and 1984 was 11,[63] whilst 17 such judgments were delivered between 1985 and 1991.[64] And second, in those cases where legislation was found by the Court (or the Commission) to be contrary to the Convention, the prior consideration of that legislation in draft form by the Government or Parliament for compliance with the Convention was almost invariably non-existent or negligible. As the accounts in Chapters Three and Four demonstrate, in most cases the relevance of the Convention, even at a general level, has simply not been recognized. There was little chance, therefore, that the potential for infringement of the Convention lying within these provisions would have been detected. It is perhaps an even more lamentable fact that on the one occasion (in 1979) when a concerted effort was made to establish in advance the conformity of certain prospective legislative provisions with the Convention, the resultant strongly expressed caveats were summarily rejected by the Government, and the legislation (a new set of Immigration Rules) was introduced unamended. The specific aspect of the Immigration Rules which had caused the most concern for many of those experts examined by the investigating Home Affairs Sub-Committee was subsequently held by the European Court of Human Rights to be in violation of the Convention.[65]

Within the current parliamentary legislative procedure there exists no mechanism by which prospective legislation is scrutinized for conformity with the European Convention. Similarly, until recently, no formal preventive measures operated in government's process of drafting legislative proposals. Traditionally, governments have relied wholly on the departments responsible for the preparation of legislative proposals to seek advice from the Foreign and Commonwealth Office or the Law Officers where there was a

---

60 A comparative survey made by the Council of Europe, of the total numbers of applications made to the Commission, hearings of the Committee of Ministers and judgments of the Court for all the member countries, is reproduced in the Standing Advisory Commission on Human Rights, *Annual Report 1986-7*, HC 298 (1987-8), p.6. The United Kingdom has the largest total of any member State in all three categories. See, also, *The Independent*, 30 Nov. 1988.
For a concise account of the relationship between, and the procedures of, the organs responsible for the administration and adjudication of the European Convention, see R Beddard, *Human Rights and Europe* (1980, 2nd edn), pp 36-49.

61 P Thornton, *Decade of Decline* (1989), p.92.

62 Mr Rolvi Ryssdal, Speech to an Informal Ministerial Conference on Human Rights, Council of Europe, *Cour* (90) 289, p.2.

63 Source: HL Deb. Vol.469, col.192 (10 Dec. 1985), Lord Glenarthur.

64 This figure excludes the *Soering* case *supra*, n.59. Principal source: *European Court of Human Rights Survey of Activities 1959-1990*, Council of Europe, 23 Jan. 1991, pp 24-30 & 55.

65 *Abdulaziz, Cabales & Balkandall v United Kingdom*, ECHR Series 'A', No.94 (28 May 1985). This matter is discussed in detail in Chapter 4, *infra*, pp 86-7.

possibility of conflict. The Government's justification for placing the onus of detecting potential conflicts on the departments has been stated, glibly, as being that "departments are aware of the points at which provisions of the Convention touch on their responsibilities, so far as this was clear on the face of the Convention or is apparent from the rulings of the Court".[66] The evidence of European Court judgments on United Kingdom legislation does not bear out this optimism.[67] Indeed quite the reverse is the case. As the Standing Advisory Commission on Human Rights has declared, the number of the United Kingdom's appearances before the European Court creates "a clear impression that the Government is reluctant to meet the standards set by the Convention until forced to do so by Strasbourg".[68]

Perhaps in recognition of this poor record, the Government decided that these rather casual arrangements required restating in a more formal guise. In July 1987 the Cabinet Office issued a pair of Circulars to all departments entitled *Reducing the Risk of Legal Challenge*, and *The Judge over your Shoulder – Judicial Review of Administrative Decisions*.[69] The former is of especial interest. In addition to setting out a general condition that departments should be aware of the need to minimize the risk of legal challenge when preparing legislative proposals, it establishes a specific procedure for minimising the risk of a successful challenge in the European Court of Human Rights. In the context of this book the two most important conditions of this procedure are that departments are urged to "consider the effect of ECHR jurisprudence on any proposed legislative or administrative measure, in consultation with their legal adviser", and that "[a]ll Cabinet Committee memoranda on policy proposals and memoranda for Legislation Committee should include an assessment of the effect, if any, of ECHR jurisprudence on what is proposed".[70] No further specialized assistance is offered to the departments in the execution of these tasks beyond the seeking of "*ad hoc* guidance from the Foreign and Commonwealth Office".[71] The indications from subsequent legislation, however, as to the efficiency of these reconstituted preventive measures are far from encouraging. A Notice of Derogation had to be lodged with the Council of Europe in respect of the detention provisions of The Prevention of Terrorism (Temporary Provisions) Act 1989 *after* its enactment (see Chapters Three and Four), while s.28 of the Local Government Act 1988, the Security Service Act 1989 (for both, see Chapter Seven), the media restrictions on the broadcasting of representatives of certain Northern Irish organizations, and the modifications to the "right to silence" (see Chapter Eight), all clearly provide grounds for concern in respect of their conformity with the Convention. Yet despite these positions of questionable compliance, little consideration of the

---

66   *Minutes of Evidence*, House of Lords Select Committee on a Bill of Rights, *supra*, n.30, p.101.
67   See Chapters 3 & 4, *infra*.
68   *Annual Report 1984-5*, HC 394 (1985-6). The history of the Prison Rules before the European Court is a quintessential illustration of this minimalist attitude; see Chapter 4, *infra*, pp 67–82.
69   The first is dated March 1987, and the second dated 6 July 1987. For a general commentary on these memoranda see AW Bradley, "The Judge over your Shoulder" [1987] PL 485; and "Protecting Government Decisions from Legal Challenge" [1988] PL 1.
70   Paras 4(1) & (2).
71   *Ibid*, Annex II, para.6. For the position with respect to the tendering of general legal advice to departments, see HC Deb. Vol.124, col.781 (w) (18 Dec. 1987).

impact of the European Convention on these Acts and measures was given in Parliament. It is difficult not to conclude that they received similarly cursory treatment during their formative stages within Government. In respect of the last-mentioned instance, it is hardly credible that the Government could rush through this measure, which has patently serious implications for the conduct of criminal trials in Northern Ireland, without even previously informing the Standing Advisory Commission on Human Rights of its intentions, let alone seeking its counsel.[72] It may be the case that "full account is taken of the United Kingdom's obligations under the European Convention" when considering legislative proposals – as the Home Office (at least) maintains[73] – in which case it is possible that what the Government understands to be its "obligations" under the Convention do not correlate with the position taken by the European Commission and Court. In which case the reforms suggested in this book will serve their purpose through indirect means, as an educative force, as much as in their direct impact on proposed legislation that appears in conflict with the Convention.

In many other jurisdictions there exist a number and variety of methods by which prospective legislation is scrutinized for conformity with constitutionally protected rights, or rights enshrined in a treaty to which a State is bound. In Chapter Five a selection of examples are considered, some of which operate within government, some within the legislature, and others independently of both. Varying degrees of success are achieved by the systems in all three categories. However, in respect of the operation of the United Kingdom's legislation-making process, it concluded that the most effective type is that which would operate within Parliament.[74] A principal reason for this conclusion is that in the context of the United Kingdom, examples from the two alternative categories reveal deficiencies inherent in either group. Any "independent" scheme would exist, by definition, outside the main organ or organs of the legislative process, and, therefore, would lack the necessary influence over it.[75] Any "intra-government" scheme would lack the independence required to scrutinize objectively its own legislative proposals.[76] Within the "intra-parliamentary" category, the scrutiny system operating in Australia provides an effective basis upon which to build. Though possessed of certain unfamiliar characteristics, the basic apparatus and procedure of the Australian scheme would not be alien to British parliamentary procedure.[77]

The precedent exists, therefore, for establishing in the United Kingdom an analogous scheme for the pre-legislative scrutiny of all legislation, proposals for which are submitted in Chapters Seven and Eight. In providing a more effective means by which to reduce the possibility of legislative breaches of

[72] See Standing Advisory Commission on Human Rights, *Annual Report 1987-9*, HC 394 (1988-9), p.9. The Government later had the audacity to declare that in respect of human rights issues in Northern Ireland, its policy is to consult the Commission, HC Deb. Vol.146, col.786 (w) (9 Feb. 1989).
[73] HC Deb. Vol.119, col.220 (w) (13 July 1988).
[74] See Chapter 6, *infra*, p.16 & pp 124-8.
[75] What is more, no Government would tolerate any direct interference with its policy proposals from an external source, and Parliament is constitutionally protected from any such intrusion on its sovereign authority.
[76] The failure of the current system, whereby the Government claims to operate a process of self-censorship, tends to support this point.
[77] See Chapter 5, *infra*, pp 98-103.

the Convention the United Kingdom would, for the first time, be taking a direct step towards fulfilling its obligation under Article 1 to "secure to everyone ... the rights and freedoms defined ... in the Convention". Prevention of infringements of the Convention is infinitely preferable to amending legislation once a breach had been detected by the Commission or the Court. Ultimately it would lead to a reduction not only in the number of United Kingdom cases coming before the Convention's adjudicative institutions, but also in the cumulative impact of the considerable disadvantages of conducting and (especially) losing such cases. For instance, in addition to the time taken to pass through the domestic courts, each case takes, on average, four years from the moment of lodgement of the application to its being considered by the Commission, and, if referred to the Court, a further two years.[78] And as a consequence of adverse rulings from either the Court or the Commission the Government inevitably suffers considerable political embarrassment in both the domestic and international arenas.[79]

The scrutiny scheme here suggested adopts the same committee-based structure as that which characterizes the Australian model, whilst, in addition, incorporating certain existing elements of the United Kingdom's parliamentary procedure. Consideration of the scheme is divided into two parts according to type of legislation: the scrutiny process for primary legislation is detailed in Chapter Seven, and that for secondary legislation in Chapter Eight. Though a separate committee would be responsible for the examination of each legislative type, the two would operate in much the same way and both would rely largely on consensual authority rather than censorial powers to achieve their aim. The existing departmental select committees have acted in a like role to good effect, so that the Government's awareness of, and respect for, their task and performance has resulted in its own policy-making processes being adjusted accordingly.[80] To solicit a similar response from the Government in respect of legislative conformity with the European Convention would provide the most effective means of enhancing such conformity. In addition, however, as the committees would lay the reports of the results of their scrutiny before both Houses, the Government would also come under pressure in Parliament to justify any legislative proposal marked by the committees as apparently infringing the Convention.

The case for ensuring greater compliance with the Convention is fortified by the strengthening relationship between the Convention and European Community law. Since 1974 when France (the last of the Community's founding member countries to do so) ratified the European Convention on Human Rights, the provisions of the Convention have increasingly been recognized as generally binding in Community law.[81] Under ss 2(1) and 3(1)

---

78 *Report on Seminar on the Merger of the European Commission and European Court of Human Rights*, by Professor DC Greer, for the Standing Advisory Commission on Human Rights, *Annual Report 1985-6*, HC 151 (1986-7), p.54.
79 See, for example, Zander, *supra*, n.3, pp 37-8.
80 See Chapter 6, *infra*, p.127.
81 See for example, *Nold v EC Commission* [1974] ECR 491,507-8; *Rutili v The French Minister of The Interior* [1975] ECR 1219; *R v Kent Kirk* [1984] ECR 2689, 2718 and *Union Nationale des Entraineurs et Cardes Techniques Professionnels du Football v Heylens* [1987] ECR 4097, at 913. See also, AZ Drzemczewski, *European Human Rights*

of the European Communities Act 1972, of course, Community law
(including the decisions of the European Court of Justice) is directly
incorporated into the law of the United Kingdom, as a consequence of which
the Convention might in some areas already be construed as more than
merely an aid to statutory interpretation.[82] There has also been a strong
movement within the European Community itself to accede to the
Convention,[83] which has been energetically supported by the Council of
Europe.[84] The preamble to the Single European Act (1986), furthermore,
specifically refers to a determination of the member states to promote the
fundamental rights recognized in the European Convention on Human
Rights. The European Parliament has reinforced this intention with the
adoption of its own Declaration of Fundamental Rights and Freedoms in
April 1989 which is largely based on the European Convention.[85] As a
consequence of these initiatives, together with the completion of the
dismantling of European trade barriers by the end of 1992 (or later) under
the Single European Act, it is reasonable to presume that Community law
(and through it the Convention's provisions also) will play an increasingly
important role not only in the government of the United Kingdom, but in the
interpretation of domestic law in United Kingdom courts and in the
European Court of Justice.[86] Undoubtedly, the United Kingdom would be
better able to accommodate this process of legal integration if there existed a
system by which its legislation was thoroughly vetted during its formative
stages for conformity with the European Convention.

Convention in Domestic Law (1983), Chapter 9.

[82]   P Karpenstein & SA Crossick, "Pleading Human Rights in British Courts – The Impact of
EEC Law" (1981) 78 Law Soc. Gaz., 90–91; and P Allott's submission to the Lords Select
Committee on the European Communities, HL 362 (1979–80), para.8.

[83]   See the Bulletin of the European Communities: Supplement 5/76 (especially para.28);
and Supplement 2/79 (especially para.10). (For the House of Lords' consideration of the
latter, see the *Report of the Select Committee on the European Communities*, HL 362
(1979–80), (especially para.34)). The latest call was made in November 1990, see the
24th General Report of the European Commission, 1990, points 873 & 899.

[84]   Speech by Mr Rolvi Ryssdal, President of the European Court of Human rights, *supra*,
n.62, p.1. Even without accession it is important to note that it remains "quite feasible
that the operation of a Community provision at the national level could be challenged in
Strasbourg for compliance with the Convention", A Clapham, *Human Rights and the
European Community: A Critical Overview* (1991). p.52; see also JHH Weiler, "Methods
of Protection: Towards a Second and Third Generation of Protection" in A Cassese,
A Clapham & J Weiler (eds), *Human Rights and the European Community: Methods of
Protection* (1991), p.620. No such challenge has yet been made.

[85]   The Declaration is merely declaratory and is itself legally unenforceable; it is intended
rather to be reflective of rights already broadly in existence in the Community, see
Weiler, *supra*, n.84, pp 621–8. Indeed, for at least as long as the Declaration remains
thus, and, equally, the European Community's Charter of Fundamental Social Rights of
Workers remains merely a "solemn declaration" by 11 of the 12 member states (the
exception is the UK) with no legally binding force and therefore no jurisprudence, the
European Convention on Human Rights, with its vast body of jurisprudence, will
continue to be a significant point of reference on human rights issues in general for the
adjudicative organs of the European Community.

[86]   At least one commentator has argued further that since the coming into force of the
Single European Act the European Court of Justice has displayed a willingness "to
emphasise the Convention as a *direct* source of Community law" (emphasis supplied),
N Grief, "The Domestic Impact of the European Convention on Human Rights as
mediated through Community Law" [1991] PL 555, 556 and accompanying footnote.

2 PARLIAMENT, GOVERNMENT AND LEGISLATION

In broad analytic terms this book is concerned with the twin issues of legislative procedure and legislative compliance with the European Convention. An analysis of the first is necessary to establish the foundations for the pursuit of the second. It is the purpose of this chapter to provide such an analysis. The chapter is divided into two parts. The process by which legislation is made in the United Kingdom is examined, in respect, especially, of the opportunities for, and the efficacy of, parliamentary scrutiny within that process. This more general discussion, however, is preceded by a consideration of the discrete question of pre-legislative scrutiny, in regard especially to the compliance of legislative proposals in the United Kingdom with the European Convention.

PART I

PRE-LEGISLATIVE SCRUTINY: INTRODUCTORY ARGUMENTS

The use of a pre-legislative scrutiny scheme as a means specifically to aid the compliance of legislation with the European Convention has not previously been considered seriously in the United Kingdom. That is not to say, however, that there has been no discussion of the matter whatsoever; rather that it has been either more general in scope or much less detailed in nature, or both. Indeed, it is worth noting at the outset that as a consequence of the undeveloped nature of the issue there exists in many of the critics of the concept of pre-legislative scrutiny a degree of equivocation. Whilst they may appear antagonistic towards any design of pre-legislative assessment, some are equally adamant that something ought to be done to eliminate the costly errors, oversights and indiscretions (especially in the field of human rights) from the legislative process. Illustrations of this ambivalence are to be found in the following discussion.

As it is a purpose of this book to present an argument in favour of establishing just such a scrutiny scheme, it is necessary to address those objections raised against *any* notion of pre-legislative scrutiny, and in particular those few referring specifically to scrutiny for compliance with the European Convention. In pursuit of this aim this part is divided into brief discussions of four relevant points. Initially, I shall discuss the two principal arguments raised against the idea of pre-legislative scrutiny; this is succeeded by an analysis of relevant issues spawned by the debate on the use of pre-legislative committees within the United Kingdom's legislative process; and, finally, a survey of the basic principles upon which is to be built the argument for a pre-legislative scrutiny procedure in respect of the European Convention is provided.

The claim that pre-legislative scrutiny is unnecessary

The basis of this criticism might be traced to Lord Hailsham, in his submission of evidence to the 1977 House of Lords Select Committee on a Bill of Rights. Partly in anticipation of his subsequent "elective dictatorship" thesis he pointed to a crucial weakness in the United Kingdom's model of government, namely that "Parliament is constantly making mistakes and could, in theory, become the most oppressive instrument in the world.

Sometimes a stage comes when things cannot be left alone any longer."[1] It would appear, however, that concomitantly he does not consider a process of pre-legislative examination operating within Parliament to be the answer to this problem of safeguarding fundamental rights, but rather merely adds a quite superfluous tier to an already overwrought system of parliamentary law-making. His summary dismissal of such a process, however, is unwarranted, for if the idea had been considered in the context of the problem of Parliament's deficiencies, its merits might have been more apparent. As it was, the former Lord Chancellor was dismissive of the idea both as a proposition for some general scrutiny of all legislation, and in respect specifically to a means for ensuring legislative conformity to the European Convention. Lord Hailsham's view was that any body charged with pre-legislative scrutiny of all legislation is no more likely to discern the presence of some constitutional infringement than Parliament. What is not uncovered in Parliament in the course of its normal legislative stages of debate and amendment, in his Lordship's opinion, will no more be uncovered by a special committee "because", quite simply, "it is not humanly possible to foresee the consequence in every case of what it [parliamentary legislation] is doing".[2] Similarly, with regard to scrutiny for compliance with the Convention, he stated, when answering questions put to him by the Select Committee:

> ... I do not believe that a Committee set up for the purpose [of detecting inadvertent breaches of the European Convention by draft legislation] would necessarily be more provident than Parliament itself, or the various Government Committees which go through legislation before it is produced before Parliament, or the parliamentary draftsmen who strive with considerable skill, but not to perfection, to give effect to the real intentions of Government. I am not sure that you would add much by such a Committee ... .[3]

The supposed superfluity of intra-parliamentary scrutiny, in either its general or specific respects, has attracted considerable, though largely unjustified, support. The House of Lords Select Committee wholly adopted the Hailsham view, in its report, stating that it was "sceptical of the usefulness of a parliamentary committee", on the grounds that it was unlikely to do better than the existing ordinary parliamentary process.[4] Lord Allen, the Chairman of the Lords Committee, in agreeing with Lord Hailsham's view made a curious attempt to support his stance. He maintained that as "... one did not know with certainty what the meaning of the Convention was", its provisions were extremely difficult to apply.[5] Such

---

1   Lord Hailsham in an article printed in *The Observer* in 1970, quoted by the Earl of Arran during the second reading of the latter's Bill of Rights Bill - HL Deb. Vol.313, col.249 (26 Nov. 1970). Lord Hailsham reiterated the point some years later in *The Dilemma of Democracy* (1978), p.13.
    On the demise of Parliament as a body able to exercise control over the Executive, see S A Walkland, *The Legislative Process in Great Britain* (1968) p.92; and also, J Grigg, "Making Government Responsible to Parliament" in R Holme & M Elliot (eds), *1688-1988 Time for a New Constitution* (1988), pp 167-80.
2   *Report of the House of Lords Select Committee on a Bill of Rights*, HL 176 (1977-8), p.23.
3   *Ibid*.
4   *Report of the Select Committee on a Bill of Rights, supra*, n.2, p.39. Michael Zander agrees,. having commented, "I would not myself recommend such machinery"; *A Bill of Rights?* (1985, 3rd edn), pp 86-7.
5   *Minutes of Evidence taken before the House of Lords Select Committee on a Bill of Rights,*

an argument is sophistry. It is based on the premise that in order for the provisions of a charter such as the European Convention to play any part in the United Kingdom's legislative process, one must first gain a clear idea of its intention. Yet that constitutes the essential reason why a relatively small but specialized scrutiny committee, rather than members of either or both Houses sitting *en masse*, should be entrusted with this task of initial examination of legislative proposals. Upon receiving reports and advice from such a committee Parliament would then be in a better position to make an informed decision in any specific instance as to the impact of the relevant demands of the Convention.

The Standing Advisory Commission on Human Rights has had similar reservations. In a report assessing means by which human rights may be protected, it pronounced that "[l]ike the committee on the preparation of legislation, we do not think that there is any practical scope for introducing a new scrutiny stage as part of the parliamentary process itself because of the undue strain which it would impose on a parliamentary machine which is already under great pressure."[6]

It is implicit in both the opinions of Lord Hailsham (and the Lords' Committee) and the Standing Advisory Commission – that the adoption of another level of scrutiny as quite unnecessary – that Parliament, through its present mode of operation, detects all irregularities that it is reasonably possible to detect. Clearly, this is not the case. As indicated above, Lord Hailsham himself notes that the parliamentary scrutinizing process is far from perfect. And whilst it may be accurate to say that "it is probably unlikely that a government would deliberately introduce some Bill which flagrantly went against the Convention on Human Rights; but it might well introduce something that was an inadvertent breach",[7] it does not alter the regrettable fact that breaches, however caused, nonetheless frequently occur.[8] It cannot be overlooked that a violation of the Convention, even if unintended, is no less serious for those who have to suffer the consequences and no less damaging to the protection of fundamental rights in general than if the breach were intended. This being so, Lord Wade has asked, "would it help if there were a committee that would examine bills that might fall foul of the European Convention, and be under a duty to report to the House that there was a possibility in a particular clause, of a breach so that as a result of that, there would not be this inadvertent breach at the legislative stage?"[9] I think Lord Wade's question (rhetorical though it may be) must be answered in the affirmative. As it is imperative that preventive action needs to be taken to ensure that negligence, or poor judgement, on the part of Government or Parliament does not result in legislative infringements of the European Convention, then the demands of legislative expediency, whilst not without

---

HL 81 (1977–8), p.221.

6   *The Protection of Human Rights in Northern Ireland*, Cmnd 7009 (1977), para.7.17. The opinion of the Committee on the Preparation of Legislation referred to in the quotation is to be found in its 1975 Report: Cmnd 6053, para 18.33. Note, however, that in this report the concern was not specifically related to compliance with the European Convention or any other treaty or statute, but rather whether scrutiny was to be directed at the general form and drafting of bills.

7   *Report of the House of Lords Select Committee, supra*, n.2, p.22 (*per* Lord Wade).

8   See Chapters 3 & 4, *infra*.

9   Report, *supra*, n.2, p.22.

importance, must be subordinate to that aim.

The claim that pre-legislative scrutiny is impracticable

The second objection to be addressed might be viewed as an extension of the supposed inefficacy of a further level of scrutiny. The Standing Advisory Commission on Human Rights maintained that the implementation of such an examination scheme would be impossible within the present confines of the legislation-making system. That is, despite welcoming the proposal in principle – "it is an example of a desirable reform ..." – the Commission considered the institutional obstacles that stand in its way to be such that to this statement there must be added the qualification: "... which would be dependent on wider constitutional changes".[10] It is suggested, however, that the problem is exaggerated. To begin with, the Commission openly acknowledged that it had based its opinion on the conclusions of an earlier report of the Select Committee on the Preparation of Legislation[11] which, with all due respect to the Commission, dealt with the issue of pre-legislative scrutiny from a very different angle. It was concerned solely with the demands of the structure and drafting of bills. The Standing Advisory Commission correctly pointed out that the Select Committee rejected the idea of implementing a system for the scrutiny of drafting technique during the passage of a bill through Parliament, but what is of much greater significance to our present concern is the Select Committee's rider that the present procedure may be altered if "it can clearly be demonstrated that it would be beneficial to do so".[12] The question of pre-legislative scrutiny of legislation with the object of ensuring compliance with a set of internationally protected human rights exists at a completely different level from that of the supervision of legislative form, and by virtue of that fact alone would, it is suggested, qualify to be considered as of such demonstrable benefit. Politically, there may indeed be a number of storms to be weathered, but in terms purely of mechanical feasibility of such scrutiny, the outlook is not as inclement as some would have us believe. Indeed, Chapter Six of this book is devoted to the consideration of suggestions that have been advanced as to how a pre-legislative system of examination might be established and operate in the United Kingdom; and a detailed proposal of how one scrutiny scheme might operate is provided in Chapters Seven and Eight. Suffice it to say, for the time being, that a case for the incorporation of some sort of examination system can be constructed on much more stable foundations than can the case against.

In spite of the irrefutable proposition that legislation which inadvertently violates certain human rights can and has been passed by Parliament, it is not beyond all doubt that infringements of a less fortuitous nature might become law when the demands of political expediency prove stronger than those of the strict adherence to the letter (and indeed spirit) of the European Convention. It must be borne in mind that the real danger of such an occurrence comes not from Parliament *per se*, but rather from the often oppressively powerful hand of the Executive that may effectively direct

---

10   Cmnd 7009, (1977), *supra*, n.6, para.7.17.
11   *Report of the Select Committee on the Preparation of Legislation*, Cmnd 6053 (1975) (the "Renton Committee").
12   *Ibid*, para.18.34.

Parliament in its legislative role.[13] The truism that Parliament has been reduced from its erstwhile function of providing a forum for relatively independent Members to introduce legislation and initiate debates, to that of being little more than an instrument in the hands of the most dominant party in the House of Commons, need not be reiterated here. The literature on this topic is vast,[14] but perhaps the point I am trying to make was captured most succinctly in a report from the Select Committee on Procedure in 1977 which stated that

> ... the balance of advantage between Parliament and Government in the day to day working of the Constitution is now weighted in favour of the Government to a degree which arouses widespread anxiety and is inimical to the proper working of our Parliamentary democracy.[15]

A little later in the same report it was declared that "... a new balance must be struck...", to be achieved not by rearrangement of the formal powers held by the three arms of government but rather by a fundamental change in the procedures and practices that interlink them. The aim, it was said, should be to "...enable the House as a whole to exercise effective control and stewardship over ministers and the expanding democracy of the modern state...".[16] The most maligned of all "control procedures" – ministerial responsibility – is in urgent need of redesign. As a basis for the United Kingdom's system of control over the operations of the Executive, it is now widely conceded to be outmoded and thoroughly inadequate, capable today of providing little more than "technical accountability".[17] It "fails as an interpretation of the constitutional promise of accountability for the exercise of public power because a Parliament dominated by the Executive cannot effectively call ministers to account".[18]

The paucity of opportunities, through formal procedural channels or otherwise, for Parliament to superintend the Government has also been noted and condemned at length in the Kilbrandon Commission's mammoth report on the constitution in 1973. Such is the continuing authority of the argument in a section of the Memorandum of Dissent to the report that, despite the fact that it is nearly 20 years old, it is worth quoting at length:

> In a modern democracy it is not enough for the great majority of the elected representatives of the people to be limited, for the most part, to essentially negative carping criticism of, and post facto investigation of, departmental decisions which they had no chance to shape. This means, therefore, that Parliamentarians must be able to make their contribution to policy-making while policies are still being worked out in the departments and before ministerial decisions have been taken. This is in line with the report from the House of Commons Select Committee on Procedure in 1967 [HC 539] which said that 'the

---

13   For an analysis of this phenomenon in respect specifically of the legislative process, see Part II of this chapter, *infra*, pp 29–32.
14   The field is simply too broad for justice to be done in citing even all the leading works, so I will simply indicate three distinctive interpretations of the problem: Lord Hailsham, *The Dilemma of Democracy* (1978); I Harden & N Lewis, *The Noble Lie* (1987); and, P McAuslan & JF McEldowney (eds), *Law, Legitimacy and the Constitution* (1985).
15   *First Report of the Select Committee on Procedure*, HC 588, (1977–8), para.1.5.
16   *Ibid*, para.1.6.
17   *The Economist*, 4 February 1985, p.25, commenting on the refusal of the Secretary of State for Northern Ireland to resign after the "Maze Breakout" in 1983. For a thorough analysis of the issue see, CC Turpin, "Ministerial Responsibility" in J Jowell & D Oliver (eds), *The Changing Constitution* (1989, 2nd edn), pp 53–85.

House should be brought in at an earlier point in the legislative process so as to allow discussion by Parliament of subjects and details of potential legislation before the Government finally prepares a Bill'. And this was endorsed by the second report from the Select Committee on Procedure in 1971 [HC 538], which recommended that 'regular use should in future be made of pre-legislation committees, to consider matters with a view to consequent legislation.'[19]

Clearly the intention of any proposal to involve the House of Commons (or at least a committee representing the parties within it) at a much earlier stage in the legislative process is to allow a greater breadth of opinion to bear on the actual policy-making, antecedent to the drawing up of legislative proposals.[20] Not only would this be highly controversial, but for the purpose of trying to establish a precedent for a system of pre-legislative scrutiny for compliance with Convention-protected rights, this goes much further than is necessary. Of course, greater involvement of the House at this stage might indeed help to ensure that prospective legislation of an iniquitous character would not reach the final stages of parliamentary debate or even the statute book. However, such an effect would be of no more than welcome assistance to the examining bodies suggested in this book which could not themselves properly be involved in the actual creation or scrutiny of *policy*. It would not, therefore, be an essential pre-requisite to their establishment.

Nonetheless, there is something to be gained from the rich debate that has surrounded the topic of pre-legislative committees which is periodically discussed with such vigour in the reports of the Select Committee on Procedure. In its sixth report of the 1966–7 session, one of the experts to be called in and examined commented:

> ... everyone knows that a minister preparing a Bill is consulting all sorts of outside organisations and indeed must do so inevitably. The one lot of people he never consults in any way before he prepares it are members of the House of Commons, the Members of Parliament generally. All too often the Bill is produced in a form agreed outside, and is then given to the House on a much more 'take it or leave it' basis than sometimes members would wish it to be.[21]

Indeed, most legislation, once introduced to Parliament, is rarely rejected or even substantially amended. This *fait accompli* is apparent even at the point of first reading, as it has been suggested that by then "the policy-making process is so far advanced that it is difficult for parliamentary debate to have any significant effect on the principles underlying the Bill".[22]

A system of pre-legislative committees for the purpose of advising and informing both Houses of Parliament might provide the basis for the creation of a process of pre-legislative scrutiny of legislation in the context of the European Convention, in that it would be but a relatively small procedural step to incorporate a review of the demands made by the Convention into such a process of pre-legislative scrutiny. But as, after a number of unsuccessful attempts, it seems unlikely that they will be introduced, the

---

18   Harden and Lewis, *supra*, n.14, p.118.
19   *Report of the Royal Commission on the Constitution* (1969–73), Cmnd 5460, Vol II: Memorandum of Dissent by Lord Crowther-Hunt and Professor AT Peacock, para.292.
20   See generally Sir Douglas Wass, "Checks and Balances in Public Policy-Making" [1987] PL, 181; and Harden and Lewis, *supra*, n.14, pp 231–5.
21   Rt Hon William Whitelaw (then Opposition Chief Whip), *Minutes of Evidence taken before the Select Committee on Procedure* 1966–7, HC 539, para.279.
22   Harden and Lewis, *supra*, n.14, p.103.

development of a separate, though not dissimilar, scrutiny scheme for legislative compliance with the Convention might prove more promising. Still, as indicated above, some aspects of the debate over general pre-legislative scrutiny committees are relevant to the development of this separate and specific scheme.

The debate over pre-legislative scrutiny committees

In respect of the prevention of potential infringements of the European Convention by statutes, it is easy to see how the reason used by the Renton Committee on the preparation of legislation to reject the call for the establishment of pre-legislative committees might also be relied upon in opposing the claim that a form of pre-legislative scrutiny is imperative to the protection of human rights under the European Convention. The rationale behind the Renton Committee's stand was that such pre-legislative involvement would place "... undue strain on a parliamentary machine already under great pressure and would also add to the labour of the draftsmen who have enough to do as it is to keep pace with the legislative programme".[23] This argument, however, is unconvincing. As regards the first limb of the Committee's reasoning – if we are to reject an attempt to try to restore Parliament to being more than merely a legitimizing instrument of the party in government by allowing the whole body of members of both Houses to have some impact on the formulation and implementation of policy on the grounds that it clogs the bureaucratic wheels of Westminster, then we must ask ourselves what is the true purpose of the legislature. Is it merely to strive towards a point where the whole process of passing legislation is simplest to manage, and where there is a minimum of administrative inconvenience? Surely not. The whole point of Parliament's existence as a legislation-making forum is to allow elected representatives to participate in, and provide impetus for, the execution of democratic government. According to one former leading civil servant who has first hand experience of the shift in power from Parliament to the Executive, this is an aim too readily subverted. As a result, he claims that

> ... there is no statutory requirement for the Government to give reasons for most of its decisions; no duty is laid upon it to publish or give access to information on which decisions are made; no rules apply to the internal processes followed in reaching decisions or govern the mechanisms by which deals are struck between public authority and private interest groups. There is no prescriptive procedure for the consultation of wider 'constituencies' than those the government chooses to identify and prefer. The only hard obligation on the government is to seek the endorsement of the electorate at large when Parliament is dissolved.[24]

Admittedly, there are limitations as to how far this "democratic" ideal can be taken in attempting to rectify these shortfalls, perhaps the most obvious of which is that the essentially political choice of which policy to adopt must always ultimately lie with the Executive.[25] But these limits cannot include the spurious claim (explicitly made by at least one senior politician)[26] that

---

23   Cmnd 6053, *supra*, n.11, p.19.
24   Sir Douglas Wass, in the foreword to Harden and Lewis, *supra*, n.14, p.xl.
25   See *Second Report of the Select Committee on Procedure*, HC 538 (1971), para. 8.
26   Mr Gerald Kaufmann MP (then a Shadow Minister) declared, when asked in 1980 to give his assessment of the new select committee system during its first year of operation, that

the exigencies of administrative expedition are to take precedence over the demands for wider parliamentary scrutiny of those policies the Government has chosen to follow, especially, that is, if such rights as those protected by the European Convention are at issue. This is surely a legitimate expectation.

The second limb of the Committee's argument is even less persuasive. Should the establishing of a pre-legislative committee increase the workload of the parliamentary counsel who are responsible for the drafting of prospective legislation, then the problem could be remedied relatively simply by the addition of more counsel. In fact, it is submitted that the introduction of a system of pre-legislative scrutiny for compliance with the European Convention is unlikely to add significantly to the task of the drafters. The preventive influence of a pre-legislative scrutiny committee, it is later argued, is likely to take effect either through the committee's active involvement at the policy formulation stage or by the Government's anticipation of subsequent scrutiny by the committee.[27] Whilst it may lengthen slightly the time between the conception of an idea or policy and it being presented to the drafters for translation into legislative form, that should not itself add anything to their job. In any event, the use of pre-legislative scrutiny as a sort of safety net, whether before or during the drafting, is surely beneficial, for as HW Arthurs commented in support of the Canadian pre-legislative vetting system, "... even the most vigilant draftsmen must surely slip once or twice over a ... [long] period".[28]

Pre-legislative scrutiny and the European Convention

Of much greater significance than accidental transgression of the Convention-protected rights through imperfect drafting is an attitude of indifference, or even disregard, to the rights and procedures enshrined in the European Convention on the part of those responsible for the policy behind legislative proposals. As the detailed examples in Chapters Three and Four demonstrate, United Kingdom legislation has been found too often to infringe the provisions of the European Convention, so it is by no means certain that governments, particularly those holding a large majority in Parliament, would be consistently vigilant in their respect for the Convention in the face of pressing political goals. Lord Gordon-Walker's observation, whilst sitting on the House of Lords Select Committee on a Bill of Rights, in response to

---

"[I]t [the Government] was elected by a very large majority last year and I believe it has the right to carry them [its policies] out - however misguided and indeed evil I believe these policies to be, and I do not believe that Parliament should create trip wires for these policies because I would not like it if Parliament created similar trip wires for a Labour Government in whose policies I thoroughly believed." Far from seeing select committee scrutiny as an aid to the House in its quest to exercise some control over the actions of the Executive, Mr Kaufmann views such inquiry as little more than an impediment to an Executive's commitment to implement whatever measures it chooses, apparently irrespective of any moral, let alone human rights, obligations. BBC "Analysis" programme 1980; quoted by A Davies, *Reformed Select Committees: The First Years* (1980), pp 62-3.

27 The Government may request the opinion of the Committee (or Counsel to the Committee) at a much earlier stage, in an effort to avoid subsequent adverse reports from the Committee; see, for example, the suggestion in Chapter 7, *infra*, p.148 & pp 150-2.

28 *Minutes of Evidence*, House of Lords Select Committee, *supra*, n.5, p.242.

the suggestion that Lord Reid's claim that it is inconceivable that Parliament would enact legislation which ran contrary to the articles of the European Convention,[29] is soberingly trenchant: "... when judges say 'inconceivable', they do not know about how Parliament works".[30]

In particular, the potential for breaches of the Convention through indifference or ignorance of its demands lies in those instances where apparent legislative denials of protected rights are held by the Government to be justified under the appropriate derogating provisions in the Convention. This was the position with the Prison Rules and immigration legislation (both primary and secondary),[31] both of which were subsequently found to violate the Convention. There exist examples of such potential in more recent legislation which also failed to attract critical analysis on this point due, apparently, to inadequate appreciation of the relevance of the Convention. For instance,[32] certain aspects of the Public Order Act 1986 provide some grounds for concern. The general purpose of the Act is to preserve public order at the limited expense, if need be, of freedom of public protest and assembly. The prescribed means, however, by which this is to be achieved leave great potential for abuse. Quite apart from the creation of four specific new offences consequent upon disobeying a police officer's instructions,[33] an entirely new charge of offensive conduct has been introduced which, in contrast to the usual position in English criminal procedure, and possibly also inconsistent with Article 6(2),[34] requires the defendant to prove that his behaviour was not likely to cause distress to others.[35] Additionally, the provisions empowering the police to impose conditions as to route or location of assemblies and processions on the new ground of likely disruption to community life, though strongly defended,[36] may nonetheless effectively negate the very point of the demonstration by removing the inconvenience through which it gains recognition, and thereby impinge upon the Convention-protected right to freedom of peaceful assembly. These points notwithstanding, the form in which the Government addressed its *obligations* under the European Convention in the White Paper which preceded the Act amounted to a bare assurance that it had borne them in mind during its deliberations.[37] What little the Government added to this

---

29   *Waddington v Miah* [1974] 1 WLR 683, 694.
30   *Minutes, supra*, n.5, p.130. See also Lord Scarman's caveat over "instant legislation, conceived in fear and prejudice", *English Law – The New Dimension* (1974), p.20.
31   See Chapters 3 & 4, *infra*, pp 45-7 & 67-89.
32   Further examples are discussed in Chapters 7 & 8, *infra*, pp 141-9 & 162-70.
33   Ss 5, 12, 14 & 39.
34   Article 6(2) reads: "Everyone charged with a criminal offence shall be presumed innocent until proved guilty according to law". Whilst it has been recognized that placement of the onus of proof on the accused is not necessarily contrary to the demands of this Article (see JES Fawcett, *Application of the European Convention on Human Rights* (1987, 2nd edn), p.180), the fact the new legislation may be inconsistent (as was declared in the early case of *Austria v Italy* (1963) 6 Yearbook ECHR 740, 782-4) was not even recognized by the Government; see *infra*, n.36 & 39. Note also that the similarly worded s.11(d) of the Canadian Charter of Human Rights and Fundamental Freedoms which enshrines the right to be presumed innocent until proven guilty has been understood to include the prerequisite that in criminal cases the state must bear the burden of proof, *R v Holmes* [1988] 1 SCR 914, 933 (*per* Dickson CJC, dissenting).
35   For a discussion of the problems for the courts of applying statutory obligations of proof placed on defendants see, P Mirfield, "The Legacy of *Hunt*" [1988] Crim. LR 19-30.
36   *Review of Public Order Law*, Cmnd, 9510 (1985), paras 4.23-4; see also, para.5.3.
37   *Ibid*, para.2.15.

statement concentrated rather on the *limitations* to the right to peaceful assembly provided in Article 11.[38] Lamentably, however, despite the fact that the Government's exaggerated concern for the maintenance of public order may have stretched the permitted derogation of the protected right of assembly to an unsustainable degree, the question of the Bill's conformity to the Convention was never pressed in the House of Commons during its second reading.[39]

In circumstances such as this, a pre-legislative scrutiny committee might alert, or more fully inform (as with the Public Order Bill), both Government and Parliament as to the relevant provisions of the European Convention. So powerful would be the threat of such unwelcome and politically damaging exposure that a bill's promoters would be unlikely to support recognized potential violations of the Convention, and even where they did, they would necessarily do so under scrutiny. With reference to the Canadian examination system (the first form of which was established in 1960),[40] this point is borne out, despite the fact that it is a governmental rather than parliamentary based system. It has been maintained by the Senior Legislative Counsel in the Canadian Department of Justice that bills are not usually found to present problems, since the examination provisions have had an earlier prophylactic effect – an effect which was the principal reason for setting up the examination in the first place.[41]

The informative and educational effect that accrues from the publicized scrutiny of a proposed piece of legislation through a pre-legislative vetting procedure might permit the electorate (which, of course, possesses ultimate authority over both Parliament and the Government) to appreciate the importance of the Convention. Such a scrutiny scheme in the United Kingdom would unequivocally advance the earnest sentiment expressed in the Preamble to the Convention that, "[F]undamental Freedoms ... are best maintained on the one hand by an effective political democracy and on the other by a common understanding and observance of Human Rights upon which they depend". It is on this basis that the argument for the creation of a pre-legislative scrutiny committee empowered to examine prospective legislation for adherence to the articles of the European Convention is constructed. For in alerting Parliament to the possibility of any inconsistencies with the Convention in legislation before it, the scrutiny committee would provide the stimulus for an enlightened discussion, within and without Parliament, of the relevant human rights issues, with the result that these rights would be better appreciated and protected.

---

38   *Ibid*, paras 1.8 & 2.15.
39   HC Deb. Vol.89, cols 792–869 (13 Jan. 1986); see also, ATH Smith, *Offences Against Public Order* (1987), pp 10–11.
40   For further consideration of international examples of pre-legislative scrutiny (including the Canadian system), see Chapter 5, *infra*.
41   Mr Donald Maurais, correspondence with the author. See also EA Driedger, "The Meaning and Effect of the Canadian Bill of Rights: A Draftsman's Viewpoint" (1977) 9 Ottawa L Rev. 303, at p.311.

PART II

LEGISLATION: PASSING BY PARLIAMENT?

There is hardly any part of our national life or of our personal lives that is not affected by one statute or another. The affairs of local authorities, nationalised industries, public corporations and private commerce are regulated by legislation. The life of the ordinary citizen is affected by various provisions of the statute book from the cradle to grave. His birth is registered, his infant welfare protected, his education provided, his employment governed, his income and capital taxed, much of his conduct controlled and his old age sustained according to the terms of one statute or another. Many might think that as a nation we groan under this overpowering burden of legislation and ardently desire to have fewer rather than more laws. Yet the pressure for ever more legislation on behalf of different interests increases as society becomes more complex and people more demanding of each other. With each change in society there comes a demand for legislation to overcome the tensions which that change creates, even though the change itself may have been caused by legislation, which thus becomes self-proliferating.[42]

This was how the Renton Committee viewed what it called the "mass of legislation" in the United Kingdom in 1975. The predictions it made with respect to the further growth of legislation continue to be borne out. The omnipresence of legislative provisions has been reached on the strength not only of primary (i.e. "parliamentary") legislation, but also, and increasingly, by way of secondary (or "executive") legislation. The extraordinary growth of the latter in particular has contributed enormously to the aggrandizement of legislation.

In respect of both types, however, it is clear that the scope of legislation is broad and the issues it deals with complex. It is in this context, therefore, that we must consider the role and influence of Parliament in the process of the enactment of legislation in respect, in particular, of the opportunities for its scrutiny of the legislative proposals laid before it. Within the parameters of this book the fulfilment of these opportunities refers only to the object of ensuring that legislation made either directly by Parliament or by an authority to which it has delegated legislative powers, complies with the provisions of the European Convention on Human Rights. It is to an exploration of this proposal that the subsequent chapters are in the most part devoted. The sole concern of this section, however, is with the subject of legislation itself, its origins, formulation, and scrutiny. A prerequisite

---

[42]   Report of the Renton Committee, *supra*, n.11, para.7.3.

knowledge of the nature of legislation, including (very generally) the mechanics of its actual creation, is made all the more necessary within this book if it is accepted that any scrutinizing scheme would be most effectively applied either immediately before, or during the initial stages of the legislative process. Before approaching the matter of how best to adapt the legislative process so as to achieve the present objective one must first look at what constitutes that process.

The enactment of legislation, it is to be presumed, lies in the preserve of the legislature. And, in fact, in the strictly formal sense of the requirement that legislation does not gain legitimacy until it has been passed or endorsed by the legislature (or its delegates), Parliament clearly plays the principal role in the legislative process in the United Kingdom. But this involvement of Parliament by no means constitutes the full scope of the legislative process. Parliament's authority, it is argued, is exercised at a level of no more than the superficial scrutiny and validation of legislation which in all essential respects is already complete.[43] It is claimed that "today's conventional wisdom is ... that Parliament has relinquished any capacity for legislative initiative it may once have possessed to the executive in its midst".[44] It is considered, furthermore, that "[l]egislation is now an almost exclusively executive function",[45] where the Government dominates the legislative timetable, and where nearly all public bills (and invariably any of significance) are government-sponsored or supported. The organization and ranking of government bills performed by the Cabinet's Legislation Committee effectively determines which bills are to occupy Parliament's time in any session, and, where the Government is supported by anything more than the barest of majorities, determines which of those are to become law.[46] Even the success of the occasional non-executive (that is, from the Opposition or the backbenches) sponsored legislation[47] must be qualified by recognizing that without government support, or at the very least neutrality, none of these bills would have any chance of survival. What is more, government support is often secured only at the cost of bills being completely restructured, with the effect that it is "little exaggeration to say that ... [they] ... are really a special sub-species of government legislation".[48] The Executive, it is clear, provides the main impetus for the enactment of legislation, a role which is today not merely accepted but expected.

Policy formation remains, as indeed it must, the prerogative of the Executive. The point of contention, therefore, is how can the exercise of this prerogative and the implementation of the resultant strategies be supervised

---

43   See Harden & Lewis, *supra*, n.14, p.103; also, G Drewry, "Legislation" in MT Ryle & PG Richards (eds), *The Commons Under Scrutiny* (1988), p.126, and JAG Griffith, "The Place of Parliament in the Legislative Process" (1951) 14 MLR 279

44   G Drewry, "Legislation" in MT Ryle & SA Walkland (eds), *The Commons Today* (1981), p.91.

45   SA Walkland, *The Legislative Process in Great Britain* (1968), p.20.

46   For evidence of the overwhelming success of government-sponsored legislation, see G Drewry, *supra*, n.43, p.133.

47   See G Drewry, *supra*, n.44, pp 96 & 113; see also his table on the size of private members' Acts relative to those of the Government, p.98, and also *supra*, n.43, pp 137-8. For a survey of the parliamentary time spent on government and non-government bills, see the *Second Report of the Select Committee on Procedure*, HC 350 (1986-7), Table 1, p.xxxiii.

48   G Drewry, *supra*, n.43, p.135.

and checked in accordance with the demands of a system of responsible government in a parliamentary democracy. If Parliament is not to legislate, then it must legitimate, but in order to do so effectively it must have the opportunity as well as the information to intervene. How, when, and to what extent this should occur in respect of legislation generally as well as that specifically affecting rights protected by the European Convention, are all questions that can only be answered once it is established what is the current influence of Parliament in these respects.

The influence of Parliament[49]

1 Primary legislation

Any attempt to assess the impact that Parliament has on the legislative process[50] must begin with an examination of how the process itself is regulated. As already indicated, the introduction of legislation and its passage through Parliament are clearly activities dominated by the Government. In so far as the Standing Orders of the House of Commons lay down formal provisions for consideration of legislative proposals by the House, these are arranged so as to give precedence to government business.[51] In addition, the Government possesses the power to dictate the length of time that Parliament spends on any bill, and, thereby, the quality of scrutiny to which it is made subject. Allocation of time orders (or "guillotine" motions) are used to limit the amount of time that is to be spent on any stages of a bill.[52] Bills made subject to a guillotine motion are often passed with many clauses not considered at all, often in the case of the most controversial legislation. Use of the motion has risen sharply over the last two decades, and where it was once seen as a wholly exceptional measure it is now considered the "normal" method for ensuring the passage of an important bill if any degree of opposition to it is detected.[53]

The two crucial stages of a bill's passage where an exhibition of this government strength, if required at all, is likely to be employed are at second reading and during committal. Successful completion of a bill's second reading all but guarantees its enactment – at least in respect of its basic principle, if not the minutiae of its elaboration. In committee a government's majority (either proportionally reflected in the membership of a standing

49 The widespread concern over Parliament's waning authority led directly to the establishment in 1979 of a whole new range of Departmental Select Committees. Whilst it is recognized that this development has had some effect on the general process of parliamentary scrutiny I do not herein consider this consequence except where it is of specific relevance.

50 For thorough analyses, see DR Miers & AC Page, *Legislation* (1990, 2nd edn) pp 68–97; Erskine May, *Parliamentary Practice*, CJ Boulton (ed), (1989, 21st edn), pp 461–519; and M Zander, *The Law–Making Process* (1985, 2nd edn), pp 45–49.

51 HC S.O. No.13(1). Ten days per session are allocated for consideration of Private Members' Bills (HC S.O. No.13(4) & (7)); and, a total of only twenty days per session are allocated to the opposition parties (HC S.O. No.13(2))

52 See generally, Erskine May (1989, 21st edn), *supra*, n.50, pp 409–15. The less controversial but more commonly adopted closure motion is also available, see *ibid*, pp 405–9.

53 P Silk, *How Parliament Works* (1987), p.140; note the overwhelming support amongst MPs that the motion appears to enjoy in the results of a 1985 survey quoted by Silk on p.141.

committee, or *in toto* if the bill is being considered in a committee of the whole House) has the predictable effect of facilitating a high proportion of government initiated amendments to be carried, and a correspondingly low proportion of opposition amendments being accepted. This is in spite of the fact that almost three times as many amendments are moved by the Opposition as by Government.[54] Still, as "proceedings in committee ... certainly absorb most of [parliamentary] time spent on legislation",[55] it can be fairly claimed that in terms of influencing the shape of a bill the committee stage provides the most effective opportunity, with the second reading stage being little more than a primer for the business of the committee.[56]

On the face of it, therefore, government's exercise of its prerogative to govern is little impeded – indeed it is amply supported by – the rules and conventions of the legislative procedure. But these formal steps in the legislative process belie a whole network of informal agreements, understandings and conventions. Colloquially referred to as the "usual channels", these private and informal lines of communication are at least as important to the effective operation of all parliamentary functions, including that of legislation-making, as those which are public and formal. In short, the "usual channels" refer to the working relationship between the whips and the business managers of the main political parties. It is a system of compromises, designed to ensure that normally there will exist a common understanding between the parties as to how the legislative process will be conducted, what proposals will be considered, and when and for how long that consideration will take place. Disruptive and delaying tactics, therefore, are employed by the Opposition only when it is unable to pursue its objectives satisfactorily through the "usual channels". Similarly, the Government will often resort to such vigorous tactics as the moving of closure or guillotine motions only when it has failed to secure agreement through the "usual channels".[57] It should be noted in passing, however, that it is a curious paradox that when a guillotine motion is in operation, the quality of debate (if not its length) is often enhanced as the limited time available impresses upon both the Government and the Opposition the need to be concise and to the point.[58]

Although government has pre-emptive control over the introduction of legislative proposals into Parliament, as well as control over the time to be allotted to each proposal, it has been argued that in practice the Opposition and groups of private members are frequently instrumental in the actual determination of these questions. This is particularly so in respect of the time spent debating a certain issue, or a certain aspect of an issue. Quite apart from the days set aside for use by the opposition parties, Erskine May concludes that "the manner in which [items of business] are debated and the

---

54   JAG Griffith, *Parliamentary Scrutiny of the Government Bills* (1974), Table 3.8, p.93 (the sessions monitored were those between 1967–71).
55   JAG Griffith & MT Ryle, *Parliament* (1989), p.231.
56   See Griffith, *supra*, n.54, p.30.
57   Indeed, as Griffith has pointed out, party leaders and Chief Whips "take great personal pride in getting difficult bills through without a guillotine and feel correspondingly disappointed when they have to resort to one," *supra*, n.54, p.21. Note, however, that it is unusual for guillotine motions to be agreed to through the "usual channels".
58   *Ibid*, p.22.

time taken to complete the necessary proceedings are to a large extent influenced by the actions of the opposition".[59] Instances illustrating this include the large number of amendments moved by the Opposition in committee which effectively determine not only what will be considered, but what will be excluded from consideration, even if such amendments are seldom adopted. Similarly, the issues concentrated on during second reading are usually chosen by those who wish to raise their objections to them. It has been remarked that "[i]n a sense all Government time is equally opposition time, and the opposition's use of multifarious opportunities available to it for influencing the way in which the proceedings of the House in Government time are conducted is thus of the first importance in the distribution of time available for business in any session".[60]

There can be little doubt that these opportunities to influence debate exist and, if used carefully, that they make a valuable contribution to the process of legislative scrutiny. In the specific instance of scrutiny for conformity to the European Convention on Human Rights, it is considered that should an appropriate scrutiny scheme be introduced, not only would these opportunities be increased in number but the influence thereby exerted would be greatly enhanced. The overarching qualification clearly remains, however, that such opportunities – either as they presently stand or subsequent to the introduction of the suggested scheme – will never of itself provide the Opposition with the power of veto. For if the Opposition's objections to any fundamental aspects of a bill are not successfully countered by the imposition of procedural limitations on time available for scrutiny, then the conclusive authority of a government majority will almost certainly provide the means to do so. As almost invariably a bill, or at any rate its principal element, is presented to Parliament as a *fait accompli*, the Opposition is left thereby with perhaps plenty of opportunities to register its disapproval, but with little hope of seeing its complaints acted upon. What is more, this problem is accentuated when the legislative proposal at issue is highly controversial. In this event, should the Government be determined, the fate of the Opposition's resistance to the bill is effectively sealed before it has started, leaving open to the Opposition the sole course of obstinately obstructing the bill in its passage through Parliament.[61] When this path is taken the resulting recalcitrance on both sides ensures that nearly all hope of any effective scrutiny is lost. Both the Government and the Opposition unfortunately force themselves and each other into a position where "rational and systematic consideration of and the reflection upon the principles and details of proposed measures may be subordinated to essentially political considerations".[62] The potential for such destructive intransigence over controversial legislation cannot be easily removed from an essentially bipartisan parliamentary system. It might, however, be mollified. It can be justly argued that a conspicuous benefit of the institution of a pre-legislative scrutiny scheme based on the European Convention would be that

---

[59]   Erskine May, *Parliamentary Practice* Sir Charles Gordon (ed) (1983, 20th edn), p.303.
[60]   *Ibid*, p.304.
[61]   See the Memorandum submitted by the Study of Parliament Group to the Select Committee on Procedure, HC 49–IV (1984–5), p.72.
[62]   Miers & Page, *supra*, n.50, p.77. This was the position, for example, with the Industrial Relations Act 1971, and more recently the Local Government Act 1985.

where contentious 'legislative provisions had some bearing on Convention-protected rights, parliamentary consideration of these aspects of the bill would be less likely divided according to party political sympathies. Information and comment provided by a parliamentary committee such as the one here advocated might be considered more objectively by members both of the Government and the Opposition. Reports of the scrutiny committee, therefore, might possess the potential in certain instances to mitigate the disabling polarization of debate in Parliament over particularly controversial legislative proposals.[63]

2   Secondary legislation

Secondary, or delegated, legislation can be viewed as the result of striking a constitutional bargain;[64] that is, in return for approving only the principle of a legislative proposal, and leaving to the Executive's discretion the details of its implementation, Parliament is relieved of the time-consuming duty of examining the minutiae of these administrative issues.

The category is comprised principally of statutory instruments, a body which through the broadly drafted provision of s.1 of the Statutory Instruments Act 1947 includes all Orders in Council and regulations made under legislative authority. In respect to the last mentioned, however, there has developed a growing class of administrative rules ("quasi-legislation") which do not fall within the definition of statutory instrument. The peculiar nature of quasi-legislation receives separate discussion below.

Over 2200 Statutory Instruments are brought into effect each year, affecting an enormous range of issues. The extended and increasing[65] use of delegated legislation has generally been accepted as being inevitable; the focus of concern, therefore, has shifted from the quantity to the substance of Statutory Instruments. In theory, the division between policy or principle and the detail of its implementation is coterminous with that which separates primary from secondary legislation. In practice, however, the dividing line is notoriously difficult to determine with any degree of precision. The problem of "where 'detail' ends and 'principle' begins remains unresolved and [is] probably unresolvable".[66] Here then we have the grounds for that perennial dilemma for delegated legislation. The acknowledged necessity of secondary legislation coupled with the attractive practical advantages of speed, flexibility and adaptability lead inexorably to conflict over the proper boundaries by which its use ought to be restricted. Increasingly, there is concern over the extent to which the authority to determine issues of principle is being delegated to the Executive.[67] The prevalence of this

---

63 See Chapter 7, infra, p.139.
64 TSt.JN Bates, "Scrutiny of Administration" in *The Commons Under Scrutiny, supra*, n.43, p.200.
65 On the simple comparative analysis of numbers of pages of Statutory Instruments in relation to those of the statute books, in 1935 there existed almost parity, by 1975 – though both figures had increased dramatically – pages of Statutory Instruments now outnumbered those of statutes by a ratio of 3:1, and by 1987 this had risen to more than 4:1. These are conservative estimates as the figures for statutes do not include the often significant number of pages devoted to consolidation statutes.
66 G Drewry, *supra*, n.43, p.139. See also, *Report of the Committee on Ministers' Powers*, Cmd 4060 (1932), p.19, and PS Atiyah, *Law and Modern Society* (1983), p.125.
67 See, for example, the extensive power granted to the Secretary of State for the Environment to set rates limits under s.4 of the Rates Act 1984.

practice of wide delegation is due largely to the fact that it clearly suits the Executive to press for broad discretionary powers when an enabling statute is before Parliament. This ploy, it has been noted before the Select Committee on Procedure, is especially worrying as ministers sponsoring a bill "very often ... do not know themselves quite what use they intend to make of the powers".[68] Later in the same submission of evidence to the Committee the same witness proclaimed that "there are a great many cases in which the principle is not stated in the Bill; all that is stated in the Bill is that this shall be whatever the minister says in the Statutory Instrument".[69] Furthermore, there is little Parliament can do to alter or control this potential for executive legislation when faced with the potent combination of a strong government majority in Parliament, a long and complex legislative programme, and a limitation on the time available for scrutiny.

Although the level of parliamentary scrutiny of delegated legislation is determined ultimately by the enabling Act, considerable latitude is allowed the Executive during the drafting procedures of delegated legislation. Unlike primary legislation, which receives the attention of the Parliamentary Counsel, secondary legislation is drafted, almost exclusively, within the relevant Government Department.[70] A Minister's own departmental lawyers are clearly held on a much tighter rein when issued with drafting instructions for Statutory Instruments than are the staff of the more independent and centralized Parliamentary Counsel.

In addition to the system of drafting, the validation procedure for secondary legislation (that is, Statutory Instruments) has few of the techniques of scrutiny that exist for primary legislation. There are, in fact two procedures, known as affirmative and negative.[71] The former requires the positive consent of both Houses (or only the Commons, should the parent Act so direct), and this option (in theory at least) is usually reserved for the most important or controversial instruments.[72] Additionally, the Government is obliged to find time for the consideration of instruments subject to affirmative resolution. On account of this obligation, the less stringent negative procedure for secondary legislation is increasingly preferred by governments, with the result that relatively few affirmative motions are made and fall to be considered by Parliament. Consistently fewer than 17% of all Statutory Instruments laid before Parliament are subject to the affirmative procedure.[73] The negative procedure, on the other hand, permits all instruments made under it to obtain the force of law unless there is tabled a motion for annulment (a "prayer") within forty days of the instrument being laid. However, few prayers are even discussed in Parliament, let alone achieve their objective.[74]

[68] Mr Henry Knorpel, Speaker's Counsel, in *Minutes of Evidence submitted to the Select Committee on Procedure*, HC 350 (1986-7), p.9.
[69] *Ibid.* The Social Security Bill 1985, and the Education Bill 1986-7 were cited as examples of this practice. And indeed, when the latter was enacted in 1988 it contained a provision empowering the Minister to amend the Act itself, ss 232(5) & 236(8) & (9).
[70] TSt.JN Bates, *supra*, n.64, p.201, and Atiyah, *supra*, n.66, p.130.
[71] A small number of "general instruments" need only be laid before Parliament, no further action being necessary.
[72] For example, the annual renewals of the Prevention of Terrorism Acts between 1976-1989.
[73] Based on a table compiled by Paul Silk, *supra*, n.53, p.151
[74] The Government is under no obligation to find time for any of the large numbers of

Once the decision has been taken – and incorporated in the enabling Act – as to which procedure is to be adopted, instruments subject to either are first laid before Parliament and then pass through a two-tiered system of examination. First, the "technical" aspects of a Statutory Instrument are scrutinized by the Joint Committee on Statutory Instruments, or, where appropriate, by the Commons Select Committee on Statutory Instruments.[75] Both committees are required to determine whether a particular instrument should be brought to the special attention of the House, according to certain criteria. Presently, there are nine stipulated grounds upon which any instrument may be so referred. These include: if the instrument purports to exclude challenge by the courts; if it purports to have retrospective effect; if it appears not to be *intra vires* the parent Act; and other lesser conditions of delay, or inconclusive drafting.[76] Should it be considered necessary, as a consequence of this scrutiny, either committee may report to the appropriate House that the instrument be accorded its special attention. The fact that such reports are seldom made[77] is a reflection of the considerable and largely successful efforts of the committees (in reality, their assisting counsel) through the responsible departments to reconcile the demands of the Standing Order with the objects of the instrument (even, exceptionally, if this means the withdrawal of the instrument)[78] *before* the need arises to report to the relevant House. The significance of this point is enhanced in view of the fact that when a committee is pressed to report to the House in this way there is no procedural guarantee that its conclusions will be debated or recognized, even, that is, when *vires* is in doubt.

Usually after one or other of the scrutiny committees has reported, the merits of the Statutory Instrument are considered either by the House, or by a standing committee. The overwhelming majority of "negative" instruments, however, receive no such parliamentary attention, and even those that do are subject to stringent limitations if debated on the floor of the House; instruments requiring the affirmative resolution are normally limited to a 1½ hour debate, initiated, usually, late at night. Those few instruments subject to annulment which are granted a debate are nearly always completed before 11:30 p.m.[79]

prayers tabled each session. In the eight sessions between 1974/5 and 1982/3, only 134 hours were spent debating negative motions when the number of Statutory Instruments subject to the negative procedure for that period was 6990, *ibid*, p.152.

75   Though the latter is a separate committee its membership consists of the same MPs as sit on the Joint Committee. The Joint Committee, which is the busier of the two, is composed of seven members from each House; it is chaired by an MP, and is assisted by senior counsel from each House (the Speaker's Counsel from the Commons, and Counsel to the Lord Chairman of Committees from the Lords); see further, Chapter 6, *infra*, pp 160-1.

76   See HC S.O. No.124. Note, however, the "catch-all" criterion: "... or on any other ground which does not impinge on its merits or on the policy behind it".

77   TSt.JN Bates, *supra*, n.64, p.202, has calculated that only 2% of instruments are so reported.

78   P Silk has calculated that in the three sessions 1980-3, 11 instruments were withdrawn, prior to the Committee's report being made, *supra*, n.53, p.154. It appears that withdrawals and relaying of instruments on the basis largely of drafting difficulties is a more common occurrence, *Record of Proceedings of the Third Commonwealth Conference on Delegated Legislation* (1989), p.6 (*per* Mr Bob Cryer MP).

79   Increasingly, however, where time is short and the subject is considered to be too narrow or technical, affirmative instruments before the Commons, in particular, are increasingly referred to a standing (or "merits") committee.

The twin disadvantages of the inconvenient time of day at which the debates are conducted and the severely limited time that is available are compounded by the inability to amend Statutory Instruments during the parliamentary debate on their merits – the question is put on a take it or leave it basis. This has the result that many Statutory Instruments possessing a number of provisions acceptable to the majority of MPs, but also some that are extremely contentious, present members with an uncomfortable dilemma. More often than not, in this event, the entire instrument – "warts and all" – becomes law.[80]

The detrimental effect of these restrictions is of even greater significance given the increased use of delegated authority not only in a purely quantitative sense but also qualitatively, where issues of policy are now not uncommonly decided at this level. Yet for as long as the assertion that delegated legislation "is conceptualized by most parliamentarians as being the government's rather than Parliament's business"[81] remains accurate, these restrictions are unlikely to be eased.

3   Quasi-legislation

Since 1944 it has been recognized that there exists a third tier of "legislation" known – since Robert Megarry adopted the term – as "quasi-legislation".[82] It is a term used to denote that amorphous area between formal, judicially recognized "law", and pure administrative direction or guidance with no legal base. So far, the delineation of this category is far from complete, partly because of the enormity of the field it covers and partly because of its inherent ambiguity. Something that claims to incorporate "laws–which–are–not–laws" necessarily provides grounds for confusion as well as concern. The fundamental problem – as Ganz, in one of the very few works of any substance on the subject, points out – is that "the line between law and quasi-legislation [is] blurred because there are degrees of legal force and many ... rules ... do have some legal effect".[83] Even the procedural division that most readily jumps to mind – namely, that it comprises all legislation that has some legal authority but which is not implemented by way of an Act of Parliament or Statutory Instrument – is inappropriate. "A legally binding provision may be contained in a circular," it has been noted, "whilst a code of practice may be embodied in a Statutory Instrument."[84]

The unsupervised nature of quasi-legislation permits a huge diversity of forms to exist, from statutorily provided codes of practice, including directives merely referred to (that is, not detailed in delegated legislation),[85] through departmental circulars, to codes of conduct and ethics.[86] Not

[80]   The Select Committee on Procedure, however, has recommended that amendments to Statutory Instruments should be permitted. *Second Report (together with the Minutes of Evidence) from the Select Committee on Procedure*, HC 350 (1986–7).
[81]   P Byrne, "Parliamentary Control of Delegated Legislation", Parliamentary Affairs, 29 (1976) 366, 375.
[82]   "Administrative Quasi-legislation" (1944) 60 LQR 125.
[83]   Gabriele Ganz, *Quasi-Legislation: Recent Developments in Secondary Legislation* (1987), p.1.
[84]   *Ibid.*
[85]   *R v Secretary of State for Social Services, ex parte Camden LBC* [1987] 1 WLR 819; see further, AIL Campbell, "Statutory Instruments – Laying and Legislation by Reference" [1987] PL 328.
[86]   See R Baldwin & J Houghton, "Circular Arguments: The Status and Legitimacy of

surprisingly, therefore, there is a corresponding diversity in the levels of legal authority that are considered to inhere in these various forms.[87] Furthermore, whilst such rules, of course, may be declared by the courts to be *ultra vires*,[88] it appears less certain whether such a conclusion might be based on the notion of reasonableness.[89]

In many respects the *raison d'être* of quasi-legislation is similar to that pleaded for Statutory Instruments – namely, speed of implementation; flexibility, but with the addition of widespread use of non-technical language (in particular, non-legal jargon); and unification of existing codes or practices. What is distinctive, perhaps, about quasi-legislation is that one of its principal aims is to obtain order and compliance through persuasion rather than compulsion. This consensus, or voluntary approach, is nearly always cited as a main reason for adopting quasi-legislation; indeed, more often than not, consensus is an absolute precondition to the effectiveness of such administrative ordinances. Proof of the rule is provided by the exceptions to it. Thus the strongly opposed Code of Practice on Picketing introduced under the Employment Act 1980 was repeatedly flouted during the 1984-5 miners' strike and had eventually to be dispensed with and a statutory provision introduced in its stead.[90] The establishment of a set of quasi-legislative rules is often the result of a compromise bargained for during the parent bill's parliamentary passage, between the imposition of a statutory obligation and leaving the position as it is.[91]

In this event the importance of the concessions made by the Government are qualified in (at least) three different respects. First, as we have already established, the degree to which quasi-legislation can be enforced in the courts is a far from settled matter. Second, though the minister responsible for piloting a bill through Parliament may be forced to agree to a code, for example, it nevertheless falls to the Minister and his or her department to decide the details of its contents. Third, the public availability of the code or rules may be so restricted as effectively to exclude those interests the rules are intended to affect. With respect to the publication of quasi-law, it has been observed that "[i]t would be impossible to devise a more bizarre and haphazard system than the one which has grown up from a maze of

---

Administrative Rules" [1986] PL, 240-45 for an indication as to their variety.

87   For an account of the incoherent body of judicial pronouncements on the legal status of quasi-legislation, see Baldwin & Houghton, *ibid*, pp 245-67. Indeed, in respect of the Immigration Rules alone, there exist a number of opposing judicial interpretations as to their legal authority; see, IA Macdonald, *Immigration Law and Practice* (1987, 2nd edn), pp 25-31.

88   *R v Waverney DC, ex parte Bowers* [1982] 3 WLR 661; see also, *R v Chief Immigration Officer, Gatwick Airport, ex parte Kharazzi* [1980] 1 WLR 1396, 1402.

89   For a general account of this issue, see Baldwin & Houghton, *supra*, n.86, pp 252-60 and K Puttick, *Challenging Delegated Legislation*, (1987), pp 235-43. Compare the limiting interpretation in this respect of the House of Lords in *Gillick v West Norfolk & Wisbech Area Health Authority* [1986] AC 112, at 192 (*per* Lord Bridge), with the more expansive approach of the Privy Council in *Attorney-General of Hong Kong v Ng Yuen Shiu* [1983] 2 AC 629, 638 and the Court of Appeal in *R v Secretary of State for the Home Dept, ex parte Khan* [1984] 1 WLR 1337, 1347 (*per* Parker LJ).

90   The Public Order Act 1986, s.14, provides the police with the power to limit the size of public assemblies, of which picketing is an example. Another instance is provided by the Prime Minister's unilateral decision to disallow trade union membership at GCHQ under authority of Article 4 of the Civil Service Order in Council 1982.

91   Ganz, *supra*, n.83, p.105. Ganz provides a long list of notable examples where this has happened.

individual provisions with very little attempt at consistency or systemisation".[92] In some cases they are published by HMSO and so are readily available,[93] but in others they are published only by the relevant department (which can severely restrict access),[94] and with some they are not published at all.[95]

The existence of these factors raises serious doubts over the impact of extra-departmental scrutiny, parliamentary or otherwise, to which quasi-law is subject. "Parliament's influence on many areas of quasi-legislative activity", according to one commentator, "is virtually non-existent."[96] Codes of practice, for instance, receive no formal parliamentary consideration. The Departmental Select Committees are provided with some opportunities for scrutiny of proposed codes and circulars at their formative stages, but only on the initiation of the Department. In any case, they have power only to advise and suggest and not to compel changes. Indeed, much of the supervision of the drafting and subsequent implementation of quasi-legislation is administered by extra-parliamentary bodies.[97] But in many cases there is not even any external supervision of this kind.

The paucity of parliamentary scrutiny in respect of quasi-legislation has important consequences. The compliance of a significant number of examples of quasi-legislation with the European Convention on Human Rights has been questioned before the European authorities, including codes of practice made under the Police and Criminal Evidence Act 1984; mental health codes; immigration rules; circulars and standing orders made under the Prison Rules; and the code of practice on access to children in care made under the Health and Social Services and Social Security Adjudications Act 1983. All of these examples are discussed at length in Chapters Three and Four, below. The profusion of quasi-legislation alone ought to be sufficient to necessitate the implementation of improvements in the system of parliamentary control, and the fact that some have been proved to have been contrary to certain basic human rights can only add significantly to the strength of this argument.

It has been suggested that these improvements might be achieved by way of a combination of means, the most significant of which in the present context is the argument for extending the terms of reference of the Joint Committee on Statutory Instruments with respect to non-statutory instruments beyond the current limitations stipulated in House of Commons Standing Order 124.[98] This would have the conspicuous advantage of

---

[92] *Ibid*, p.36.

[93] For example, the Highway Code; Equal Opportunities Codes; and Health and Safety at Work Codes.

[94] For example, the codes under the Employment Act 1980; and those few Home Office Circulars that are published.

[95] For example, the Standing Orders and Circulars under the Prison Rules - a matter which has led in part to repeated adverse rulings from the European Court (see Chapter 4, *infra*, pp 67-82); and the majority of Home Office Circulars. See also Ganz, *supra*, n.83, p.39, and further, *Record of Proceedings of the Third Commonwealth Conference on Delegated Legislation*, *supra*, n.78, p.24.

[96] G Drewry, *supra*, n.43, p.121.

[97] For example, the Council on Tribunals; the Gas and Electricity Councils; the Commission for Racial Equality; the Equal Opportunities Commission; the Countryside Commission; and the Monopolies and Mergers Commission.

[98] Ganz, *supra*, n.83, p.107; see also, *Record of the Proceedings of the Third Commonwealth*

providing a basis for incorporating quasi-legislation into the system of pre-legislative scrutiny proposed later in Chapter Eight, since it is by the extension of the terms of reference of the Joint Committee on Statutory Instruments that I seek to achieve the enhanced parliamentary scrutiny of all secondary legislation for compliance with the European Convention. It must be conceded, however, that any development in this regard is likely to encounter many difficulties. The quantity and variety of administrative rules and regulations, if such a body can be satisfactorily determined (itself an extremely complex exercise), would place enormous strain on the already limited resources devoted to the parliamentary scrutiny of secondary legislation. An understanding of the nature of the whole problem of the supervision of quasi-legislation (both in respect of its creation and implementation) is only beginning to be developed; unsurprisingly, therefore, how best to address it – even in respect of the limited concerns of this book – remains to some extent a matter of supposition.

Conclusion

It is clear that Parliament is not responsible for the Acts to which it lends its name – certainly not, that is, with respect to their conception and formulation, now the preserves of government – and contributes little in the way of scrutiny. Still less effective is its involvement in the making of subordinate legislation, and with many areas of quasi-legislation even a nominal role in supervision is absent.

The sheer size and diversity of modern legislative programmes and the consequent pressure that puts on the time available have undoubtedly played a significant part in creating this position. In response, alternative modes of assessment and examination have been developed. New or revitalized systems of both select and standing committees are increasingly shouldering the burden of scrutiny as a sustained effort is made to try to make more time available on the floor of the House. Also, it is argued, there has been a massive increase in negotiation and consultation with outside interest groups at the policy stage of legislative initiatives,[99] and although the opportunities to influence thereby afforded are considerable, they ultimately rely on the benevolence of the Government. Moreover, the courts appear unwilling to compel government departments to consult affected interests, to the extent that they will accept a plea of inconvenience from the Department as sufficient reason not to consult.[100]

As the efficacy of scrutiny of primary, secondary, and quasi-legislation is questionable, so, *a fortiori*, pre-legislative examination designed specifically to ensure compliance with the European Convention on Human Rights is thoroughly inadequate. In this case, having established the basis of the problem of Parliament's ability to call the Government to account in respect

---

Conference on Delegated Legislation, supra, n.78, p.23. Ganz's other suggestions include an attempt to impose consistency and order on all forms of quasi-legislation by issuing a code of practice to regulate codes of practice, *supra*, n.83, p.107, and a statutory requirement for the publication by HMSO of all quasi-legislation affecting the public, *ibid*, p.41.

99   See Miers & Page, *supra*, n.50, pp 136-7, and Puttick, *supra*, n.89, Chapter 8.

100 *R v Secretary of State for Social Services, ex parte Association of Metropolitan Authorities* [1986] 1 WLR 1.

of legislation as a whole, we are now in a position to address the particular problem of legislative compliance with the European Convention.

3 INFRINGEMENT OF THE EUROPEAN CONVENTION BY PRIMARY LEGISLATION

Parliament left to its own devices has proved singularly inept in detecting possible breaches of the European Convention in bills laid before it. In this chapter there is detailed the most prominent examples of statutes which have contained provisions subsequently found to be incompatible with the European Convention.[1] In most cases these accounts are relatively brief, but considerably more attention has been devoted to some examples – especially the former legislation on homosexuality in Northern Ireland, and the succession of Prevention of Terrorism (Temporary Provisions) Acts since 1974. These examples have been emphasized for two closely related reasons. Both are issues which are especially controversial and have excited much interest and argument not only within Westminster but also throughout influential and well-informed extra-parliamentary circles – notably the media; academics; civil rights organizations; and occasionally the wider audience of the general public. At the time when Parliament was considering each of these legislative proposals there existed an extensive array of informed opinion upon which it could have drawn. It might have been supposed, in this case, that both the Government and Parliament would have been sufficiently acquainted with all the relevant issues, including the demands of the European Convention, and have conducted its deliberations accordingly. In common with the other examples considered, however, this was not the case with the legislation governing either homosexuality or the prevention of terrorism. The lamentable conclusion, therefore, is drawn that if the pertinence of the rights enshrined in the European Convention is not

---

1   For a complete list of all transgressions involving both primary and secondary legislation see Appendix 1, *infra.*

adequately appreciated either by government or the legislature in respect of issues of such prominence, what comfort is to be had with respect to ensuring compliance with the Convention of the vast majority of statutes which fail to attract the same intensity of interest?

The justification for the disparity in treatment between the instances chosen for discussion in this chapter might be summarized in one sentence. Whereas the purpose of the shorter recitals of legislative transgression of the Convention is largely illustrative of the breadth of the problem, that of the more detailed accounts of the other issues is demonstrative of its depth. It is maintained that this combination provides crucial support for the weight of argument for a change in the present system of legislative scrutiny.

Trade union legislation on "closed shops"

The provisions regarding a union membership agreement (or "closed shop") in s.30, together with Schedule 1 para.6(5), of the Trade Union and Labour Relations Act 1974 permitted an employer to dismiss an employee (by virtue of s.24) if they refused to join a trade union on grounds other than those of religion. When brought before the European Court of Human Rights in the case of *Young, James and Webster*[2] these provisions were considered to be in violation of the rights of the three applicants freely to join or abstain from joining trade unions under Article 11 (right to freedom of association) of the European Convention. The legislation was considered by the Court to be incapable of justification under the exception of its being "necessary in a democratic society", as provided by Article 11(2). Despite the fact that the cited sections, in particular, were strenuously debated in both Houses, the possibility that they might contravene the European Convention was not once raised.[3] Nor was any mention of the Convention made in relation to their provisions during the Bill's committee stage.[4] Yet had the relevant requirements of the Convention been explicitly recognized and conscientiously examined, then it is not unreasonable to assume that the dichotomous nature of the Article's guarantee that everyone has the "right to freedom of association ... and to join trade unions" would have been better appreciated. It should have been clear, as the European Court subsequently insisted in this case,[5] that the inclusion of the word "freedom" thereby grants to the individual the choice whether or not to exercise the right that follows it. Equally, therefore, irrespective of how politically unwelcome the result, it ought to have been reasonably clear that legislation effectively compelling one to exercise that right would be in violation of the implicit right to choose protected under the terms of the Article.

---

2   See *Young, James and Webster v United Kingdom*, ECHR Series 'A', No.44 (26 June 1981).

3   For example, see generally the two second readings: HC Deb. Vol.873, cols 228–338 (7 May 1974); and HL Deb. Vol.353, cols 1011–20, 1025–63, 1066–108, 1109–14, (16 July 1974). Not even when amendments to these clauses of the Bill concerning precisely this question of the legal protection given to closed shops were tabled was the Convention invoked: HC Deb. Vol.867, cols 1699–1716 (11 July 1974). Provisions in the Universal Declaration of Human Rights relevant to closed shops, however, were mentioned by Mr David Mitchel MP. Curiously, he did not corroborate his argument by referring also to the European Convention on Human Rights, despite the fact that the enforcement machinery of the latter is far superior; *ibid*, col.1708.

4   Minutes, Standing Committee E, cols 821–6 (27 June 1974); cols 941–961 (2 July 1974).

5   *Young et al, supra*, n.2, para.62.

In view of the Court's condemnation of the impugned legislation, how much more effective the parliamentary debate might have been had, prior to the event, advice and information of the pertinent conditions of the Convention been made readily available to Parliament. As it was, consequent on the European Court's decision, Parliament was forced to go through the undignified and wasteful process of amending something which through ignorance or indifference was initially passed by the legislature in contravention of the European Convention.[6] With the institution of an appropriate scrutiny procedure it is probable that such apparently straight-forward interpretative difficulties as these would be better understood, anticipated and prevented.

Legislation on corporal punishment

The European Court, in the *Tyrer* case, held ss 8 and 10 of the Summary Jurisdiction (Isle of Man) Act 1960, which allowed judicial corporal punishment (in this case birching), to be contrary to Article 3 of the Convention (protection from torture, inhuman or degrading treatment or punishment).[7]

Although legislation passed by the Manx legislature is not subjected to further debate in Westminster before becoming law – rather, it comes to the mainland only to receive Royal Assent from the Queen (on advice of the Privy Council) – questions on the proposed legislation may be raised in Parliament. However, on the single occasion that the provisions of this Bill were raised in Parliament, there was wanting any recognition of the significance for the Bill of the related guaranteed rights in the Convention.[8]

Despite the decision in the *Tyrer* case, the argument for introducing legislation in the United Kingdom for the administering of corporal punishment (especially for juvenile offenders) has never waned. Even subsequent to the *Tyrer* decision, when the issue has been addressed by Parliament it is not unusual for some members to exhibit a remarkable disdain for, and ignorance of, the provisions of the European Convention and the decisions of its adjudicative institutions. The subject was broached in Parliament during the (unsuccessful) attempt to add a new clause to the Criminal Justice Bill 1987, providing for the whipping of young offenders. The amendment's sponsor (Mr Warren Hawksley MP) seemed oblivious to the fact that as a signatory to the Convention, the United Kingdom is obliged, under Article 53, to abide by the decisions of the European Court no matter how disagreeable they may seem. Though Mr Hawksley wasted no words in illustrating his dislike for the United Kingdom's association with the Convention,[9] he did not insist that as a prerequisite to the adoption of his corporal punishment clause the United Kingdom should lodge an appropriate Notice of Derogation with the Council of Europe, or, indeed, withdraw its ratification of the European Convention. Many of those who supported the clause seemed to consider that as "some of the [European

---

6   Initially amended, when the *Young et al* case was still in progress, by the Employment Act 1980, s.7; more substantial amendments were made by the Employment Act 1982, s.3.

7   *Tyrer v United Kingdom*, ECHR Series 'A', No.26 (25 April 1978).

8   HC Deb. Vol.621, cols 844–54 (8 April 1960)

9   HC Deb. Vol.113, col.923 (31 March 1987).

Court's] decisions are most extraordinary" (the *Tyrer* case being singled out amongst them), then the United Kingdom need not abide by them.10

If it is the case that even those who energetically support changes in the law that are conspicuously contrary to a decision of the European Court are not conversant with the demands of the Convention, then it is unlikely that the general level of understanding throughout Parliament will be any better.11 It is not immoderate to suppose that simply by explicitly bringing Parliament's attention to provisions of the Convention relevant to legislative proposals before it, many such potential violations would be intercepted.

Child care legislation

In a collection of five cases concerning the taking into care of children by local authorities, the European Court found United Kingdom legislation inadequately fulfilled the demands of the European Convention.12 The central issue was that of parental access to children who had been taken into care. The Court held that certain elements of the governing legislation regarding this matter (and its corollary of processes of appeal, should access be denied) were in violation of Articles 6(1) and 8 of the Convention.13 The significance of the legislation in this example is that although the impugned provisions were contained in a statute enacted some years prior to the United Kingdom's ratification of the European Convention, in 1980 the Child Care Act, which consolidated all existing child care law, was passed by Parliament without debate.14 Clearly, neither Parliament nor the Government were aware of the potential therein for violation of the Convention. And yet barely a year after the enactment of the 1980 Act, the first of the five almost identical complaints concerning certain of the consolidated provisions was lodged with the European Commission.15

Article 8 enshrines the right to respect for family life and in the European Court's opinion this right was not sufficiently protected under s.2(1) of the Children Act 1948 (now replaced by s.3(1) of the Child Care Act 1980) under which the local authority can transfer parental rights and duties (including the "right of access") with regard to a child from the child's natural parents to the authority. The failing, in the Court's view, was that this section, by virtue of its broad scope, allowed the local authority a degree of discretion when deciding this issue, exercise of which had potentially serious adverse effects on relations between parents and children. The Court concluded in one case (which is representative of the judgments in all five) that this

10 *Ibid.*
11 At least it can be said with respect to this instance that the Government apparently recognized its obligations under the Convention and declined to support the clause; *ibid*, col.939.
12 *'O' v United Kingdom*, and *'H' v United Kingdom*, ECHR Series 'A', No.120 (8 July 1987); and *'W' v United Kingdom*, *'B' v United Kingdom*, and *'R' v United Kingdom*, ECHR Series 'A', No.121 (8 July 1987).
13 This was so in all cases except in *'O'* in which only Article 8 was held to have been violated, and in *'H'* Article 6(1) was violated by virtue of the delay in proceedings concerning access.
14 HC Deb. Vol.977, col.1289 (29 Jan. 1980). The Joint Committee on Consolidation Bills reported that the Bill was pure consolidation and added nothing new to the law; no further consideration of the Bill was held to be necessary. See the *Third Report of the Joint Committee on the Consolidation of Bills*, HC 256 (1979–80).
15 *'W' v United Kingdom*, Application 9749/82 (18 Jan. 1982).

provision was used by the local authority to exclude the applicant parent from its decision-making process, thereby denying him the "requisite ... protection of his interests" under Article 8.[16] As a result of this ruling the Government was obliged to issue a new code of practice under the Child Care Act 1980, stressing the importance of involving the child's natural parents in the local authority's determination of where parental rights should lie.[17]

Article 6(1), which entitles everyone to the right of having their civil rights determined in a hearing conducted before an independent tribunal within a reasonable time, was also held to be inadequately protected by domestic child care legislation. With respect to the transfer of parental rights (including that of access) to the local authority, the parents' right of challenge lies in an application for judicial review to the High Court as provided by s.4A of the Children Act 1948, as amended by s.58 of the Children Act 1975 (now replaced by s.6 of the Child Care Act 1980). In the Court's opinion the inability of the English courts under this procedure to review the "merits" of a local authority's decision[18] made it impossible for an applicant to have their rights properly determined in accordance with the requirements of Article 6(1).[19] The new code of practice, indicated above, now also provides parents whose access has been terminated with an opportunity to apply for an access order and have their application examined before a juvenile court, with an appeal, if necessary, to the Divisional Court.[20]

Though these alterations would appear now to bring United Kingdom child care legislation on this matter into line with the Convention, they, of course, came too late to prevent the infringement of Convention-protected rights suffered by these five applicants, and likely by many more in similar cases.[21]

Immigration legislation

Another serious legislative transgression of the Convention came to light after the European Commission received hundreds of applications from aggrieved East African Asians unable to gain admission into the United Kingdom after the enactment of the Commonwealth Immigrants Act 1968. What is remarkable about this case is that under the terms of the British Nationality Act 1948 all the applicants were citizens of the United Kingdom and Colonies. Under Article 3(2) of the Fourth Protocol to the European Convention on Human Rights admission to the country of which you are a national is guaranteed. The admission of the East African Asians could not have been refused, therefore, if the United Kingdom had ratified the Fourth Protocol, but as this was not (and remains not) the case, the applicants had

16 'W' v United Kingdom, supra, n.12, paras 68 & 70 (to be read in conjunction with para.38). The issues involved were much the same in all cases, so in order to avoid unnecessary duplication I shall give references only for the 'W' case.
17 Code of Practice on Access to Children in Care (Dec. 1983), para.6, issued under the provisions of s.12G of the Child Care Act 1980. Sub-ss 12A – 12G of the Act, which deal generally with the involvement of parents in the decision to make a care order, were introduced by the Health and Social Services and Social Security Act 1983, s.6, Schedule 1, Part 1, para.1.
18 For an account of the effect this has had, see D Hersham, "Access to Children in Care: Challenging the Local Authority" (1987) 17 FL, pp 399–404.
19 'W' v United Kingdom, ECHR, supra, n.12, paras 82–83.
20 Sub-ss 12B and 12C.
21 See A Holden, "Access and the Courts" (26.7.83) Vol.14, Social Work Today, No.44.

to rely on different provisions of the Convention in seeking relief.[22]

In a combined case of twenty-five applications, the Commission found certain provisions of the Act to be in violation of three Articles of the Convention.[23] After deciding that the legislation discriminated against the applicants, "on the grounds of their colour or race",[24] the Commission stated that it thereby "constitutes an interference with their [the applicants'] human dignity which ... amounted to 'degrading treatment' in the sense of Article 3 of the Convention".[25] The Commission also concluded that the refusal of admission to the applicants under the terms of the 1968 Act constituted "an interference with the applicants' 'family life' in the sense of Article 8 of the Convention in that it prevented, against their will, the reunion in the United Kingdom of the members of the applicants' families, who were all citizens of the United Kingdom and colonies".[26] It was further considered that this infringement was "contrary to Article 14 read in conjunction with Article 8 of the Convention, in that it discriminated against male immigrants on the ground of their sex".[27]

It is not unreasonable to assume that the European Court would have followed the Commission in finding against the United Kingdom, but in the event the case was effectively foreclosed by the Government after it made the appropriate amendments to the legislation and granted entry to the complainants.[28] In so doing, it has been stressed, "the Government was able to avoid any binding precedent being established [ie. through a judgment of the European Court] to the effect that the exclusion of citizens of the United Kingdom and Colonies from the United Kingdom could involve a violation of Article 3".[29]

The enactment of the Commonwealth Immigrants Act 1968 provides another penetrating example of the inadequacies of the United Kingdom's system of parliamentary scrutiny of legislation. The apprehensive circumstances surrounding the introduction and subsequent passage of the Bill through Parliament[30] cannot excuse the lack of understanding amongst

---

22   The most cursory reasons for the Fourth Protocol not being ratified were given in Parliament, HC Deb. Vol.768, cols 10–11 (8 July 1968).

23   *East African Asians v United Kingdom*, (Groups I & II) Report of the Commission, 14 December 1973; (1981) 3 EHRR 76 (NB The Commission's decision was never officially published and remains confidential). For further comment on this case, see FG Jacobs, *European Convention on Human Rights*, (1975), p.33.

24   *Ibid*, paras 201 & 207.

25   *Ibid*, para.208.

26   *Ibid*, paras 231–2.

27   *Ibid*.

28   A quota system for the admission of East African Asians was introduced. The Committee of Ministers declared itself satisfied with this outcome in its report of 21 October 1977; see, 20 YB, ECHR (1977) 642.

29   AC Evans, "United Kingdom Immigration Policy and the European Convention on Human Rights" [1983] PL 91, 94. Nonetheless, the Commission's report apparently continues to be cited with approval; see the submission of Anthony Lester QC to the Home Affairs Sub-Committee on Race Relations and Immigration, HC 434 (1979–80), para.19; and Chapter 4, *infra*, p.85.)

30   Fears of the United Kingdom being swamped by political refugees fleeing oppression in Kenya were fuelled by widespread media reports; even the Cabinet, it appears, became overly anxious when confronted by top-secret reports telling the same stories of mass expulsion (see Richard Crossman, *The Times*, 6 October 1972, quoted in V Bevan, *The Development of British Immigration Law* (1986), p.81). See also D Steel, *No Entry* (1969), Chapter 11, "Mounting Hysteria". The Bill received Royal Assent barely one week after

politicians, of all parties, of the Bill's consequences for human and civil rights in general, and those protected by the European Convention in particular. Indeed, if anything, the emotional atmosphere surrounding the whole question of immigration in the 1960s should have alerted the Government to the possibility of passing what Sir Leslie Scarman later warned against: "instant legislation, conceived in fear or prejudice and enacted in breach of human rights".[31] From the recollections of Richard Crossman, a senior member of the Labour Government at the relevant time, it appears that this much was realized when the bill was being pushed through Parliament, but only, it would appear, at an "academic" level – political expediency ensured that this argument gained no further significance. Thus, Mr Crossman was able to record with apparent equanimity the feeling amongst his cabinet colleagues that with regard to the contemplated legislation, "we realized [it] would have been declared unconstitutional in any country with a written constitution and a Supreme Court".[32]

It is, in this light, quite remarkable that throughout the lengthy deliberations on the Bill, and the undoubted gravity of the provisions it contained, the question of possible violations of the European Convention was mentioned only once in Parliament. Sir Dingle Foot observed that having preliminarily signed the Fourth Protocol to the Convention (which, inter alia, secures rights of entry to nationals of the state), should the Government force the passage of the bill, it "never shall be able to ratify that protocol".[33] His remarks, however, were barely acknowledged, and far from adequately addressed, by the Home Secretary or Home Office ministers in their contributions to the debate.[34]

So, once more, repressive legislation was allowed to reach the United Kingdom's statute book with only a whisper of warning being raised against it of the possible contravention of the European Convention. And, in the absence of any effective preventive measures, the familiar course of having later to alter legislation in the face of an adverse decision of the European Court had once more to be taken.

Detention under mental health and criminal justice legislation

Under s.66 of the (now superseded) Mental Health Act 1959 the Home Secretary was invested with the power to decide whether or not to discharge a mentally disordered offender held in detention. His discretion was complete and, for all practical purposes, non-justiciable, for though he was able to receive advice from medical officers and the Mental Health Tribunals he was

---

being introduced.

31 Stated in support of the argument that some constitutional constraint should be placed on the legislature, in *English law - The New Dimension* (Hamlyn Lectures, 1974), p.20. See also, the trenchant criticisms of British immigration law in general in an independent report which immediately preceded the 1968 Act: H Street, G Howe & G Bindman, *Report on Anti-Discrimination Legislation* (1967).

32 As quoted by V Bevan, *supra*, n.30.

33 HC Deb. Vol.759, cols 1269-70 (27 Feb. 1968). Sir Dingle Foot (together with Anthony Lester QC) was later to act as counsel for the applicants in the *East African Asians* case before the Commission.

34 *Ibid*, col.1354.

under no obligation to accept any recommendations from either.35

In 'X' v United Kingdom,36 the conformity of this legislation with Article 5 of the Convention was successfully challenged. The point at issue was whether review by the Home Secretary under the 1959 Act adequately protected the right of a detained person to have the "lawfulness of his detention ... decided speedily by a court". It had previously been decided by the European Court in the Winterwerp case (which involved mental health legislation in the Netherlands) that in mental health cases "special procedural safeguards" may, in fact, be necessary to ensure that a detained person suffering from a mental disorder enjoys the same right of access to the courts as everyone else.37 It was suggested that there ought to exist a process whereby restricted patients could have the lawfulness of their detention periodically reviewed by a court.38 Unfortunately, it would appear that the lessons of this case were not heeded, or even recognized, by the United Kingdom Government. There is no doubt that this attitude of apparent indifference was (and, in the case of analogous criminal justice legislation, it is later argued, continues to be)39 sustained by the Government's mistaken, if not rather arrogant, belief in the assurance provided by the doctrine of ministerial responsibility that the Secretary of State will always be prevented from acting beyond his or her statutory powers. The Government argued, in its submission to the Court in the 'X' case, that by this process, in combination with other extra-judicial methods of holding a minister accountable, conformity with the Convention is ensured.40

This, however, was to miss the point; the fact that these safeguards operate outside the courts is precisely what prevents them from meeting the requirements of Article 5(4). Merely to comply with domestic law in no way guarantees the protection of Convention rights. In the case, the European Court decided that the regular review of the reasons for the detention of a mentally ill offender must be performed by the courts. Indeed, as the wording of Article 5(4) is explicit on this very point, it is difficult to understand how the Government hoped to justify not making provision for judicial control in the first place. We might accept the Government's argument that as it had never anticipated such an expansive construction of the breadth of reviewable areas under Article 5(4), it had seen no need to provide for review by the courts of the detention of mentally disordered patients.41 But this is a shallow explanation in view of the burgeoning public debate in the United Kingdom during the relevant period concerning the fairness of mental health legislation.42 The highly pertinent conclusions of

---

35 In one domestic case it had been declared that the Home Secretary was not under a duty to act judicially or fairly, *R v Secretary of State for the Home Dept, ex parte Powell* (unreported) QBD 21 December 1978, reproduced in LO Gostin, "Human Rights, Judicial Review and the Mentally Disordered Offender" [1982] Crim. LR 787.
36 ECHR Series 'A', No.46 (1981)
37 *Winterwerp v The Netherlands*, ECHR Series 'A', No.33 (24 Oct. 1979), para.60.
38 *Ibid*, para.55.
39 Certain criminal justice provisions, procedurally similar to those of the former Mental Health Act, have been recently successfully challenged before the European Court of Human Rights in the cases of *Weeks* and *Thynne. Wilson & Gunnell, infra*, nn 50 & 51 and accompanying text.
40 *'X' v United Kingdom*, ECHR Series 'A', No.46 (24 Oct. 1981), paras 55 & 60-1.
41 *Ibid*.
42 Articulate warnings had been made in a number of publications – for example, a report

the European Commission (later endorsed by the Court) in the *Winterwerp* case cited above had been available since the publication of its report on 15 December 1977. The reproval of Dutch law in this case – on the grounds that it did not adequately provide for periodic judicial review of the lawfulness of the detention of mentally unstable individuals – could equally have applied to English law at the time. Indeed, just such a censure was already being sought through the application of 'X' to the Commission lodged over three years previously, in 1974.[43] Yet, in spite of the pertinence of these two prominent factors, the Government remained unmoved until it was obliged to take action to rectify the position following the European Court's judgment in the 'X' case.

Had the Court, in 'X', merely reiterated the rulings it made in the *Winterwerp* case (which would not have been improper) – that is, the necessity for judicial review, or at least, review by a specialized body with quasi-judicial powers, in cases of this kind – it would not have much advanced the cause of many aggrieved mental health patients in this country. Previously, when called upon to review mental health cases through the issue of writs of *habeas corpus*, the domestic courts had made it abundantly clear that they were prepared to review only the procedural propriety, and not the substantive merits or reasonableness, of the exercise of the powers vested in the Secretary of State.[44] So, in order to provide an adequate judicial test of the legality of a patient's internment, it was necessary for the European Court to rule that the scope of judicial review be extended beyond mere procedural conformity. It held that the review should "be wide enough to bear on those conditions which, according to the Convention, are essential for the lawful detention of a person on the ground of unsoundness of mind".[45] As it is also required by Article 5(4) that the review body is to be independent,[46] the Government was effectively faced with a choice between modifying the remedy of *habeas corpus* as administered in the ordinary courts, or altering the terms of reference of the Mental Health Tribunals. It chose the latter course, largely on the strength of the greater expertise and informality of the tribunals, though it has been provided that they are to be chaired by a lawyer – typically a circuit judge or a recorder.[47] Tribunals today are required to conduct periodic reviews (at least one a year) of the legality of the continued detention of a mentally impaired offender.[48]

Domestic legislation on this issue would appear now to have been brought into line with the requirements of the European Convention, but this fact notwithstanding, the necessary changes were made many years after the

---

compiled for MIND by LO Gostin, *A Human Condition*, Vols I & II (1975), especially Vol.I, pp 68-74; also, "Editorial Comment", NLJ, 5 October 1978, p.967; and even in the Government's own *Review of the Mental Health Act 1959*, Cmnd 7320 (1978), para.5.18.

43   Application No.6998/75 (14 July 1974).
44   *Ex parte Powell, supra*, n.35; indeed, it has been calculated that since the enactment of the 1959 Act there have been no reported cases of the courts being willing to consider the substantive issues at stake. See LO Gostin, *supra*, n.42, p.788 (see also pp 788-90 for an account of some cases demonstrating this unwillingness).
45   *'X' v United Kingdom*, ECHR, *supra*, n.40, para.58.
46   *Ibid*, para.61.
47   Mental Health (Amendment) Act 1982, Schedule 1, para.8; consolidated in the Mental Health Act 1983, s.78(2)(c).
48   1982 Act, *ibid*, s.28 (& Schedule 1); and, 1983 Act, *ibid*, ss 72 & 73.

deficiencies had become apparent, and then only as a consequence of an unfavourable judgment of the European Court.

However, despite the clear analogy with the review procedures of the Mental Health Act 1959, provisions under the Criminal Justice Act 1967 concerning the review of custodial sentences for *crimes* committed by persons with mental disorders remained unaltered. For although the detention of such persons is in part punitive, once the period of time (known as "the tariff" period) associated with that part has elapsed, the rationale for the continued detention of the individual to be made subject to an adequate system of review is the same as that pertaining to the continued detention of a mentally ill patient – namely, that mental instability is, by its very nature, "susceptible of change with the passage of time".[49] In predictable consequence, successful challenges to the 1967 Act were brought before the European Court of Human Rights by a number of applicants. In the cases of *Weeks*[50] and *Thynne, Wilson & Gunnell*[51] (both of which were *initiated after* the Court's judgment in *'X'*),[52] the Court held that the provisions of the Act relating to the powers of the Parole Board to review indeterminate life sentences (being served in these cases by mentally disturbed prisoners), and the effective unavailability of judicial review of such sentences[53] were in breach of the requirements of Article 5(4) of the Convention. In common with the previous mental health procedures for review of an individual's continued detention, under ss.61 and 62 of the Criminal Justice Act 1967 the Secretary of State is granted ultimate discretionary authority to deny the release on licence of a detainee serving a life sentence. Under s.59 the Parole Board is duty-bound to advise the Secretary of State in this respect, but the latter is not obliged to follow the advice tendered. This fact drew the European Court to the conclusion that "the Board therefore lacks the power of decision required by Article 5(4) when dealing with this category of case", both in respect of providing effective periodic review of cases and the release on licence of individuals serving life sentences.[54] The most regrettable aspect of these two cases is that it is clear from the Court's judgments that there existed a distinct line of reasoning originating in *'X'* and running through both *Weeks* and *Thynne et al*.[55] The manifest relevance of *'X'* to the legislation impugned in the later cases may not have been evident to the Government or (more likely) was disregarded by it, but in either event the Government's apparent resolve to leave the relevant provisions of the Criminal Justice Act unaltered is inexcusable.[56]

---

49   *Thynne et al*, *infra*, n.51, para.70.
50   ECHR Series 'A', No.114 (2 March 1987).
51   ECHR Series 'A', No.190 (25 October 1990).
52   Applications were lodged with the European Commission, in respect of the former, on 6 April 1982, and in respect of the latter, on 3 June 1985. The judgment in *'X'* was handed down on 24 October 1981.
53   See the Court's observations in *Weeks*, *supra*, n.50, para.69.
54   *Weeks*, *supra*, n.50, para.64; for a similar conclusion in the *Thynne et al* case, see *supra*, n.51, para.80.
55   In respect of *Weeks*, see *supra*, n.50, paras 61–8; and in respect to *Thynne et al*, *supra*, n.51, the Court concluded, after quoting both *'X'* and *Weeks* (paras 60–70), that it saw "no reason to depart from its finding in the *Weeks* judgment ...", para.80.
56   Notwithstanding this point and the fact that the House of Lords Select Committee on Murder and Life Imprisonment recommended in 1989 that executive discretion in respect of the release of life sentence prisoners be replaced by an independent tribunal – see *Report* of the Committee (1988-9), HL 78-1, para.154 - a large measure of executive

Homosexuality legislation in Northern Ireland

A challenge as to the compatibility with the Convention of certain domestic statutes governing the traditionally controversial issue of homosexuality has also been successfully mounted. Until relatively recently, all homosexual acts in Northern Ireland, whether performed in private or in public, or even between consenting adults, were prohibited. This was in contrast to the rest of the United Kingdom where, in England and in Wales (effectively since the Sexual Offences Act 1967) and in Scotland (since the Criminal Justice (Scotland) Act 1980), such sexual behaviour was permitted between adults in private. Under the twin enactments of the Offences Against the Person Act 1861 and the Criminal Law Amendment Act 1885, homosexuality, *per se*, continued to be an offence in Northern Ireland. Mr Dudgeon, a homosexual living in Northern Ireland, complained to the European Commission that the continued existence of these restrictions in the province violated his right to privacy guaranteed by Article 8 of the European Convention.[57]

As the legislation at issue in this case was enacted last century, long before the birth of the European Convention, some explanation is required as to their relevance to my thesis. Clearly the Acts could not have been made subject to any scrutinizing process for conformity with the Convention. On the face of it, therefore, it would appear that their censure by the adjudicative institutions of the Council of Europe provides no corroboration for the contention that presently not enough care is being taken to ensure that legislation does not contravene the Convention. What the *Dudgeon* case does provide, however, is a most revealing indication of the status accorded to the Convention by government in its policy-making process, with respect to this important social issue. In the case it was decided by both the Commission and the Court that Article 8's protection of the right to privacy extended to the sexual activities of homosexuals. Both bodies agreed that the prohibition of "private consensual homosexual acts"[58] involving male persons over 21 years of age caused Mr Dudgeon (who was 35 at the time) "to suffer an unjustified interference with his right to respect for his private life".[59] Accordingly, it was declared that there had been a breach of Article 8. The decriminalization of such acts in England and Wales in 1967 can be seen as being preemptory of just such a violation of civil rights. So it cannot be said that the British Government had been oblivious to the restrictions on civil liberties that remained in Northern Ireland (and Scotland) after it was decided that the Sexual Offences Act 1967 was to apply only to England and Wales.

---

discretion in this respect was retained in the Criminal Justice Act 1991. Whilst, in response to the *Thynne* case, the Parole Board may now operate more like a court (s.32 & Sched.5) and the Minister is now *obliged* to release a prisoner where (the prisoner having served the "tariff" of his sentence) the Board so directs (s.34(3)), considerable discretion remains available to the Minister to make rules and give directions to the Board as to how it is to execute the tasks assigned to it (ss 32(5) & (6) and 34(4). Once again, the Government has demonstrated its reluctance to comply with European Court rulings beyond what is the (questionable) minimum necessary alteration to impugned legislation. For evidence of this minimalist approach during passage of the Criminal Justice Bill, see HC Deb. Vol.186, col.360 (20 Feb. 1991), HC Deb. Vol.193, cols 902 & 904 (25 June 1991) and HC Deb. Vol.195, cols 309-10 (16 July 1991).

57   *Dudgeon v United Kingdom*, ECHR Series 'A', No.45 (22 Oct. 1981)
58   Words of the Commission, as reported by the Court, *ibid*, para.35.
59   *Dudgeon v United Kingdom*, *supra*, n.57, para.63.

The reason for this restriction in respect of Northern Ireland stemmed from the province's peculiar constitutional position, whereby under the Government of Ireland Act 1920 the power to legislate on certain matters – including social issues such as sexual morality – was delegated to the Northern Ireland Parliament at Stormont. This remained the case until 1972 when the Northern Irish Parliament was prorogued and direct rule reinstated. Since that time (except for one brief and ill-fated devolution experiment in 1974),[60] the United Kingdom Parliament has been directly responsible for legislation in Northern Ireland. Upon the resumption of direct rule, the main problem facing Westminster in the present context was the intolerance towards homosexuals exhibited by a considerable proportion of the province's population. The strength of this feeling was made clear in 1976 when the Government began to make tentative suggestions as to how the legal position on this issue in Northern Ireland might be brought into line with that of the rest of the United Kingdom. Merlyn Rees, the then Secretary of State for Northern Ireland, announced that it was the Government's intention to seek views on the question of amending Northern Ireland's homosexuality laws.[61] The then recently established Standing Advisory Commission on Human Rights located in Belfast responded to the Government's declared interest by publishing a report in April 1977. Partly on the basis of the rather surprisingly favourable indications in the report the Legislation Branch of the Northern Ireland Office issued a proposal for a draft Homosexual Offences (Northern Ireland) Order on 27 July 1978 which sought to extend the mainland homosexuality laws to Northern Ireland. It was apparent, however, even from the foreword to the explanatory document of the draft proposal, that the Government was sensitive to the strength of opposition within Northern Ireland to any relaxation of the law in this field. The proposal was published and comments on its provisions were invited. Untypically, the usual sectarian divides in the province did not dictate the outcome, and Roman Catholics, Presbyterians, and Unionists all expressed concern over the "inevitable" lowering of moral standards that would result from these changes in the law. There were, of course, forcefully argued submissions in favour of the reforms, notably from organizations representing homosexuals and social workers as well as the Standing Committee of the General Synod of the Church of Ireland, and indeed an opinion poll conducted on the issue in January 1979 indicated an even divide between those for and those against the change. But ultimately the Government bowed to the vociferous pressure of the anti-reform lobby and in July 1979 the draft proposal was suspended. Humphrey Atkins, the new Secretary of State for Northern Ireland, announced that as "it is clear that a substantial body of opinion [in Northern Ireland] (embracing a wide range of religious as well as political opinion) is opposed to the proposed change ... the Government propose (sic) to take no further action ... but we should be prepared to reconsider the matter if there were any developments in the future which were relevant".[62] Two years later, after the European Court's judgment in the *Dudgeon* case, such a reconsideration was effectively forced on the Government, and an Order in Council very similar to that

---

60   The Northern Ireland Assembly had legislative competence in certain devolved areas.
61   HC Deb. Vol.916-i, cols 856-7 (29 July 1976).
62   HC Deb. Vol.969, col.466 (w) (2 July 1979).

promulgated in 1978 came into force in December 1982.[63]

The essential point of this brief history is that, in familiar fashion, it took an adverse decision of the European Court before the United Kingdom Government was able to appreciate the consequences of the inconsistency, not to say injustice, of its failure to extend the law to Northern Ireland. This is not to deny that successive governments were faced, as is so often the case in Northern Ireland, with an almost intractable dilemma. On the one hand, they were under pressure to admit the claims of the majority (or at least a very sizable minority) of Northern Irish citizens to determine their own legal solution to this contentious social phenomenon,[64] whilst on the other it was appreciated that making Northern Ireland an exception in this matter was to run the risk of denying certain basic civil rights (recognized elsewhere in the United Kingdom) to some of those who live there. It must be noted with respect to the second point that concern over a possible breach of obligations to protect the rights enshrined in the European Convention was never raised during the parliamentary deliberations on the subject of homosexuality law in Northern Ireland. Faced with this difficulty of balancing competing interests, in addition to the loose convention that legislation on an issue like this is usually left to the initiative of private members rather than government,[65] and Britain's general reluctance and unease over conducting the affairs of Northern Ireland from Westminster, the Government's lack of conviction in reforming the law in the province is perhaps understandable. However, as all the examples in this chapter illustrate, if the United Kingdom is to pay the respect that is due to an international treaty on human rights to which it is party, then it must not yield to the demands of political expediency, even when mounted by such a united body of opinion as the anti-homosexuality lobby in Northern Ireland.

In this case the Government could not claim ignorance of the gravity of the continued curtailment of certain freedoms to homosexuals living in a part the United Kingdom, when since 1967 all governments had been persistently urged to amend this anomaly. What is more, recognition of the severity of the criminal sanctions that existed in Northern Ireland prior to 1982 is surely implicit in the deliberate leniency with which the Royal Ulster Constabulary enforced those sanctions against homosexuals. In the *Dudgeon* case it was noted that although there was no stated policy to the effect, "so far as the Government are (*sic*) aware from investigations of the records, no one was prosecuted in Northern Ireland during the period in question [1972–80] for an act which would clearly not have been an offence if committed in England and Wales".[66]

The conclusion to which we are drawn in this episode is as inescapable as it is familiar. To have allowed such an iniquitous situation to have persisted in the United Kingdom, especially in view of the opportunities that were available for the appropriate changes to have been made, reflects badly on the efficacy of the United Kingdom's legislative machinery in taking account of, let alone honouring, the obligations under the European Convention.

---

63   Homosexual Offences (N.I.) Order 1982. S.I. 1982/ No.1536 (N.I. No.19).
64   See Foreword to Proposal for Draft Homosexual Offences (Northern Ireland) Order, 1978 (27 July 1978).
65   *Supra*, n.62.
66   *Supra*, n.57, para.30.

Anti-terrorist legislation – the PTAs and the EPAs[67]

Perhaps the least surprising of all pieces of legislation to have been assailed with infringing rights enshrined in the European Convention on Human Rights have been the successive Prevention of Terrorism (Temporary Provisions) Acts (hereafter the PTAs) of 1974, 1976, 1984 and 1989, and the Northern Ireland (Emergency Provisions) Acts (hereafter the EPAs) 1973, 1975, 1978, 1987 and 1991. In spite of the indubitable restrictions on individual liberty that these Acts have imposed, however, there is only one instance of a successful direct challenge to each of the two sets of legislation.[68] Naturally, the grievous terrorist threat existing within, and emanating from, Northern Ireland, could not be allowed to run unchecked, as plainly terrorism itself curtails many civil rights. Nevertheless, it has been often argued that the original PTA, born of the devastating bombings of two Birmingham pubs by the IRA in 1974, and pushed through all its parliamentary stages in only 48 hours, was not the best possible response to this growing menace.[69] It was indicative of this particular concern that the 1974 Act was made subject to six-monthly renewal, culminating in complete re-enactment in 1976. Since then the United Kingdom has never been without a PTA,[70] albeit always subject to annual renewal, as well as a succession of Select Committee investigations. The controversial nature of some of the provisions in the Act as to their effect on civil liberties – in particular, power to detain for up to seven days and the power to serve exclusion orders – makes the scrutiny of its operation especially important. It might be expected, therefore, that conformity with the European Convention would have been an issue featuring prominently in the numerous parliamentary debates and reviews of the Acts which have been conducted since 1974. This, unfortunately, has not been the case.

There are two aspects of the legislation which the European Commission and European Court have found it necessary to censure. They are, first, the provisions for the extension of detention of suspects under s.12 of the PTA 1984 (re-enacted in s.14 of the 1989 Act) which, with the permission of the Secretary of State, allowed up to five days to be added to the initial maximum of 48 hours; and second, detainees' access to friends, relatives and solicitors during their detention which under the Judges' Rules was imprecise, especially with respect to the permissible maximum length of time that access could be denied. In spite of the fact that both these issues have been continuously examined and questioned by civil rights organizations, academics, MPs, and by successive select committees established to assess

---

67   The Prevention of Terrorism (Temporary Provisions) Acts and the Northern Ireland (Emergency Provisions) Acts respectively. See also the discussion of PTAs in the context of secondary legislation in Chapter 4, infra, pp 89–94.

68   One indirect challenge (detailed later in the section) to the provisions for detainees' access to friends, relatives and legal advisers contained jointly in the PTA 1984 and Police and Criminal Evidence Act 1984 was successful before both the European Commission and the European Court. The case of Ireland v United Kingdom, ECHR Series 'A', No.25 (1978), of course, concerned interrogation techniques used by the RUC which were not legislatively endorsed.

69   It was claimed that the Bill had "a ring of desperation about it", HC Deb. Vol.882, col.687 (28 Nov. 1974), per Mr John Lee MP. See also, ibid, col.672.

70   Like that other infamous "temporary" Act – the Official Secrets Act 1911 – Governments of all political hues have shown a marked reluctance to repeal an Act which provides them with such sweeping powers; see also, The Independent, Editorial, 17 Feb. 1988.

the operation of terrorism legislation, seldom has the European Convention been invoked in support of the doubts raised. Still less have those few arguments that have included use of the Convention as a gauge against which to measure the restrictions of the legislation received the parliamentary attention they so patently deserved. Once more we are confronted with examples reflecting the regrettable lack of appreciation of the European Convention's significance within the United Kingdom's law-making process. Moreover this cannot be due to a want of opportunities for these questions to be properly addressed either by the specially established review bodies or by members of either House of Parliament. Between 1974 and 1988 there were no fewer than 15 reviews and reports on the subject of anti-terrorist legislation laid before Parliament,[71] and four full-scale debates on the four PTA Bills which have passed through Parliament in that time.

It must be said that from the very outset the severe nature of the anti-terrorist legislation has always been acknowledged. Indeed, Roy Jenkins, who was responsible as Home Secretary for the introduction of the first Prevention of Terrorism (Temporary Provisions) Bill in 1974, openly referred to the "encroachment – limited but real – on the liberties of individual citizens".[72] Government spokesmen have consistently recognized this draconian character of the PTAs, but equally they have been satisfied that the case justifying their existence has always been unquestionable. What is more to the point, Parliament has always endorsed this view by large majorities in all three re-enactments of the legislation, and all the intervening renewal debates. Reference, however, to the pertinence of the European Convention in this context has been almost non-existent during the second reading and committee stages of the Prevention of Terrorism (Temporary Provisions) Bills, 1974, 1976, 1984 and 1989. Indeed, the only direct reference was made during the latter stages of the 1984 Bill, when Mr Gerald Bermingham emphasized the necessity of "having laws which comply with the European Convention on Human Rights", and this observation was completely ignored by the Government.[73] Major select committee reviews of the anti-terrorist legislation preceded all three re-enactments,[74] but not even in these was the European Convention accorded any significant attention. No doubt these review bodies were hampered by the restrictive terms of reference that they were invariably required to work within,[75] but in

---

71 In 1983, CP Walker noted that there had been 9 reviews conducted (excluding re-enactment in 1976); since then the Baker Report: *Review of the Operation of the Northern Ireland (Emergency Provisions) Act 1978* (Cmnd 9222 (1984)), four annual reports by specially appointed commissioners which reviewed the operation of the PTA 1984 (see Chapter 4, *infra*, pp 93-4), and the Colville Report which preceded the PTA 1989 (Cmnd 264 (1987), *infra*, n.74) have all been completed.

72 HC Deb. Vol.882, col.634 (27 Nov. 1974)

73 HC Deb. Vol.52, col.954 (25 Jan. 1984).

74 PTA 1976: preceded by the *Report of the Committee to consider, in the context of civil liberties and human rights, measures to deal with terrorism in Northern Ireland*, Cmnd 5847 (1975) (the "Gardiner Report"); PTA 1984: preceded by the *Report of the Committee to Review the Operation of the Prevention of Terrorism (Temporary Provisions) Act 1976*, Cmnd 8803 (1983) (the "Jellicoe Report"); PTA 1989: preceded by the *Report of the Committee to Review the Operation of the Prevention of Terrorism (Temporary Provisions) Act 1984*, Cm.264 (1987) (the "Colville Report").

75 With the possible exception of the Gardiner Committee (*ibid*), the Committees' briefs demanded only that they should review the operation of the anti-terrorist legislation, not to evaluate the need for its continuance.

none would a detailed assessment of the demands of the European
Convention with respect (especially) to the provisions for arrest and
detention and access to relatives and solicitors have been inappropriate.
Indeed, quite the contrary would be true. The status of these committees
placed them in an ideal position to broach the question of how best to
ensure compliance with the Convention associated with the above matters,
possibly by using the sizable body of European Court jurisprudence – on the
subject of detention without trial in particular – as an indication of the
required standards.[76]

The absence from these reviews of *any* consideration of the impact of the
European Convention, however, has not been complete. Conspicuously, the
Baker review of 1984 (which though primarily concerned with the operation
of the EPAs, nevertheless devoted some time to the implementation of the
PTA 1976) was a little more attentive to the demands of the Convention.[77] In
response to Amnesty International's submission urging his committee to
take due account of all the international human rights treaties to which the
United Kingdom is party, including the European Convention on Human
Rights, Sir George Baker asserted in his Introduction that "I have had them
in mind throughout".[78] Specifically, he assessed the arrest and detention
provisions of the two Acts in light of the tenets of Article 5 of the Convention.
Parts (1)(c) and (3) of this Article he interpreted as requiring that an arrest
must be made with reasonable suspicion of an offence having been
committed; and that the arrest should be for the purpose of bringing the
suspect promptly before the competent court. With respect to s.11 of the
EPA 1978 he noted that neither criterion was fulfilled: a constable was
empowered to arrest anyone "he suspect[ed] of being a terrorist", and detain
him for up to 72 hours without charge (sub-s.(3)).[79] The continued existence
of such a subjective criterion by which an arrest might be made has always
been curious, as well as regrettable, in view of the fact that the comparable
provision in the PTA (s.12 in the 1984 Act and s.14 in the 1989 Act) has
always required the more objectively determined arrest criterion of
"reasonable grounds" for suspicion of a terrorist-related offence under the
Act having taken place. The Baker Report was unequivocal on this point
when it concluded that "*reasonable* suspicion should be required when a
constable arrests without a warrant [emphasis supplied]".[80] The caveat and
recommendations offered by the remarks in the Baker Report were not
immediately heeded by the Government; that is, despite the fact that barely
four months later the derogation provision which the Government had
lodged with the Council of Europe in respect of all of the EPAs was
withdrawn,[81] thereby laying open to challenge the peculiarity of this

---

76 See *infra*, nn 104 & 105, and accompanying text.
77 *Supra*, n.71, Cmnd 9222 (1984). The late Sir George Baker was chairman. It should be
    noted that in the *Report of the Commission on Legal Procedures to Control Terrorist
    Activities in Northern Ireland*, Cmnd 5185 (1972) (the "Diplock Report"), the provisions of
    the Convention (Article 6 in particular) were explicitly recognized. It was summarily
    concluded, however, that special arrangements under the "Diplock Courts" (as they
    became known) would not violate these demands. (para.14).
78 *Ibid*, para.30.
79 Note, however, that this section is now seldom used; see *infra*, n.89, and accompanying
    text.
80 *Supra*, n.71, para.283.
81 See (1984) 128 SJ 600 for the statement of withdrawal, which was lodged with the

provision against the requirements of Article 5(1) of the Convention. The repeal of s.11 of the EPA 1978 and its replacement with the arrest criterion of "reasonable grounds for suspicion" did not occur until 1987,[82] fully three years after the publication of the Baker Report. In the meantime (on the 16 June 1986) three persons arrested and detained under the provision on suspicion of being terrorists had lodged applications with the Commission, alleging that s.11 of the 1978 Act was in violation of Article 5(1)(c) of the Convention.[83] Both the Commission and Court agreed with the applicants, in concluding that, even given the terrorist nature of the alleged offences, the fact that the Government did not demonstrate to the Court that there existed any grounds for reasonable suspicion, as specifically provided in Article 5(1)(c), for the arrest of the applicants, amounted to a breach having occurred. In the words of the Court: "... at least some facts or information capable of satisfying the Court that the arrested person was reasonably suspected of having committed the alleged offence", must be provided. "This", it continued, "is all the more necessary where, as in the present case, the domestic law does not require reasonable suspicion, but sets a lower threshold by merely requiring honest suspicion."[84] For the Government not to have amended s.11 of the EPA accordingly, *before* it withdrew the relevant notice of derogation (the lodgement of which had been precisely to excuse this section from the demands of Article 5) is reprehensible in the extreme.[85] It is indeed difficult to interpret this episode as anything other than an example of the Government's disdain for the requirements of the Convention, for it can hardly be argued that it was nothing more than a mere oversight.[86]

Whilst, in contrast, it is correct to point to the PTAs' use of "reasonable grounds" as a basis for arrest under s.12, that itself does not absolve the provision from all criticism. For as Baker trenchantly observes, an arrest under the PTA need not be "necessarily for the purpose of bringing before a court".[87] The statistics related to detentions under the PTAs bear this point out. The annual percentage of those detained under the Acts in Northern Ireland who were released without a charge being brought against them was consistently above 70% in the period 1984–7, the yearly average figure was 74.5%; and the corresponding figures for the rest of the United Kingdom are even higher: more than 74% each year, with a yearly average of 80%.[88] With

---

Council of Europe on 22 August 1984. Indeed, the withdrawal of the derogation notice was something advocated by the Baker Report, but *only* when accompanied by the appropriate amendment to the legislation that rendered derogation unnecessary; *supra*, n.71, para.264

82 EPA 1987, s.6; re-enacted in s.16 of EPA 1991.
83 *Fox, Campbell & Hartley*, ECHR Series 'A', No.182 (30 August 1990), para.24.
84 *Ibid*, para.34.
85 In this light, the rather pious claim of the Government in its statement withdrawing the notice of derogation in 1984, that it was then "satisfied that the [anti-terrorist] measures ... in the United Kingdom are fully in accord with ... the Convention ...", (*supra*, n.81), is scarcely credible.
86 Furthermore, the outstanding inconsistency of s.11 under the EPA 1978 with the Convention was acknowledged neither by the Secretary of State when introducing the EPA 1987 Bill (which repealed the offending provision), nor by any members during the ensuing debate; HC Deb. Vol.107, cols 1079–1124 (16 Dec. 1986).
87 *Supra*, n.71, para.264.
88 Of the total number of persons charged with an offence (whether under the PTAs or not) in Great Britain in the same period as a result of *detention* under the PTA, the annual percentage of those charged with offences under the PTAs ranged between 39% and 61%; in Northern Ireland, however, less than 2.5% per year were so charged; source: the

such a high proportion of those detained not being charged and therefore not brought before a court, it is difficult to avoid the conclusion that the implementation of the arrest and detention provisions under s.12 of the Act is not primarily, in the words of Article 5(1)(c), "for the purpose of bringing [the suspect] before the competent legal authority". This proposition is further supported by the fact that s.12 of the PTA 1984 and the subsequent, almost identical s.14 of the 1989 Act have virtually completely replaced s.11 of the EPA 1978 as the principal instrument by which arrests for suspected terrorist-related offences are effected.[89] The preference for the use of the former provision appears, in fact, to relate more to the gathering of intelligence and general screening than to the apprehension of suspected terrorists for predetermined offences. In a leading case concerning this issue, the Lord Chief Justice for Northern Ireland declared that "no specific crime need be suspected in order to ground a proper arrest under s.12(1)(b) ... [as the arrest] ... is usually the first step in the investigation of the suspected person's involvement in terrorism".[90] The same point has since been strongly reiterated, once in the Jellicoe Report,[91] and once by Leon Brittan (when he was Home Secretary) in a radio interview when he stated, with reference to government policy on the detention of terrorist suspects, that "the object of the exercise is not to secure convictions but to secure information".[92] Another specific warning of the possible infringement of Article 5(1)(c) of the Convention by the s.12 detention powers was given by the Standing Advisory Commission on Human Rights in its *Annual Report for 1984-85*: "[w]e remain concerned that this provision [arrest under s.12 of the PTA 1976] appears to confer power to arrest for questioning and may therefore infringe Article 5(1)(c) of the European Convention on Human Rights".[93]

More general analyses of the doubtful compliance of certain aspects of the PTAs with the European Convention cannot have escaped the attention of the Northern Ireland and Home Offices. On the eve of the introduction of the first EPA in 1973, for instance, and a year or so before the first PTA, one academic commentator adumbrated a number of principles which should, in his opinion, "govern the approach to emergency powers".[94] One of these was

---

Colville Report, Cm.264 (1987), *supra*, n.74, Tables 1 and 3 (pp 5 & 7, respectively).
In so far as the following statistics are capable of interpretation this trend appears to be continuing: of the 11,289 persons detained under the PTAs between 1985 and 1991 (inclusive) 36.6% (ie. 4,137) were subsequently charged with offences (presumably, under the PTAs and other Acts); source: HC Deb. Vol.203, cols 519-20 (w) (12 Feb. 1992).

[89] Though the preference for the use of s.12 of the 1984 PTA has been steadily increasing over the past few years, its use was immediately extended when s.11 was rendered otiose, except in circumstances where the arrest is accompanied by search and seizure, by s.6 of EPA 1987. See the Colville Report, Cm.264 (1987), *supra*, n.74, para.5.2.1.

[90] *Ex Parte Lynch* 1980 NILR 126, at 131, *per* Lord Lowry LJC. There appears to be a certain degree of confusion as to the official policy adopted by the police on the use of s.12. In the Baker Report it was indicated "that the police are now trained to treat arrest for terrorist offences as requiring similar suspicion as for all other offences", *supra*, n.71, para.283 - which contradicts the *Lynch* judgment. But in Viscount Colville's 1987 review, the *Lynch* approach was reinstated, Cm.264 (1987), *supra*, n.74, para.4.1.1.

[91] *Supra*, n.74, para.112.

[92] This was quoted by the Government in its submission to the European Court in the case of *Brogan et al v United Kingdom*, *infra*, n.101, para.46.

[93] HC 394 (1985-86), para.65.

[94] WL Twining, "Emergency Powers and Criminal Process: The Diplock Report", [1973] Crim. LR 408.

that "the creation and exercise of emergency powers should comply with
international law and with internationally accepted standards of civilised
government as set forth in such documents as ... [inter alia] ... the European
Convention for the Protection of Human Rights".[95] The Standing Advisory
Commission on Human Rights has also consistently pointed to the value of
the European Convention to the legislature as some sort of "touchstone" in
the enactment of emergency legislation.[96] Writers have repeatedly remarked
on the danger of emergency legislation transgressing protected civil rights.[97]
Also a substantial list of examples of abuse of the detention provisions under
the PTAs (many of which involved the holding of "suspects" incommunicado
for days without charging them, and sometimes without any serious
questioning) were compiled for the National Council for Civil Liberties (as it
then was).[98] Further still, some of the less desirable consequences of
detention without trial were brought to the fore through the notorious case
of *Ireland v United Kingdom*.[99] Although here the legislation itself was not
under direct challenge, it was the facility to detain for prolonged periods
available to the police under the emergency legislation which provided them
with the opportunity to employ the impugned interrogation techniques. And
finally, both Labour and Conservative Governments have recognized the
extreme nature of some of the powers granted to the security forces under
emergency legislation by invoking the European Convention derogation
provision under Article 15; but only (and this is an important point further
discussed below) with respect to the EPAs and not (until 1989) the PTAs.[100]

The *Brogan* case[101]

In view, therefore, of this "public" awareness of the relevance of the
Convention, it is a matter of some regret that the United Kingdom
Government should have found itself in the invidious position of having the
European Court rule in the *Brogan* case that the seven-day detention
provision of s.12 of the PTA 1984 is an infringement of the Convention.[102] In
this case, which was in fact a combination of four complaints (identical, save
in respect of the length of time for which each applicant was detained), the
European Court held that even the shortest of these periods – four days and

---

95   *Ibid*. And although in his article Twining acknowledged the Diplock Commission's
     attempt to observe this cardinal rule, subsequent observance of this rule by Parliament
     whilst enacting anti-terrorist legislation has never been made explicit and so is difficult
     to determine.
96   *Annual Report 1982-83*, HC 262 (1983-84); see also *Annual Reports: 1983-84*, HC 175
     (1984-85), paras 8-38; and *1985-86*, HC 151 (1986-87), pp 8-10; and generally, *The
     Protection of Human Rights by law in Northern Ireland*, Cmnd 7009 (1977). See also the
     recent proposal for a new EPA, *Annual Report 1990-1*, HC 488 (1990-1), pp 86-107.
97   For example: D Bonner, *Emergency Powers in Peacetime* (1985), pp 83-90; DPJ Walsh,
     The Use and Abuse of Emergency Legislation in Northern Ireland (1983), generally; and K
     Boyle, T Hadden and P Hillyard, *Law and State: The Case for Northern Ireland* (1975), pp
     6-26 & 153-161.
98   See C Scorer and P Hewitt, *The Prevention of Terrorism Act: The Case for Repeal* (1984),
     pp 39-54; and C Scorer, S Sencer and P Hewitt, *The New Prevention of Terrorism Act: The
     Case for Repeal* (1985), pp 36-51.
99   ECHR Series 'A', No.25 (1978)
100 Though in 1984 even this (EPA) derogation was withdrawn, see (1984) 128 S.J. 600; and
     further, see *supra*, n.118.
101 *Brogan et al v United Kingdom*, ECHR Series 'A', No.145 (29 Nov.1988).
102 A set of 12 further challenges to s.12 of the PTA were declared admissable by (a chamber
     of) the Commission: *McEldowney et al v United Kingdom*, March 1991.

six hours – was contrary to the requirements of Article 5(3) (that a detainee be brought promptly before a judicial authority).[103] A notable feature of the decision was the emphasis placed by the Court on precedent in reaching its conclusion. Both the Commission and the Court had decided in previous cases that in normal criminal cases a person should be detained for no longer than four days before being brought before a judicial authority.[104] In its report the Commission identified no fewer than five terrorist–related cases in which the Commission and the Court had found extended periods of detention without charge incompatible with the requirements of promptness in Article 5.[105] The main issues in these cases were similar to those in the *Brogan* case, but not identical. The Commission acknowledged that in considering the *Brogan* case it had to bear in mind "the context in which the applicants were arrested and the reality of problems presented by arrest and detention of suspected terrorists".[106] The European Court agreed,[107] though it considered "that the scope for flexibility in interpreting and applying the notion of 'promptness' [in the context of Article 5(3)] is very limited".[108]

It is submitted that even a marginal improvement on the Government's and the legislature's awareness of relevant issues in previous cases brought before the European Commission and Court might have been sufficient for the impact of each of the Prevention of Terrorism (Temporary Provisions) Bills on rights protected by the European Convention to have been better appreciated in Parliament before their enactment. It has always been a declared principle, as the Commission noted in *Brogan*, that "it is inherent in the whole of the Convention that a fair balance has to be struck between the general interest of the Community and the interests of the individual".[109] Yet, as the foregoing account establishes, even at this general level Parliament's and apparently the Government's willingness to investigate the relevance of the European Convention to an issue as threatening to the preservation of civil rights as detention without charge or trial is inadequate.

Amidst considerable controversy, the United Kingdom Government chose to respond to the European Court's ruling in the *Brogan* case by registering with the Council of Europe a "Notice of Derogation" in respect of the seven-day detention provision (now s.14 of PTA 1989).[110] A challenge to the derogation has since been declared admissible by the European Commission.[111]

---

[103] *Supra*, n.101, para.62. In this respect the Court disagreed with the Commission, as the latter held that the two shortest periods (four days and six hours, and four days and eleven hours) did fall within the permissible limits of Article 5(3). Report of the Commission, *Brogan et al v United Kingdom* (14 May 1987), para.107.

[104] Report of the Commission, *ibid*, para.103; and ECHR, No.145, *supra*, n.101, para.57.

[105] *Supra*, n.103, para.104. In all, ten periods of varying length were considered (a number of cases involved more than one complaint), three of which were for, or just below, the seven–day maximum available under United Kingdom law. The warning these cases served was not, it appears, heeded by successive United Kingdom Governments.

[106] *Supra*, n.103, para.106.

[107] *Brogan et al v United Kingdom*, ECHR, *supra*, n.101, para.61.

[108] *Ibid*, para.62.

[109] Report of the Commission – *supra*, n.103, para.80.

[110] Statement by the Home Secretary (the Rt. Hon. Douglas Hurd), HC Standing Committee. B, sixth sitting, col.235. (22 Dec. 1988)

[111] *Brannigan & McBride v United Kingdom*; declared admissible by the Commission on 28 Feb. 1991.

The *McVeigh* case

A second example of terrorist–related legislation transgressing the Convention is even more blatant. In the case of *McVeigh, O'Neill & Evans v United Kingdom*, the European Commission found, in the case of two applicants, that detention for 45 hours without access to their wives was in breach of the applicants' rights protected under Article 8.[112] At the time (1977) rights of access to solicitors and relatives were not covered by statute, but by the Judges' Rules, which were indeterminate on the question of length of time for which access could be rightfully denied. The Rules stated only that every person in custody had a right to be provided with the opportunity of contacting his friends, relatives and a solicitor, except where in so doing it was reasonably likely that the process of investigation would be hindered. The Police and Criminal Evidence Act 1984 established a statutory provision concerning rights of access, but in setting the maximum permissible length of time for which a terrorist suspect might be detained without contact with friends, relatives or solicitors at 48 hours,[113] the Act clearly contradicted the conclusion of the Commission in the *McVeigh* case reported fully three years previously. In the context of the present argument it matters little that the disparity is just three hours; the fact that an opinion of the Commission should be disregarded at all is yet another disturbing example of what is at best indifference, or at worst deliberate defiance, on the part of the Government. It is impossible to believe that the Home Office in drawing up either of the Police and Criminal Evidence Bills[114] was not fully aware of the conclusion of the Commission in the *McVeigh* case, as three members of its staff actually represented the Government in the case![115]

The Home Secretary never offered, and was not asked to provide, an explanation for this unequivocal contradiction as the matter was not raised in the many hours of debate, in both Houses and in the committee rooms, during the passage of the Police and Criminal Evidence Act 1984.[116] This is surprising given the continuous and serious interest in the conditions of detainees with respect to legal advice and access to friends and relatives that was evident throughout all parliamentary deliberations of the Prevention of Terrorism Bills and renewal orders, and the two Police and Criminal Evidence Bills.[117] The conclusions in the *McVeigh* case in respect of rights of

---

112 *Report of the Commission* (18 March 1981), para.240. The Committee of Ministers concurred with the Commission's decision in its *Resolution DH (82)1* (24 March 1982), reported in 5 EHRR 71, para.113.

113 Ss 56(11)(b) (access to friends and relatives), and 58(13)(a) (access to solicitor) provide for the denial of access for a terrorist suspect only for a period "beyond which he may no longer be detained without the authority of the Secretary of State", as presently determined by s.14(4) of PTA 1989 (ie. 48 hours). See also s.44 of EPA 1991 for similar restrictions of access.
The Government was unable to provide statistics on the use of the PTA 1989 version of this provision when asked: HC Deb. Vol.193, col.367 (w) (24 June 1991).

114 The first was introduced into the House of Commons on 17 November 1982 (HC Deb. Vol.32, col.280) – it failed with the General Election in June 1983; and the second was introduced into the House of Commons on 26 October 1983 (HC Deb. Vol.47, col.284).

115 Report of the Commission – *supra*, n.112, "Introduction".

116 Nor was the matter picked up by M Zander in his examination of the Act: *The Police and Criminal Evidence Act 1984* (1985).

117 Note the *Report of the Committee of Inquiry into Police Interrogation Procedures in Northern Ireland*, Cmnd 7497 (1979) (the "Bennet Report"), in which it was stated that in Northern

access for detainees might have been better appreciated and duly acted upon had there existed some formal scrutinizing machinery to bring the views of the European Commission and Court to the attention of Parliament during the passage of the 1984 Act. The *McVeigh* case again demonstrates the evidently unsatisfactory operation of the present arrangements for the screening of legislation for compliance with the European Convention. For even should the direct consequences of this particular infringement be not too grave, the real danger lies in the fact that it was allowed to happen at all.

The partial use of derogation

It would appear that for some time there has existed in Government an attitude which facilitates occurrences such as the above. Perhaps this is best illustrated by the United Kingdom's use of derogation notices under the European Convention. It was always something of a mystery that the United Kingdom chose to invoke the derogation provisions of Article 15(1) of the Convention only with respect to the EPAs when comparable powers were available under the PTAs.[118] The inconsistency in treatment between the two sets of Acts in this respect is all the more incomprehensible in view of the fact that the EPAs have applied only to Northern Ireland whilst the PTAs have extended to all parts of the United Kingdom despite it being at least arguable that the circumstances in Great Britain, being less serious than in Northern Ireland, do not warrant such extreme powers. In regard to their respective detention provisions the maximum period for which a suspect may have been detained under the EPA was only three days (until the relevant section of the EPA 1978 was effectively removed by the EPA 1987)[119] compared to seven days under the PTA (s.12). Furthermore, it has been suggested that the limitations on the use of s.12 of the PTA were actually less stringent than those on s.11 of the EPA 1978.[120] Finally, perhaps the most lamentable fact of all is the negligence of successive governments in not devoting equal attention to the relevance of the European Convention to the two sets of emergency legislation, with the result that the European Court in the *Brogan* case held s.12 of the PTA to be in violation of the Convention. It might be considered a moot point whether reliance on the derogation provisions of the Convention for the PTAs would have altered the Commission's decision to refer that case to the Court. However, this is most unlikely. The Commission already has a policy of considering the issues relevant to derogation even where the Government has not explicitly relied upon them under Article 15,[121] with the result that such issues were considered in this case.[122] Yet still the decisions of both the Commission and the Court favoured the applicants. It would appear that the Commission in particular felt compelled by the long line of precedents to find against the United Kingdom's seven-day detention legislation.

Ireland the Royal Ulster Constabulary actively pursued a policy of refusing detainees access to legal advice, para.123.

[118] For the texts of these notices, see the following Year Book of European Convention on Human Rights references: 1971 (14), p.32; 1973 (16) p.26; 1975 (18) p.18; 1978 (21) p.22. The notices were finally withdrawn in 1984 (see (1984) 128 SJ 600).

[119] See *supra*, n.82 and accompanying text.

[120] Walsh, *supra*, n.97, p.27; see also, *supra*, pp 57–8.

[121] Bonner, *supra*, n.97, p.89.

[122] *Brogan et al v United Kingdom*, ECHR, *supra*, n.101, para.48.

As already indicated, the significance of the anti-terrorism legislation to the argument for an improvement in parliamentary scrutiny of legislation lies in the very controversy that surrounds it. For, as the above account illustrates, even in this controversial matter the question of legislative compliance with the Convention is never satisfactorily raised in Parliament, let alone properly addressed through argument.

Conclusion

From the examples discussed in this chapter there emerges a pattern reflecting an almost institutionalized attitude of neglect towards the European Convention within government which, even if not wilful, is inexcusable. The pertinence of the Convention is rarely discussed during the parliamentary stages of a bill. We are assured, however, that its requirements are considered at the policy-making and drafting stages.[123] Yet if this is the case, then is it not curious that, on the rare occasions when the topic is raised, the Government should choose either simply to ignore the matter,[124] or first glibly to acknowledge the point and then to ignore it.[125] Surely the Convention warrants greater respect than this. If its provisions have been attended to by the appropriate government department prior to a Bill's introduction to Parliament, why not say as much, and perhaps also convey to Parliament the outcome of such consideration. The absence of any machinery through which the significance of the Convention might be made clearer to Parliament (and to government departments) has been conspicuous and damaging.

This fact notwithstanding, the Convention was ratified by the United Kingdom more than forty years ago since when, as we have seen,[126] there has been a steadily increasing stream of adverse decisions involving primary legislation against the United Kingdom handed down by the European Court. There have also been a number of judgments delivered in respect of legislation in other member states which were not without significance for United Kingdom law. These factors alone ought to have been sufficient to ensure a wide appreciation and implementation of the Convention's safeguards throughout the United Kingdom's law-making process. Added to this, the pressure from interest groups, official bodies, and assorted experts[127] on successive governments to recognize the full impact of their more controversial legislative proposals on Convention-protected rights should have guaranteed a higher profile for the Convention. Yet, as the above accounts of legislation relating to terrorism, homosexuality, immigration, mental health, criminal justice and child care in particular plainly illustrate, this has not been the case.

There remains no option, therefore, but to conclude that the current "process" for ensuring observance of the Convention (if, in a formal sense, one can be discerned at all) is thoroughly inadequate. Certainly, the creation of a specialized body concentrating on this scrutinizing task alone (and not,

---

123 See *McVeigh, supra*, n.112, para.157; and further, Chapter 1, *supra*, pp 12–13 and Chapter 6, *infra*, pp 130–1.
124 As, for example, with the Prevention of Terrorism Bill 1983–4, *supra*, n.67.
125 As, for example, with the Commonwealth Immigrants Bill, *supra*, n.30.
126 Chapter 1, *supra*.
127 As evidenced by my account of the prevention of terrorism legislation, *supra*.

as with policy-makers, drafters, and ordinary members of Parliament, approaching it simply as one of many) would provide a more effective assurance against inadvertent (careless, or otherwise), breaches of the rights under the Convention.

4 INFRINGEMENT OF THE EUROPEAN CONVENTION BY SECONDARY LEGISLATION

This chapter comprises a detailed examination of the compatibility with the European Convention on Human Rights of three prominent examples of delegated legislation – namely, the Prison Rules, the Immigration Rules, and the annual renewals of the Prevention of Terrorism Acts (PTAs).[1] All three have been subject to examination before the adjudicative organs of the Council of Europe, and also all possess additional peculiar characteristics which commend them to study within the context of this book. The chapter focuses on these instances in giving consideration to the general question of infringement of the Convention in subordinate legislation.

The Prison Rules have formed the central issue of concern in no less than five judgments of the European Court against the United Kingdom.[2] What is more, essentially the same aspect of the Rules was involved in each case. This record might be explained in part by the absence of any parliamentary scrutiny of the compatibility of the Rules with the Convention when they came before Parliament for approval. Partly, also, an explanation might be

---

1   This *excludes* two examples of secondary legislation in other areas that the European Court judged were in violation of the Convention – namely, *Gaskin v United Kingdom*, ECHR Series 'A', No.160 (7 July 1989) in which it was held that regulations issued in 1983 under the Local Authority Social Services Act 1970 permitting the disclosure of future care records to the individuals concerned but *not* past records (*ibid*, para.23) was a violation of Article 8 (*ibid*, paras 33–49); and, *Granger v United Kingdom*, ECHR Series 'A', No.174 (28 March 1990) in which it was held that the absence of review of a refusal of legal aid to appeal against a conviction in the Legal Aid (Scotland) (Criminal Proceedings) Scheme 1975, made pursuant to the (now replaced) Legal Aid (Scotland) Act 1967 (*ibid*, paras 30–1) was contrary to Article 6(1)(3)(c) (*ibid*, paras 42–8).

2   *Golder; Silver; Campbell & Fell; Boyle & Rice* and *McCallum*; see Appendix 1, *infra*, for full references; for discussion, see *infra*, pp 68–82.

found in the fact that as the same matter (namely, prisoners' correspondence rights) formed the basis for five consecutive cases, it would appear that there exists an unwarranted obduracy on the part of the Government in respect of its response to adverse rulings from the Commission or the Court. It cannot be emphasized too strongly that the Convention provides guidelines as to the minimum level of protection of basic human rights,[3] and is not to be viewed simply as an intrusive set of protected rights to be honoured only when the European Court so dictates.

Throughout the proceedings in the five cases before the Commission and the Court, the question of the extent of ministerial discretion, provided for by the Prison Rules, to issue operational instructions to the prison authorities was the focus of considerable contention.

The matter of discretion is also central to the continuing debate over the compliance of the Immigration Rules with the Convention. Not only is a significant proportion of immigration law administered through unpublished instructions issued by the Home Secretary directing immigration officers on how to apply the Rules, but the precise legal status of the Rules themselves is uncertain. Nevertheless, only one case directly concerning the Immigration Rules has come before the European Court of Human Rights,[4] though many applications have been made to the Commission. A remarkable feature of the relationship between the Immigration Rules and the Convention in recent years has been the pre-eminence of the question of conformity to the Convention during the formative stages of new sets of Rules and amendments to existing ones. Several factors have contributed to this position, not the least of which is that since the Commission's decision in the *East African Asians* case,[5] the Rules' comformity in this respect is now more frequently called into question both inside and outside Parliament. In spite of this heightened awareness, however, the requirements of the Convention are not always understood, still less implemented, by the Government and the legislature.

Finally, the conspicuous nature of the extraordinary restrictive provisions of the Prevention of Terrorism (Temporary Provisions) Acts fires the controversy that accompanied their annual renewals. Nonetheless, as is demonstrated in this chapter, such a high profile carries no guarantee that the impact this legislation will have on the rights protected by the Convention will even be recognized by either the Government or Parliament.

---

3   See R Beddard, *Human Rights in Europe* (1980, 2nd edn), p.178. Significant proportions of the total number of applications to the European Commission from the United Kingdom are lodged by persons held in detention. From a peak in the period between 1964 and 1976, when the average annual figure was approximately 40% (an average of 170 applications per annum), the numbers have fallen to around 15% (an average of about 80 applications per annum) in the 1980s. In part this drop reflects the relative success of a number of these applications before the European Commission and Court; see *infra*, pp 67–82.
    Source: adapted from statistics published by the European Commission (1983), as reproduced by Sir James Fawcett, "Applications of the European Convention on Human Rights" in M Maguire, J Vagg and R Morgan (eds), *Accountability and Prisons* (1985), p.63.
4   *Abdulaziz, Cabales & Balkandali* (1985), see *infra*, n.133 and accompanying text.
5   See, *infra*, n.103 and accompanying text.

The Prison Rules

The long and troubled history of the United Kingdom's complex Prison Rules contains some less than edifying exposures of their defects in cases brought before the European Court. In respect of the rules governing the censorship of prisoners' correspondence (particularly with legal advisers), the United Kingdom Government has received adverse rulings from both the European Commission and the Court in five cases.[6] Throughout these confrontations the Government has consistently argued that the restrictions on the rights of prisoners, including the vetting of their mail, are inherent features of detention. FG Jacobs, however, has pointed out that this position is especially difficult to defend, "since the restrictions imposed under the English (sic) Prison Rules appear to have no parallel in most other contracting States".[7]

The current set of consolidated Prison Rules dates from 1964 and marks the first consolidation since 1949. In the intervening years there had been numerous alterations, amendments and additions to the Rules which even in 1949 numbered a not insubstantial 207. This fact, together with the Home Office practice of issuing internal Standing Orders and Circular Instructions to all Prison Governors in an attempt to exercise some central control over the implementation of the Rules and, more generally, over the day-to-day functioning of British prisons, had led to a position of thorough obfuscation.[8] The 1964 Rules came into being as a Statutory Instrument subject to the negative procedure,[9] on a motion moved by the Secretary of State under the powers vested in him by s.47(1) (and in accordance with s.52(2)) of the Prison Act 1952. During the debate little attention was paid to the consequences of restricting the opportunity of prisoners to correspond with legal advisers, though there was some concern that the requirement that any interview between a prisoner and his legal adviser involving any legal issue (other than litigation to which the prisoner was already party) was to be held within sight and hearing of a prison officer (Rule 37(2)) was a "denial of justice".[10] This omission is surprising, given the power of the Secretary of State under the Rules to intercept prisoners' mail, on grounds of

---

6   In addition the Committee of Ministers decided in *Chester v United Kingdom* that there had been a violation of Article 8 of the Convention by the Prison Rules; the impugned provisions in this case, however, had been abolished by the time the case had reached the Commission; see *Resolution DH(90) 37* (13 Dec. 1990).

7   FG Jacobs, *The European Convention on Human Rights*, (1975), p.91. The Rules apply also in Wales.

8   Indeed, during the House of Commons debate on the new Rules of 1964, Mr William Warbey MP admitted that he had spent "many hours" along with the staff of the Commons Library trying to ascertain the full extent of all types of prison regulations. HC Deb. Vol.687, cols 1369 & 1371 (23 Jan. 1964). See also the Earl of Longford's expressions of frustration when faced with the multi-tiered hierarchy of prison regulations, while attempting to delimit the full parameters of the censorship of prisoners' correspondence, HL Deb. Vol.387, cols 2064-5 (13 Dec. 1977). See also, A Tettenborn, "Prisoners' Rights", [1980] PL 75.

9   The negative motion was criticized by Mr Niall McDermot MP for causing the debate on the Rules to be "hamstrung" on account of the fact that they could only be accepted or rejected *in toto*, and not amended. HC Deb. Vol.687, col.1384, (23 Jan. 1964).

10   *Ibid*, col.1386 (*per* Mr Warbey MP). If the prisoner is already party to an action, then such an interview may be held within sight but out of hearing of an officer (Rule 37(1)). There were also reservations expressed over the lack of any specific provision for prisoners to write to their MPs, *ibid*, cols 1359-62 & 1394-5.

both content and quantity. The scope of this discretionary power was perhaps not fully appreciated at the time, though an indication of the Government's general attitude was evident from remarks made by the Home Secretary during the debate. In response to an inquiry about the right of a prisoner to be accompanied by a friend, relative or solicitor when presenting his case before visiting magistrates on a charge of an offence against prison discipline, he declared that "one cannot go more than a certain distance in these cases. A man who has got himself into prison cannot hope to have all the advantages that a free man would have outside if he was having his case presented by a lawyer or a trade union official or someone like that".[11]

This statement would appear to disregard the provisions of Article 6(3)(c) (right to legal assistance) of the European Convention. Yet, at no point during the debate on the Prison Rules was the Convention even mentioned. As subsequent events in Strasbourg have demonstrated the danger that some of the Rules might violate certain rights in the Convention was always present.

The *Golder* case

The first case to be brought before the Commission and the Court involving the Prison Rules was *Golder v United Kingdom* in 1975.[12] Whilst Mr Golder was in Parkhurst prison there occurred a serious disturbance during which a prison officer was attacked by a number of inmates including, the officer alleged, Mr Golder. Though no charges were preferred against him, an entry describing the event remained in his record, marked with the words "Charges not proceeded with". Golder maintained his innocence from the beginning and the fact that a record of any kind, even one so qualified, remained on his file was, he claimed, to his detriment, especially in respect of his chances of gaining early parole. After petitioning the Secretary of State under Rules 33 and 34, Mr Golder was refused permission to contact a solicitor with a view to initiating defamation proceedings regarding the prison officer's statement in his prison record. Believing this to be an infringement of his rights to a fair trial (Article 6(1)), and to privacy of correspondence (Article 8), Golder submitted an application to the European Commission. Subsequently, the Commission concluded that there had been a violation of Mr Golder's rights as he claimed.[13] When the case came before the European Court, the discretion extended to the Home Secretary by Rules 33 and 34 was examined in detail. It was the opinion of the Court that

> [b]y forbidding Golder to such contact [with a solicitor], the Home Secretary actually impeded the launch of the contemplated action. Without formally denying Golder his right to institute proceedings before a court, the Home Secretary did in fact prevent him from commencing an action at that time, 1970. Hindrance in fact can contravene the Convention just like a legal impediment.[14]

In which case *access* to a court, the judgment continued, is of paramount importance, as the "fair, public and expeditious characteristics of judicial

---

11   *Ibid*, col.1314.
12   ECHR Series 'A', No.18 (21 Feb. 1975).
13   *Golder v United Kingdom*, Report of the Commission, [1973] ECHR Series 'B', No.16 (5 July 1973), paras 99 & 123.
14   ECHR Series 'A', No.18, *supra*, n.12, para.26.

proceedings are of no value at all if there are to be no judicial proceedings".[15] Accordingly, the Court concluded that the Home Secretary's denial of leave to Golder to consult a solicitor was a violation of his right under Article 6(1).[16] Equally, the Court found that Golder's right to privacy under Article 8 had been infringed.[17] The Court accepted that in certain circumstances, as provided for under Article 8(2), there is a "'necessity' for interference with the right of a prisoner to respect for his correspondence, having regard to the ordinary and reasonable requirements of imprisonment".[18] In the opinion of the Court, however, the Government's argument for the "necessity" of restricting correspondence, based largely on the ground of prevention of crime and disorder, was in this case without foundation.[19]

The Government could not let these strictures pass unheeded. In response to the Commission's Report, it amended the Prison Rules in respect of, amongst other things, prisoners' correspondence with legal advisers.[20] Rule 37 was supplemented by a provision giving inmates the right to correspond with legal advisers, but only in respect of proceedings to which they are already party. This palliative measure subsequently proved to be insufficient in the light of the European Court's judgment in the *Golder* case, where the entitlement to access to legal advice was rooted in a more general right than the one conceded by the United Kingdom in the above amendment. The Court considered that the ability of the Home Secretary to prevent a prisoner *commencing* an action amounted to an infringement of the Convention.[21] Prisoners, therefore, must be allowed access to legal assistance whether or not they are already party to an action. Once again the Government was obliged to amend Rule 37. This time it was to provide that "a prisoner may correspond with a solicitor for the purpose of obtaining legal advice concerning any course of action by which the prisoner may become a party to civil proceedings or for the purpose of instructing the solicitor to issue such proceedings".[22] Yet, even this was (and remains) qualified by being made "[s]ubject to any directions of the Secretary of State".[23] In effect, therefore, the scope for the Home Secretary to deny this right in a manner and according to criteria that may subsequently be found to be contrary to the Convention is retained. A request for government time to be provided for a debate on this amendment was refused by the Home Secretary.[24] He might have been better advised to have acceded to this request, as the hazard of retaining such a level of ministerial discretion in the Rule might then have been better appreciated and the Rule modified accordingly. Moreover, he

---

15   *Ibid*, para.35.
16   *Ibid*, para.40.
17   "Impeding someone from even initiating correspondence constitutes the most far-reaching form of 'interference' (para.2 of Article 8) with the exercise of the right to respect for correspondence," *ibid*, para.43.
18   *Ibid*, para.45.
19   *Ibid*.
20   The Prison (Amendment) Rules 1972, S.I.1972/1860.
21   See *supra*, n.13.
22   The Prison (Amendment) Rules 1976, S.I.1976/503, para.4. Both the amendments to Rule 37 remove correspondence with a solicitor from the otherwise general requirement for leave from the Secretary of State to correspond with anyone other than a friend or a relative, as provided in Rule 34(8).
23   *Ibid*.
24   Rt. Hon. Roy Jenkins, HC Deb. Vol.909, cols 611–12 (8 April 1976).

could not have been unaware of this inherent danger, for in the same year (1976) no fewer than 197 applications to the European Commission were made by persons held in detention (46% of the total number of applications made by United Kingdom citizens during the whole of 1976), though of course not all of these concerned complaints over prisoners' rights of correspondence and their rights to legal advice.[25] One such case was initiated by Mr Reuben Silver.

The *Silver* case[26]

Mr Silver's application to the European Commission was subsequently joined by six others. All applications were lodged before the laying of the 1976 amendment to the Prison Rules mentioned above. Though the applicants were concerned generally with the censorship of prisoners' correspondence on all matters, they focused primarily on the powers contained in Rule 33, and the corresponding S.O.17, which enabled the prison authorities to stop letters seeking legal advice.[27] Their complaints were based on two issues: the wide discretionary powers of the Secretary of State to censor prisoners' correspondence (Rule 33), and, secondly, the requirement that all complaints had to be first raised and settled through the appropriate internal channels before prisoners were permitted to communicate their grievances to a legal adviser – the so called "'prior ventilation rule" (S.O.17(A)). In both respects the applicants claimed that the Government was in breach of Articles 6(1) and 8 of the Convention.[28]

The discretionary power of the Secretary of State

Under the authority of Rule 33(1), (2) and (3), the Secretary of State, through his delegates, censored a number of the applicants' letters.[29] This, it was alleged, was an unjustified interference with the prisoners' right to respect for their correspondence under Article 8.[30] The Government, in response, sought to justify the censorship by way of the two–part qualification to the right of privacy provided in the Article. The right may be restricted where it is in accordance with the law to do so, and where it is necessary in a democratic society.[31] In regard to the first part, it was maintained by the Government that the relevant powers granted to the Secretary of State were within the boundaries of domestic law (though subsequently even this has

---

[25] Source: European Commission (1983), *supra*, n.6.
[26] Report of the Commission, ECHR Series 'B', No.51 (11 Oct. 1980). The Commission's report is in this section generally preferred to that of the European Court because it dealt more thoroughly with the issues involved, and in any case the Court largely agreed with the Commission and added little in its judgment; see *infra*, n.56 and accompanying text.
[27] Both the Order and the Rule originate from the same source – namely, Circular Instruction 45/1975.
[28] In not providing an effective remedy for breaches of Articles 6 and 8, breach of Article 13 was also alleged; both the Commission and the Court found subsequently that such a breach had occurred, Report of the Commission, *supra*, n.26, para.445; and for the Court, *infra*, n.56.
[29] In all, 62 letters were stopped by prison authorities, *ibid*, para.75.
[30] *Ibid*, para.101.
[31] The relevant categories that fulfil the latter criterion listed in the Article 8(2) are: in the interests of public safety or economic well–being of the country; the prevention of disorder or crime; for the protection of morals; and for the protection of the rights and freedoms of others. See also *infra*, n.42, and accompanying text.

been successfully challenged in a domestic court),[32] and as such were in accordance with the law. The applicants did not dispute the lawfulness of the Secretary of State's powers under United Kingdom law, but they did question their compliance with the provisions of the European Convention. They argued that the phrase "in accordance with the law" as used in Article 8 could not simply be reduced to "in accordance with *domestic* law", as such a subjectively determined concept would be open to abuse – a more objective orientation must have been intended. The European Commission agreed, and in so doing emphasized the requirement that the law be foreseeable in its application.[33] It followed, therefore, that the Commission also upheld the applicants' claim that "any interference with a person's right under Article 8 must be predetermined by clear substantive law in order to render any interference reasonably foreseeable, adequate safeguards being set up against a misuse of power by a public authority".[34]

In their submission the applicants presciently argued that one of the instrumental reasons why the prison regulations failed to adhere to the demands of the Convention was that they were inadequately scrutinized before coming into operation, particularly in respect of their compliance with the European Convention.[35] It was their contention that the discretionary control over prisoners' correspondence was neither "sufficiently defined by any primary or secondary legislation which has the force of law".[36] Nor was this control properly policed for abuse, there being no form of effective judicial review or parliamentary scrutiny in operation.[37]

On considering these matters, the Commission concluded that the "vast discretion" conferred on the Home Secretary and the prison authorities to censor prisoners' correspondence meant that it was "impossible to establish the limits of the power or to foresee any interference, there being, moreover, no safeguards against misuse of the discretion".[38] This lack of precision in the substantive law covering interference with prisoners' correspondence which rendered such interference less predictable, was, in the Commission's opinion, contrary to the essential elements of the phrase "in accordance with the law" as established by the European Court in its judgment in the *Sunday Times* case.[39] These are that the application of the law is to be both foreseeable ("to a degree that is foreseeable in the circumstances"), and accessible (that is, "the citizen must be able to have an indication that is adequate in the circumstances of the legal rules applicable to a given case").[40] In the view of the Commission, the Prison Rules satisfied only the

32 *R v Secretary of State for the Home Dept, ex parte Anderson* [1984] 1 QB 779, see *infra*, n.78.
33 Report of the Commission, *supra*, n.26, para.284.
34 *Ibid*, para.278, and the Commission's concurrence, para.284.
35 *Ibid*, para.116.
36 *Ibid*, para.114.
37 *Ibid*, paras 113–116. This position is accentuated in regard of the quasi-legislative nature of Standing Orders and Circular Instructions – parts of the former having become publicly available only since 1981, and the latter not made public at all. See also, G Ganz, *Quasi-Legislation: Recent Developments in Secondary Legislation* (1987), p.40.
38 *Ibid*, para.279.
39 *The Sunday Times v United Kingdom*, ECHR Series 'A', No.30 (26 April 1979).
40 *Ibid*, para.49.

second of these criteria (in that they are public and are made known to the prisoners), but not that of foreseeability, as the discretion they grant to the Secretary of State was considerable and, therefore, not easily predictable. The Standing Orders and Circular Instructions on the other hand were held to satisfy neither criteria. As they were unpublished, the extent to which they restricted correspondence could not be "reasonably deduced from the [published] Prison Rules".[41]

The second exception to the right to privacy under Article 8 is if interference by a public body is "necessary in a democratic society" on the grounds, for instance, of public safety or the prevention of crime and disorder. In the *Silver* case the Government maintained that the acts complained of could be justified under one or more of these exceptions.[42] The applicants responded by indicating that the Government's plea was undermined at the most basic level by the absence of any direct parliamentary control over the formulation and application of the administrative orders covering the vetting of prisoners' correspondence. Furthermore, it was argued that, as with all qualifications to the rights in the Convention, the invocation of those in Article 8 is "strictly limited to the requirements of public policy in the face of a 'genuine and sufficiently serious threat'".[43] It was considered by the applicants that their correspondence caused no such serious threat.

In delivering its opinion, the Commission first categorized the censored letters according to their content and purpose and then assessed the merits of the justification for censorship used in each category. In respect of all but two of the resultant thirteen categories the Commission considered that the Government had not offered sufficient reasons to justify the censorship as "necessary in a democratic society", and consequently decided unanimously that there had been a violation of Article 8.[44] The interception of letters in the categories of "containing threats of violence", and "discussing crime in general or the crimes of others", not surprisingly, were considered justified under the terms of Article 8.[45]

Article 6(1) secures for everyone the right of access to the courts in order to

---

41   Report of the Commission; *supra*, n.26, paras 283–4. This consequence was anticipated by Lord Gardiner in a Lords' debate on the rights of prisoners to communicate with members of the public, when he warned that in attempting to invoke the *non obstante* provision to the general right of privacy in Article 8, "we are in difficulty if so many of these restrictions come under Standing Orders and Circular Instructions", HL Deb. Vol.387, col.2078 (13 Dec. 1977).

42   *Ibid*, paras 131–144, for these exceptions, see *supra*, n.31.

43   *Ibid*, para.123. The Court here drew upon reasoning used in a judgment of the European Court of Justice: *R v Marlborough Street Stipendiary Magistrate, ex parte Bouchereau* [1977] ECJ 1999, at 2013–4 (paras 33–35).

44   *Supra*, n.26, paras 296–409. The eleven categories under which censorship was deemed unjustifiable under Article 8 were: complaints about prison treatment; correspondence to persons other than friends or relatives; letters dealing with legal matters without the prior leave of the Secretary of State; letters containing material intended for publication; letters containing material deliberately calculated to hold the prison authorities up to contempt; letters containing representations about trial, conviction, or sentence; letters attempting to stimulate public agitation or petition; letters which circumvent or evade prison regulations; letters containing allegations about prison officers; letters in connection with business matters without the prior leave of the Secretary of State; and letters containing grossly improper language.

45   *Ibid*, paras 410–422.

obtain a "fair and public hearing" of their case. An essential element of the exercise of this right is the freedom to seek and obtain legal advice. As indicated earlier, it was determined in the *Golder* case that a refusal of leave to seek legal advice may be a violation of the right under Article 6(1) of the Convention. Nevertheless, just such a refusal was made by the Secretary of State in relation to a petition from Mr Silver. Consequently, and for precisely the same reasons as in the *Golder* case, the Commission found in favour of Mr Silver: "... in his refusal of permission to consult a solicitor, the Secretary of State failed to respect Mr Silver's right to go before a civil court as guaranteed by Article 6(1) of the Convention".[46]

The "prior ventilation rule"

Though the *Golder* case did prompt some changes in the rules controlling the opportunities for prisoners to correspond with legal advisers (the new S.O.17(A) came into operation in 1976), the requirement that all grievances had to be both aired and settled internally before permission could be sought from the Secretary of State remained in force. The issue of the compatibility of this so-called "prior ventilation rule", in respect of correspondence seeking legal advice, with the demands of the Convention rose again in the *Silver* case.[47] The Commission's trenchant comments on the new S.O.17(A) were, as we shall see later, of a strength sufficient to prompt further change in the prison Standing Orders.

As paraphrased in a later case involving the same issue,[48] S.O.17(A) provided, *inter alia*, that:

(i)   the inmate had to have sought a solicitor's advice before he could institute proceedings;
(ii) at each stage [within such proceedings] a written application, with reasons, had first to be made to the prison Governor for the necessary facilities, which could take the form of a letter or a visit; they had to be granted immediately, *except that*, in the case of prospective civil proceedings against the Home Office (or any servant thereof) 'arising out of or in connexion with' the imprisonment, *the "prior ventilation rule" generally applied'* [emphasis supplied].

The effect of this rule was to withhold facilities to obtain legal advice until the complaint had been raised through the usual internal channels[49] and that a decision, whether favourable or not, had been reached. It was claimed that the rule was intended "to enable the prison management to provide an immediate remedy".[50]

---

46   *Ibid*, para.432.
47   The aspect of the "prior ventilation rule" to which the applicants in the *Silver* case primarily objected – that is, where a complaint raised internally was considered not to warrant the need to seek legal advice, then that was in effect the end of the matter – had been removed from the relevant Standing Order (No.17) by the time the case was considered by the Commission in 1980. The old S.O.17, however, had been in force in 1972 and 1973 when the attempts of Mr Silver and others to obtain leave to seek legal advice had been thwarted. Since the prisoners' grievances under the old Order were of an almost identical nature to those brought before the Commission and the Court in the *Golder* case, the result was, therefore, also to be the same – the Commission and later the Court (see below), found that there had been a breach of Article 6(1) and accordingly ruled against the Government, *ibid*, para.432.
48   *Campbell & Fell v United Kingdom*, ECHR Series 'A', (1984), No.80 (28 June 1984), para.44. The paraphrasing is necessary because S.O.17(A) was not publicly available.
49   Report of the Commission in the *Silver* case, *supra*, n.26, para.44.
50   *Ibid*, para.310.

The Commission considered that this restriction in the (unpublished) S.O.17(A) could not "reasonably be foreseen in the general discretion conferred upon the prison administration",[51] by Rule 33 of the Prison Rules. It therefore held that "restrictions on such letters of complaint cannot be said to be 'in accordance with the law' within the meaning of Article 8(2)".[52] It was further concluded that the broad-based and indiscriminate nature of the "prior ventilation rule" was in disproportion to its purported aims and that it had not been shown to have been "a restriction which is 'necessary in a democratic society ... for the prevention of disorder' within the meaning of Article 8(2)".[53] As the Commission was at pains to stress, the restriction was, after all, an infringement of what is considered one of the fundamental elements of a democratic society – that is, "that people may seek responsible legal advice on any subject in order to protect or enforce their rights or simply to be reasonably informed".[54] Its imposition, therefore, was permissible only in the gravest circumstances. A blanket prohibition of the seeking of legal advice before the matter has been raised with the appropriate prison authorities certainly does not meet this criterion. The Commission suggested that rather than using a "prior ventilation rule", the Government would be equally well served and would remain within the boundaries of Article 8 if, instead, a "simultaneous ventilation rule" was employed.[55]

Judgment of the European Court

In all significant respects the European Court agreed with the Commission in the *Silver* case.[56] This had become inevitable after the Government decided not to contest the vast majority of the Commission's conclusions, largely because it had already conceded most of them by modifying (in 1981) the regulations covering prisoners' correspondence in direct response to the Commission's report.[57] Furthermore, it was in the light of the result of the *Silver* case that the Government chose not to contest the challenges (thereby accepting that there had been violations of Article 8 of the Convention) in the cases of *Boyle & Rice* and *McCallum*[58] to the corresponding Prison Rules and Standing Orders in Scotland which related to the stopping of letters (in periods between 1980–1); the relevant legislative provisions in Scotland were altered accordingly in August 1983.[59]

---

51   *Ibid.*
52   *Ibid*, para.314.
53   *Ibid*, para.312.
54   *Ibid*, para.340. The censorship of letters to MPs under S.O.5(c)(2) these circumstances was also held to be a sanction that was disproportionate to the legitimate aim being pursued, and was considered unnecessary in a democratic society, *ibid*, paras 297–307.
55   Report of the Commission in the *Silver* case, *supra*, n.26, para.302.
56   *Silver & others v United Kingdom*, ECHR Series 'A', No.61 (25 March 1983), paras 82 & 105.
57   Yearbook, ECHR, 1983, European Court Case Law, p.12. Though the Court had no power to review the new regulations, it nevertheless "noted with satisfaction" the substantial changes that they had made.
58   ECHR Series 'A', No.131 (20 May 1988) and ECHR Series 'A', No.183 (30 Aug. 1990), respectively.
59   In respect of *Boyle & Rice*, see *ibid*, paras 25 & 50 (note that an additional reason for the Government's attitude in this case was that it conceded that the relevant rule had been applied in error, *ibid*, para.15), and in respect of *McCallum*, see the Opinion of the Commission in its Report, 4 May 1989, paras 49–50 and the judgment of the Court, *ibid*,

Consequences of the Silver case

With the experience of the *Golder* case behind them, the British Government was perhaps more acutely aware of the political embarrassment that might follow a second adverse judgment from the European Court on the same issue. In August 1975, therefore, long before the Commission considered the *Silver* case (but still some three years after Silver had lodged his complaint with the Commission), an amending Standing Order (S.O.17(A)) was introduced in an attempt to improve the procedure by which prisoners receive legal advice. The Commission, as was noted earlier, considered this modification insufficient in meeting the requirements of the Convention and that further amendments were necessary. The main objection was to the existence of the "prior ventilation rule", which was thought unnecessary and unjustified. The Government responded with the introduction, in 1981, of a substantially revised set of Standing Orders. Some of the new orders (Nos 5B23–5B30) allowed for less restricted prisoner correspondence with individuals and organizations, but subject always to new limitations implemented under S.O.5B34. Of particular interest was 5B34(J), which replaced the maligned "prior ventilation rule" in relation to correspondence (S.O.17(A)) with a "simultaneous ventilation rule", along the lines suggested by the Commission. It now became the case that as soon as a complaint about prison treatment had been raised with the prison authorities,[60] it could be mentioned in correspondence.

This change pre-empted much of what the European Court had to say in the *Silver* case. In fact the only alteration to the regulations consequent upon the judgment of the Court was to the Prison Rule restricting access specifically to solicitors (No.34(8)).[61] This brought the Rule into line with the above modifications to the general rights of correspondence. It effectively removed the requirement for a prisoner to have obtained the leave of the Secretary of State before he could pursue any legal communication.

The *Silver* case was remarkable because it constituted a second illustration of the continuing inadequacy of the United Kingdom's legal provisions for the protection of prisoners' rights of correspondence. To follow the *Golder* case so closely, in terms of time, substance and outcome, is distinction enough. Its principal significance, however, was that for the first time the question of how a system of pre-legislative scrutiny of delegated legislation such as the Prison Rules with respect to their conformity to the European Convention on Human Rights might aid the legislative process. The inadequacy of parliamentary scrutiny of the Rules and the absence of any process of scrutiny by Parliament of the Standing Orders and the quasi-legislative Circular Instructions were factors raised by the applicants in their submissions to the Commission.[62] The case for improvement in these respects is strengthened by the persistence with which the European Commission and the Court find against the United Kingdom in cases involving prisoners' access to legal advice. For shortly after *Golder* and *Silver*, there came yet another major case involving the same issue, that of

---

60   paras 30–1.
     That is, by means of petition to the Secretary of State, or letter to the Governor, or an application to either the Board of Visitors or a visiting officer of the Secretary of State.
61   The Prison (Amendment) Rules 1983, S.I.1983/568, r.4.
62   Report of the Commission, *supra*, n.26, para.116.

Campbell & Fell v United Kingdom.[63]

The public debate and the views of domestic courts

Before considering this case, however, it is of the utmost importance to appreciate the context of informed debate within which both the *Silver* and *Golder* cases had taken place. Concern over the rights of prisoners in general, and those protected by the European Convention in particular, increased markedly since the earliest days of *Golder*, so that by the time the *Silver* case was under way, the Government could not have failed to be aware of the issues and arguments involved. At the same time a pair of cases involving prisoners' rights of correspondence were also before the domestic courts (see below). The advent of subsequent proceedings before the European Court and Commission, therefore, on this question of compliance with the Convention was inexcusable.

Since 1973 there had existed a Council of Europe document entitled *Standard Minimum Rules for the Treatment of Prisoners*.[64] which lent strong support to the argument that the rights protected by the European Convention applied equally to prisoners as to all other members of society. A number of these rules are of particular relevance – namely, that a prisoner is to be provided with the opportunity to present his defence when charged with a disciplinary offence (R.30(3)); that he is to be informed of the prison regulations that affect him (R.35(1)); that facilities are to be provided for the making of requests or complaints to prison authorities (R.36(1) & (2)); and that access to the courts and to legal advice (R.36(3) & R.37) is to be provided. The last two mentioned rules are of particular interest. Rule 36 provides that "[e]very prisoner shall be allowed to make a request or a complaint, *under confidential cover*, to the central administration, the judicial authority or other proper authorities" [emphasis supplied]. Rule 37 states that "[p]risoners shall be allowed to communicate with their family and all persons or representatives of organisations and to receive visits from these persons at regular intervals subject only to such restrictions and supervision as are necessary in the interests of their treatment, and the security and good order of the institution". It is not difficult here to discern the echo of the European Convention: Article 6(1) (access to courts) in the first of these rules, and Article 8 (privacy of correspondence) in the second. The fact that care had been taken to relate the intentions of Articles 6 and 8 of the Convention to the position of prisoners itself provides a forthright reiteration of the need to extend to prisoners the rights therein. Such guidelines ought to have been enough to ensure that no domestic prison regulations would be drawn up without some consideration of their compatibility with these established minimum standards. After all, in the preamble to the *Standard Minimum Rules*, the Committee of Ministers directs "that governments of member states be guided in their internal legislation and practice by the principles set out in the text ... with a view to their

---

63   ECHR Series 'A', No.80, (28 June 1984).
64   *Resolution 73(5)* of the Council of Europe, Committee of Ministers (13 Jan. 1973). The Rules were intended to serve as guidelines to the Convention organs in respect specifically of cases involving the rights of prisoners that come before them; see Sir James Fawcett, *supra*, n.3, p.69. They have since been superseded by the European Prison Rules 1987.

progressive implementation". The *Standard Minimum Rules*, however, appeared not to have been fully appreciated or even understood by the United Kingdom Government. In 1980, for instance (after the *Golder* case, but whilst both the *Silver* and *Campbell & Fell* cases were before the European Commission), the Secretary of State had to be asked twice in Parliament whether all the European *Standard Minimum Rules* were applied in the United Kingdom.[65] In reply, Mr Leon Brittan, then the Home Secretary, indicated on the one hand that "all are accepted and all are implemented", whilst on the other, he refused to revise a Prison Department Circular Instruction (No.46/1978) which, according to Mr Kilroy–Silk (then) MP, explicitly stated where United Kingdom prison practice differed from the *Standard Minimum Rules*, especially in relation to prisoners' correspondence and grievance procedures.[66] Indeed, the Home Secretary stated that identifying these differences was the *very point* of the Instruction.[67] Any commitment to the adoption of the set of *Standard Minimum Rules* was later openly abandoned by the Home Office.[68]

The relation of the prison regulations with the *Standard Minimum Rules* was evaluated by *Justice* in its 1983 Report, *Justice in Prisons*. It commented on a number of points raised in the *Golder* and *Silver* cases and pre-empted some of those that were subsequently to be addressed by the European Commission and Court in the *Campbell & Fell* case. *Justice* recommended, *inter alia*, that the distinction with respect to the presence of a prison officer during legal visits concerning prospective or current actions, and those dealing with "any other legal business" (Prison Rule 37(1) & (2))), should be removed.[69]

Within Parliament also, prisoners' rights of communication had become a matter of some concern. In 1977, during a major debate in the House of Lords on the matter, the Labour peer, Lord Longford, declared: There seems little doubt – I do not think that the Home Office can seriously contest this – that our rules in this country regarding prisoner correspondence are more restrictive – I would say much more restrictive – than those which generally prevail in Western Europe. My first submission must be that we take urgent steps to put our own House in order of our own free will before we are forced to do so under pressure from decisions by the European Commission, and it may be the European Court.[70]

The problem, as Lord Gardiner pointed out, is compounded by the bewildering complexity of the panoply of rules governing prisons, where the delegation of power passes through no less than five levels – one of primary legislation, one of secondary legislation, and three of quasi-legislation.[71] Such a complex hierarchy of rules and regulations clearly does nothing to

65   HC Deb. Vol.987, col.572 (w) (2 July 1980); and HC Deb. Vol.992, col.355 (w) (13 Nov. 1980).
66   *Ibid*, (HC Deb. Vol.992).
67   *Ibid*.
68   Rt Hon. Leon Brittan in reply to Mr R Maclennan MP, HC Deb. Vol.58, col.311 (w) (12 April 1984); see also A Rutherford, *Prisons and the Process of Justice* (1986), pp 112–3.
69   *Ibid*, para.32. For further support for the relaxation of visiting restrictions, see Howard League for Penal Reform pamphlet, *Losing Touch: Restrictions on Prisoners' Outside Contacts* (1979), p.24.
70   HL Deb. Vol.287, col.2064 (13 Dec. 1977); see also col.2069.
71   The levels are: the principal statute – the Prison Act 1952; the Prison Rules made under it; the Prison Department's Standing Orders; Circular Instructions which amend them; and, finally, the Governors' Handbook, *ibid*, cols 2064–5.

ease the task of prisoners wishing to exercise their correspondence and communication rights. One of the gravest criticisms levelled at the United Kingdom's practice of censorship of prisoners' letters arises directly from this profusion of delegation and sub-delegation. It is that many of the exceptions to the general right to privacy of correspondence secured by Article 8 are not provided "in accordance with the law" (as the Article insists), but rather by unpublished administrative edicts.[72] Indeed, the extensive use of quasi- and secondary legislation in prison administration ensures that Parliament's role in the making and scrutiny of these regulations is negligible. For although the Prison Rules are established by Statutory Instrument, their consideration by Parliament is not guaranteed, as they are subject to the negative procedure. Of course, even this opportunity of parliamentary scrutiny is denied the Standing Orders and Circular Instructions of the Prison Department upon which, as was pointed out in *Silver*, "the control of prisoners' correspondence is based".[73]

Scant regard was paid to the caveats and recommendations urged by their Lordships in the debate. One experienced peer – Viscount Long – even summarily dismissed as irrelevant any question of the Prison Rules being out of line with European requirements and declared himself to be "amazed" that the issue of human rights might be involved at all.[74] The Minister of State for the Home Office – Lord Harris – was a little more aware of the difficulties concerned.[75] Yet even his remarks about the need for prisoners to be treated "sensitively and with humanity" yielded no firmer intention to reform the Prison Rules than a rather vague concession "that a great deal more [progress] is both desirable and necessary".[76]

Yet, as Lord Longford had warned, it was not until another adverse decision in Europe (the *Silver* case) that any significant modifications to the regulations on prisoners' correspondence were introduced. By that time, however, the problem had escalated. A few months after the judgment in the *Silver* case had been delivered, the Government revealed that no fewer than 30 applications to the Commission "relating wholly or partly to the control of correspondence are outstanding".[77] Furthermore, the breadth of discretion allowed to the Secretary of State and the prison authorities under the Prison Rules to censor prisoners' correspondence was being questioned in domestic courts.

Despite the replacement in 1981 of the "prior ventilation rule" with the "simultaneous ventilation rule", the latter was challenged in 1983 in *R v Secretary of State for the Home Department, ex parte Anderson*.[78] As the case was before a British court, it was principally the *vires* of the relevant Standing Orders that were in dispute and not (at least not explicitly) their merits, but nevertheless the court found it necessary to address itself to the substance of certain fundamental rights.

---

72   *Ibid*, col.2078.
73   Report of the Commission in the *Silver* case, *supra*, n.26, para.116.
74   HL Deb. Vol.287, col.2070 (13 Dec. 1977).
75   *Ibid*, cols 2102-6.
76   *Ibid*, col.2106.
77   HL Deb. Vol.443, col.639 (w) (6 July 1983). Clearly, many of these would have been initiated when previous administrations were in office.
78   [1984] 1 QB 778.

The restrictions of the "simultaneous ventilation rule" had applied equally to the Standing Orders governing legal visits and general correspondence until an exception has been made for certain legal correspondence following the case of *Raymond v Honey*.[79] In this case the House of Lords confirmed that any interference with the right to unimpeded access to the courts was unlawful (in this instance, amounting to contempt of court).[80] Shortly afterwards an amendment was introduced to the Standing Orders which removed any requirement of ventilation (whether prior or simultaneous) of complaints by prisoners in respect of "an application to a court which constitutes the issuing of proceedings" (S.O.5B33(a)). However, correspondence concerning legal issues other than the issuing of legal proceedings (S.O.5B34(j)), and all visits by legal advisers (S.O.5A34), remained subject to the "simultaneous ventilation rule", and it was on this that Anderson based his case. He alleged that S.O.5A34 and S.O.5B34(j) were *ultra vires* the Prison Act 1952 and the Prison Rules 1964, as there was no provision in s.47 of the former, or in the latter rules made thereunder, to authorize "so substantial an administrative restriction on prisoners' basic civil rights of access to legal advisers and the Courts".[81] Furthermore, it had been established only a few months before, in *Raymond v Honey*, that restrictions on the right of access to a lawyer with a view to starting a legal action were legitimate only if they were specifically and expressly authorized by the parent statute – the Prison Act 1952.[82] Section 47(1) of the Act is not so clear; it authorizes only generally the institution of rules for, amongst other things, the "discipline and control" of prisoners. Certainly this does not grant an unequivocal power to place restrictions on prisoners' access to lawyers. In seeking to determine the meaning of this vague phrase the applicant suggested that one might turn to the European Convention. Indeed, a like recourse had been advocated in an earlier case by Lord Scarman for disentangling ambiguities in domestic law;[83] and moreover, the European Court had made forthright pronouncements (in the *Golder* case) on the sanctity of the right of access to a court and its prerequisite of a right of access to a solicitor.[84] The High Court in the *ex parte Anderson* case agreed with the submission of the applicant that "any ambiguity in the very general provisions of Rule 37(2) of the 1964 Rules and s.47(1) of the Act of 1952 should be resolved by construing them restrictively so as to conform with the requirements of Article 6(1) of the Convention".[85] The court added further that "if any restriction goes beyond the scope of regulating the circumstances in which visits by legal advisers to inmates may take place ... it is ... unauthorised by the Prison Rules".[86] It was held that "a requirement that an inmate should make ... a complaint as a prerequisite of his having access to his solicitor, however desirable it may be in the interests of good administration, goes beyond the regulation of the circumstances in which

---

79   [1983] 1 AC 1.
80   *Ibid*, 12–13.
81   [1984] 1 QB, 780.
82   [1983] 1 AC 10.
83   *Pan American World Airways Inc. v Dept of Trade* [1976] 1 Lloyds Rep. 257, 261; and *Attorney-General v B.B.C.* [1981] AC 303, at 352, 354.
84   *Golder* case, *supra*, n.13, para.35.
85   *Ex parte Anderson*, *supra*, n.78, p.781.
86   *Ibid*, 793.

such access may take place, and does indeed constitute an impediment to his right of access to the civil court".[87] In consequence, the court decided that the restrictions in the Standing Orders relating to visits and correspondence were *ultra vires*.[88] It had become the case, therefore, that the compliance of the United Kingdom's prison regulations with the European Convention was being successfully challenged not only in Strasbourg but also, to a degree, in the domestic courts.

Collaterally, a third case before the European authorities concerning prisoners' rights of access to legal assistance was reaching its conclusion.

The *Campbell & Fell* case

In *Campbell & Fell v United Kingdom*,[89] the allegations centred, once again, on breaches of Articles 6 and 8 of the Convention by the United Kingdom's prison regulations.[90] The European Commission in its report,[91] and the Court in its judgment, came to the same conclusions in all essential respects.[92]

In September 1976 Mr Campbell and Father Fell, together with four other prisoners, were involved in a sit-down protest in a prison corridor against the treatment of another prisoner. A struggle ensued after a number of prison officers attempted to remove the men, during which the applicants and certain members of the staff were injured. Under Prison Rules 47–52, all six men were charged with disciplinary offences, and found guilty by the Board of Visitors. It was held, both by the European Commission and by the Court, that the relevant Prison Rule (No.49(2)), in not specifically affording to Father Fell the opportunity to obtain legal advice and assistance before, and legal representation during, the hearing of the Board, was in violation of Article 6(3)(b) and (c).[93] Additionally, the Court found that in not requiring the Board's decision to be published, the prison regulations violated Article

---

87 *Ibid*, 793–4.
88 *Ibid*, 794. Both Standing Orders have now been amended. Under S.O.5A34, a prisoner is no longer required to disclose in advance the nature of any consultation with his legal adviser except where that legal business does not involve possible proceedings. Likewise, the "simultaneous ventilation rule" has been removed from S.O.5B34(j) by S.O.5B33(b) in respect of all correspondence between an inmate and his legal adviser. The latter supplements the amendment made subsequent to the *Raymond* decision; see text at n.79, *supra*.
89 ECHR Series 'A', No.80 (28 June 1984). In a more recent case that involved, *inter alia*, very similar complaints from four prisoners concerning their access to solicitors, both the Commission (in *Byrne & Others v United Kingdom*, Report of the Commission (3 Dec. 1985)) and the Committee of Ministers, (by *Resolution DH (80) 7* (20 March 1987)), concluded that there had been a breach of Article 6(1).
90 The Court also decided that there had been a violation of Article 13 in the lack of an effective remedy for breach of other Articles; see *ibid*, para.124.
91 *Campbell & Fell v United Kingdom*, Report of the Commission, 12 May 1982, paras 139, 146, 160 and 169.
92 ECHR Series 'A', No.80, *supra*, n.89, paras 107, 110 and 128. Both also use the same arguments; to avoid unnecessary double referencing, therefore, I shall refer, except where indicated to the contrary, only to the judgment of the Court.
93 *Ibid*, para.97. These sub-paragraphs provide that everyone charged with a criminal offence has the right "to have adequate time and facilities for the preparation of his defence", and the right "to defend himself in person or *through legal assistance* of his own choosing or, if he has not sufficient means to pay for legal assistance, to be given it free when the interests of justice so require" [emphasis supplied].

6(1).[94] The European Court also supported the Commission in its conclusion that there had been an infringement of Article 6(1) by reason of the Secretary of State's delay in granting permission to the applicants to seek legal advice in connection with their claims for compensation for the injuries they sustained during the original incident.[95] It followed, therefore, as was decided previously in the *Golder* and *Silver* cases, that the operation of the "prior ventilation rule" (still in use at the time of Mr Campbell and Father Fell's application) was considered contrary to the rights protected by Articles 6(1) and 8.[96]

Lastly, on the issue of access to legal advice, it was held unanimously by the Commission and the Court that the restrictions imposed on visits by solicitors to Father Fell by Prison Rule 37 (as amended) were incompatible with Article 6(1). This Rule – though subsequently twice modified – then maintained the distinction (criticized by *Justice*, above) between conditions for visits to discuss an action to which a prisoner was already party, and other "legal business". As the instant case concerned the latter, the solicitor's visits to Father Fell had to be held "in sight and hearing of an officer" (Rule 37(2)). It was considered that the denial of an opportunity to consult a legal adviser in private "amounted to an interference with the right of access to a court".[97]

Prison Rules – an overview

Given the intensified concern amongst penal experts, pressure groups and even the United Kingdom courts for the rights of prisoners, especially with respect to access to legal advice, that followed the first adverse decision of the European Commission in the *Golder* case, it is all the more reprehensible that it took so long for just the basic requirements of access to legal representation to have been secured. Such concessions were not easily gained as successive governments were initially seemingly unaware of the problem, and later were reluctant to reform the relevant prison regulations any more than was (questionably) strictly required by the European Court. It has been suggested, ruefully, that part of the reason why these developments in the case law of the Convention were not anticipated by the Home Office was that "[t]he European Convention on Human Rights – unlike the [prison] Standing Orders – was available for all to read and ponder".[98] Whilst a number of prisoners (and their counsel) chose to apprise themselves of the rights due to them under the Convention, successive governments appear not to have paid such assiduous attention to its provisions. Likewise, a subsequent and highly relevant companion document to the Convention – the *Standard Minimum Rules for the Treatment of Prisoners* – did not receive the attention of the Government and Parliament that it warranted.[99] In what

---

94   *Ibid*, paras 89–92.
95   *Ibid*, para.107.
96   *Ibid*.
97   *Ibid*, para.111.
98   Prison Officers Association, *The Prison Disciplinary System* (1984), paras 92 & 102.
99   Indeed, there has been a general attitude of ambivalence to the implementation of the *Standard Minimum Rules*, as demonstrated by other areas of prison life – the disciplinary sanction of whipping was only removed 12 years after it was discountenanced in the *Standard Minimum Rules*, see G Zellick, "Penalties for Disciplinary Offences in Prison" [1981] PL 228.

might be considered a thinly disguised reminder to both organs of government of their responsibilities in this matter, Lord Wilberforce declared in *Raymond v Honey* that "a convicted prisoner in spite of his imprisonment retains all civil rights which are not taken away expressly or by implication".[100]

Immigration Rules

The tension that exists between the United Kingdom's immigration legislation and the European Convention on Human Rights has intensified during the past twenty-five years.[101] Three factors have contributed to this position: the progressive extension of restrictive immigration legislation introduced during that period; the United Kingdom's recognition of the right to individual petition in 1966, allowing those affected by immigration legislation to approach the European Commission directly, if they believe that their rights have been infringed; and, thirdly, the development of judicial review of administrative action, providing greater opportunities for the discretion afforded to immigration authorities by legislation to be scrutinized, and, indirectly, for the Convention to be invoked (albeit in only a persuasive role) by those seeking to challenge immigration decisions.[102]

Whilst in Chapter Three, we saw how primary immigration legislation (the Commonwealth Immigrants Act 1968) came into conflict with the European Convention, in this section we shall consider the question of conformity of the Immigration Rules, or rather one aspect of them, with the Convention. The specific aspect to be considered is the so-called "husband rule" (the right of married women in the United Kingdom to have their husbands admitted into the country), as it has long been a matter of some controversy as to whether it conforms to the Convention, and has also been subject to the scrutiny of the European authorities on two occasions.[103]

---

[100] *Supra*, n.79, at 10. It has been suggested that the current position in respect of the censorship of prisoners' mail be reversed so that censorship should occur only in exceptional circumstances – that is, "where the prison authorities have reasonable suspicion that it contains objectionable material"; Alana Jones "Prisoners' Rights to Privacy and Article 8 of the European Convention on Human Rights", Annex 1 to the Standing Advisory Commission on Human Rights, *Annual Report, 1990-1*, HC 488 (1990-1), p.259.

[101] The United Kingdom's delay in recognizing the right of individual petition until 1966 was based largely on the belief that to grant the right would be to invite "abuse" of the system by those affected by Britain's efforts to decolonize, see IA Macdonald, *Immigration Law and Practice* (1987, 2nd edn), p.291.

[102] The instances of domestic cases are too numerous to list in full, but they include the seminal cases of *Waddington v Miah* [1974] 1 WLR 683; *R v Chief Immigration Officer, Heathrow Airport, ex parte Salamat Bibi* [1976] 1 WLR 979; *R v Secretary of State for Home Dept, ex parte Phansopkar* [1976] QB 606, 626. It has been calculated that in 1986 a staggering 63% of all those applications for judicial review granted leave were immigration cases, see IA Macdonald, "The Growth and Development of Modern Immigration Law" (1989) 2 ILAP, p.56.

[103] On the first occasion it constituted part of the European Commission's report in the *East African Asians* case, where in respect of three of the applicants (who were excluded husbands) the Commission held that their right to a family life had been interfered with contrary to Article 8 be read together with Article 14 on grounds which were sex discriminatory (*East African Asians v United Kingdom* (1981) 3 EHRR 76, paras 232-3). And secondly, in *Abdulaziz, Cabales & Balkandali v. United Kingdom*, ECHR Series 'A', No.94 (28 May 1985), which is discussed below, pp 86-7.

The nature of the Immigration Rules

No doubt the very nature of the Immigration Rules contributes to the controversy that surrounds them, as they are a quintessential example of that peculiar phenomenon of quasi-legislation discussed in Chapter Two, Part II. The Immigration Rules are not delegated legislation, but rather are rules of practice established by the Secretary of State for the guidance of those authorities responsible for the implementation of the Immigration Act 1971.[104] Though a "Statement of the Rules" may be debated in Parliament[105] and may be rejected on a negative motion, any alterations made to the Rules as a consequence of such a rejection or otherwise in response to suggestions offered during debate are made at the discretion of the Home Secretary. What is more, the rules are couched in the language of an administrator, not a parliamentary drafter; "they are, therefore, to be given a purposive rather than a strict construction [by the judiciary] unless the words used are wholly unambiguous".[106] The Secretary of State's authority not only to issue Immigration Rules but also to issue a substantial body of (unpublished) instructions as to how the Rules ought to be applied,[107] provide the Minister with very considerable jurisdiction over issues which often have considerable bearing on rights protected by the European Convention.[108] The existence of this discretion, in the opinion of AC Evans, indicates a reluctance on the part of the United Kingdom "to accept respect for the rights of individuals as an issue relevant to the implementation of immigration policy". Furthermore, he contends, "it may well be the failure to accept this relevance which explains the approach of the United Kingdom towards the European Convention on Human Rights and its protocols".[109] Here Evans is referring not only to the United Kingdom's failure to ratify the Fourth Protocol and the adverse report of the European Commission in the *East African Asians* case, but also to the existence of an attitude of indifference towards the Convention as a whole.[110] The irony of this position, however, is that of all the instances of United Kingdom legislation (whether primary or secondary) that have been found to conflict with the Convention, the Immigration Rules have received thorough consideration with respect to their impact on human rights.

The "husband rule"

Since the decision in the case of the *East African Asians*, the highly

---

104 *Pearson v Immigration Appeal Tribunal* [1978] Imm.AR 212; see also *R v Secretary of State for the Home Dept, ex parte Hosenball* [1977] 1 WLR 776.

105 Immigration Act 1971, s.3(2). There is evidence, however, that there may be great difficulty in organizing time for such debates; see, for example, the comments made by Mr Alex Lyon, HC Deb. Vol.932, cols 1334–5 (24 May 1977).

106 Macdonald, *Immigration Law and Practice, supra*, n.101, p.27.

107 The majority of which are trivial and uncontroversial but some more important and invidious examples have been uncovered; see Vaughan Bevan, *The Development of British Immigration Law* (1986), pp 14–15.

108 In a House of Lords debate on the Immigration Rules, Lord Avebury quoted the Home Secretary as saying that he gets over 1000 letters per month asking him to utilize his discretionary power. See also Macdonald, *Immigration Law and Practice, supra*, n.101, pp 28–31.

109 AC Evans, "United Kingdom Immigration Policy and the European Convention on Human Rights" [1983] PL 91.

110 *Ibid*, pp 104 and 107.

controversial Rule regarding the admission of husbands has been closely scrutinized for conformity with the Convention. In August 1974, eight months after the European Commission's ruling in the case, the Immigration Rules were altered so as to grant automatic rights of entry and settlement to spouses of either sex upon their marriage to a British citizen settled in the United Kingdom.[111] This allowance was, except for an alteration disqualifying those seeking entry through bogus marriages,[112] to remain intact until 1980, when amidst much dispute, the pre–1974 restrictions on non–British male spouses was re–introduced as part of a complete overhaul of the Immigration Rules. The compliance of the proposed new Rules[113] with the Convention was repeatedly questioned in both houses,[114] during which specific caveats were forcefully argued by Lord Scarman as to the dangers of the sex discriminatory nature of the "husband rule".[115] What was so contentious about the new Rule was its principal constituent – namely, the so-called "primary purpose" test. This empowered immigration officers to refuse entry to non–British husbands of British wives settled here if they had reason to believe that the marriage was primarily a device to gain entry into the United Kingdom.[116] No such requirements were made of non–British wives who sought entry to the United Kingdom to join husbands who were commonwealth citizens settled here; indeed, the husband's right to have his wife join him was statutorily protected.[117] Throughout the parliamentary debates, the Government refused to confirm that it had sought advice of the Law Officers on the issue of compliance during the formulation of the new Rules, the Home Secretary replying glibly to inquiries on this point that such information was privileged and that, in any case, compliance with the Convention is a matter decided by the courts, not at the pre–legislative stage.[118] Quite apart from the wholly inaccurate statement that the domestic courts are entrusted with the task of determining the conformity of legislation to the Convention, this is an extraordinarily myopic view of the nature and purpose of the Convention, which is precisely to encourage preventive measures rather than to rely on *ex post facto* censorial powers. This disingenuousness was compounded by the Government's inability to appreciate that the proposed new "husband rule" was, in effect, no different

---

[111] Cmnds 5714; 5716; 5717 and 5718 (1974). It should be pointed out that the requirements for fiancés are also included in these Command papers and are broadly similar to those of the "husband rule".

[112] Cmnds 238; 239; 240 and 241 (1977).

[113] Cmnd 7750 (1979).

[114] See, for example, HC Deb. Vol.975, col.276 (Mr Merlyn Rees); col.312 (Mr Eric Deakins); col.314 (Mr Cyril Townsend) (4 Dec. 1979); and HL Deb. Vol.403, cols 1022-3 (11 Dec. 1979) (where Lord Avebury points to the numerous extra-parliamentary commentaries and reports referring to the objectionable nature of the Rules and their possible violation of the Convention, including no less than four statements issued by the Commission for Racial Equality condemning the proposed changes in the Rules. On this last point, it ought to be remembered that one of the principal functions entrusted to the Commission for Racial Equality is to give advice to the Government on race-related issues; see Race Relations Act 1976, s.43(3)).

[115] HL Deb. Vol.403, cols 1065-8 (11 Dec. 1979); see also the remarks of Baroness Sear, *ibid*, col.1061, and in the House of Commons, HC Deb. Vol.975, cols 335-6 (4 Dec. 1979) (Mr Douglas Hogg).

[116] A "British wife" in this context had to be a citizen of the United Kingdom Colonies born in the United Kingdom, or one or both of whose parents were born in the United Kingdom.

[117] Immigration Act 1971, s.1(5) (effective from 1 Jan. 1973).

[118] Rt Hon. William Whitelaw, HC Deb. Vol.975, cols 256 (4 Dec. 1979).

from the regulations on immigrant husbands denounced by the European Commission in the *East African Asians* case.[119]

The unrelenting pressure on the Government on this question of adherence to the Convention culminated in the House of Commons Home Affairs Sub-Committee on Race Relations and Immigration subsequently considering the impact of the European Convention on Human Rights on the proposed new Immigration Rules. Although in its report the Sub-Committee expressed no view of its own, it nevertheless considered that the House ought to be "aware of the opinions of a number of lawyers with a special interest in this field before making a final decision about the Rules".[120] In their submissions to, and examination by, the Sub-Committee, Professor Jacobs, Lord Scarman and Anthony Lester QC were all of the opinion that the proposed Rules were likely to be found contrary to the provisions of the Convention.[121] Both Lord Scarman and Mr Lester could see no difference between the proposed Rule and the position with respect to husband immigrants complained of in the *East African Asians* case,[122] and as there was no indication that the authority of the European Commission's adverse report in that case had been in any way diluted (indeed, if anything quite the reverse was the case[123]) the same fate likely awaited the new Rule.[124]

The Government's motive for the introduction of the new "husband rule" was based on social and political reasons. On the one hand, it was believed that male immigrant husbands were more likely to seek work than wives, and thereby add further to the chronic unemployment problem,[125] and on the other it was considered necessary in deference to prevailing public opinion that "coloured immigration" should be restricted.[126] The extent to which consideration had been given to possible consequences for rights of individuals protected by the Convention remains undisclosed.[127] The inadequacy of the Government's account of its contemplation of the demands of the Convention in this matter was attributed by Mr Lester to the specific lack of any system of pre-legislative scrutiny of legislation to ensure its accordance with the provisions of the Convention.[128] It was his contention that should any Rule be found subsequently to violate the Convention (as indeed was the case with the "husband rule"),[129] then the

---

119 The Home Secretary even tried to use the fact that the new Rules were the very same as those in operation in 1969 as an argument for their introduction, *ibid*, col.257; see Mr Alex Lyon's exposure of this remarkable nonsense, *ibid*, col.295.

120 *First Report (with Minutes of Evidence) of Home Affairs Committee*, HC 434 (1979-80), para.4.

121 *Ibid*, para.101 (Professor Jacobs); paras 107-8, 110 and 118 (Lord Scarman); and paras 8 and 23-6 of Mr Anthony Lester's submission.

122 *Ibid*, para.123 (Lord Scarman); para.27 of Mr Anthony Lester's submission, and para.131 of the Report.

123 *Ibid*, Mr Anthony Lester's submission, para.19.

124 *Ibid*, para.27.

125 Report, *supra*, n.120, para.55.

126 Submission of Mr Anthony Lester, *supra*, n.121, para.24.

127 The Home Secretary, on behalf of the Government, was prepared to say no more than "we believe that we have strong arguments with which to justify these proposals if they are challenged [before the European Court of Human Rights]", HC Deb. Vol.975, cols 351-2 (4 Dec. 1979).

128 Submission, *supra*, n.121, para.3.

129 See case considered *supra*, n.144.

significance of this failure would have been demonstrated.[130]

The case of *Abdulaziz, Cabales & Balkandali v United Kingdom* (the ACB case)

In the event, despite the warnings contained in the Sub-Committee's report laid before the House of Commons, the new Rules came into force unrevised in April 1980.[131] Within a matter of months a set of three applications from married women, who were all lawfully settled in the United Kingdom and whose non-British husbands had been prevented from entering into the country by the new "husband rule" (Rule 50), had been lodged with the European Commission. It was alleged that the Convention had been violated through the discriminatory treatment of the applicants on the grounds of race, birth and sex. In its report the Commission held that violation of Article 14 (protection against discrimination) read in conjunction with Article 8 (respect for family life) had occurred on the grounds of birth and sex but not on grounds of race.[132] In the judgment of the European Court only discrimination on the grounds of sex was deemed contrary to the two Articles.[133]

The Court noted that the existence of sex discrimination in Rule 50 was not contested by the United Kingdom Government. The dispute, therefore, centred on the justification for its existence.[134] The Government claimed that the limitation on the numbers of non-British husbands admitted to the United Kingdom was consistent with its policy of curbing primary immigration, itself a policy based on the demands of preserving "public tranquillity" and racial harmony and the protection of the domestic labour market.[135] Furthermore, it contended that the number of immigrants denied entry under the provisions of Rule 50 was significant, thereby adding greatly to the attainment of those aims.[136] The applicants contested all these purported justifications, concentrating, in particular, on the alleged need to relieve pressure on an already strained labour market. The Government, it was contended, had ignored the modern role of women in employment, and the fact that some men will be self-employed and therefore will create jobs, rather than fill them. What is more, the Government's assertion that the Rule was achieving a significant reduction in the number of immigrant husbands was based on unreliable calculations (in that an unrepresentative year had been adopted for the survey) and that in any case even the Government admitted that the decrease in the number gaining entry might be attributable to economic conditions as well as to the effects of Rule 50.[137]

The European Court accepted the contentions of the applicants. In so

---

130 Submission, *supra*, n.121, paras 3–6.
131 HC 394 (1979–80).
132 *Abdulaziz, Cabales & Balkandali v United Kingdom*, Report of the Commission (12 May 1983), paras 109, 116 & 120.
133 *Abdulaziz, Cabales & Balkandali v United Kingdom*, ECHR Series 'A', No.94 (28 May 1985), paras 83, 86 & 89. In addition, it was concluded that consequent to the violation of Articles 8 and 14, there existed "no effective remedy" as required by Article 13, *ibid*, para.93.
134 *Ibid*, para.74.
135 *Ibid*, paras 75–76.
136 *Ibid*, para.75.
137 *Ibid*.

doing, it noted the existence of the well-established doctrine of a "margin of appreciation" within which a state may determine justifiable limitations on Convention rights. But in this case it considered that in the light of current concern for "the advancement of the equality of the sexes ... very weighty reasons would have to be advanced before a difference of treatment on the ground of sex could be regarded as compatible with the Convention".[138]

Response of the United Kingdom Government

Faced first with the Report of the Commission, and then more significantly with the judgment of the European Court, the Government was forced to alter the offending Rule, though, ironically as it turned out, not to the benefit of immigrants. Its response, in 1983, to the proceedings of the *ACB* case before the Commission was inadequate, if not indeed regressive, and its reaction, in 1985, to the Court's ruling was perverse.[139]

Some months before the publication of the Commission's Report (but after the pre-hearing conciliatory discussions had been abandoned and the case had been declared admissible), the United Kingdom Government initiated a number of changes to the Immigration Rules, culminating in the introduction of a comprehensively revised set of Rules in February 1983.[140] A draft of proposed amendments to the Rules[141] laid before Parliament contained one important concession on the "husband rule" – it dispensed with the requirements that the wife of the husband seeking entry must be a British citizen born in this country.[142] The "primary purpose" test, however, remained unaltered. The change was seen as little more than a rather small step in the right direction; it did nothing to alleviate the central problem of sex discrimination inherent in the Rule. As Percy Grieve (then the Chairman of the Legal Affairs Committee of the Church of England and former Chairman of its Human Rights Sub-Committee) declared soberly, "[g]rave difficulties will be created in the Commission and the European Court of Human Rights if Britain does not give substantially the same rights to women as to men ... the European Convention obliges us to do so [under Articles 8, 12 & 14]".[143] Rather than following such advice, however, the Government introduced further restrictions, consolidating the discriminatory consequences of Rule 50. Changes to the Rules announced in December 1982 reversed the onus of proof within the "primary purpose" test, so that it now fell to the applicant's husband to demonstrate that his marriage was not primarily a device to gain entry into the United Kingdom.[144] This alteration was endorsed and supplemented – by restrictions such as the probationary period for marriage and the deportation of husbands, should the marriage break down during that time – by the wholly restructured

---

138 *Ibid*, para.78.
139 See Macdonald, *supra*, n.101, p.216.
140 HC 169 (1982–83). These changes were also due in part to the new requirements of the recently enacted British Nationality Act 1981.
141 Cmnd 8683 (1982).
142 A concession gained, it was claimed, through the pressure exerted on the Government by the *Abdulaziz, Cabales & Balkandali* case before the European Commission; HC Deb. Vol.31, col.699 (Mr Roy Hattersley) and col.717 (Mr John Tilley) (11 Nov. 1979).
143 *Ibid*, col.739.
144 HC 66 (1982–83). In addition to the "primary purpose" test, further changes required that the husband and wife must intend living together and that they had met before marriage, *ibid*.

Immigration Rules of 1983.[145] As to the principal issue of sex discrimination, the Government's stance was, if anything further entrenched. Mr David Waddington (then a Home Office Minister) sought to justify the gender discrimination of Rule 50 by way of the elliptical argument that because "we have been generous about wives does not mean that we can afford to be equally generous about admitting husbands".[146]

Upon subsequent judgment of the European Court in the *ACB* case, the Government was immediately placed under an obligation to eliminate the sex discrimination within the "husband rule"; none of the justifications offered were deemed by the Court to be of sufficient import for the provisions of the Convention prohibiting such differential treatment to be qualified. In complying with this demand, however, the Government chose to dispense with the right of entry granted to wives of United Kingdom citizen husbands rather than to grant that right to husbands seeking entry.[147] Equality between the sexes, therefore, was achieved at the expense of one of the few unrestricted rights of entry for immigrants. It was the reasoning of the Government that to give to immigrant husbands the same right as that enjoyed by immigrant wives was "absurd",[148] and would simply add to the abuse of the right through using marriage as a means by which to gain entry.[149]

Immigration Rules – an overview

The discrimination complained of in the *ACB* case, therefore, has been eradicated (albeit only at the behest of the European Court, and even then only by way of the narrowest interpretation of the Court's judgment), but there yet remain numerous instances of sex discrimination within immigration legislation.[150] Four years after the judgment in the *ACB* case, Elspeth Guild was able to identify no less than 17 further instances of sexual discrimination within immigration law, including Rules governing the admission both of female students for study in the United Kingdom and of women to work in the United Kingdom.[151] Clearly, the emphasis in the European Court's ruling on the necessity for "weighty reasons" if the right to gender equality is to be qualified has not been applied by the Home Office throughout immigration legislation.

As the Government has given no indication that it intends to rectify this position, then Mr Lester's exhortation in his submission to the Home Affairs Sub-Committee that there be installed some sort of scrutiny scheme to ensure better legislative compliance with Convention rights is, certainly in respect of immigration legislation, well directed.[152]

---

145 HC 169 (1982–83).
146 HC Deb. Vol.37, col.243 (15 Feb. 1983).
147 HC 503 (1984–85). Eventually s.1(5) of the Immigration Act 1971 which preserved the exceptional rights of entry to wives (but not husbands) was repealed by s.1 of the Immigration Act 1988, so now all immigrant husbands and wives are subject to the "primary purpose" test.
148 HC Deb. Vol.80, cols 426–8 (6 June 1985) (Mr David Waddington).
149 HC Deb. Vol.82, cols 518–9 (4 July 1985) (Mr David Waddington).
150 At the time of the 1985 changes even the Home Secretary (Rt Hon. Leon Brittan) recognized as much. HC Deb. Vol.83, col.893 (23 July 1985).
151 E Guild, "Sex Discrimination in United Kingdom Immigration Law" (1988) Vol.3, No.1, ILAP, pp 82–5.
152 *Supra*, n.121, para.3.

Anti-terrorist legislation – the Prevention of Terrorism (Temporary Provisions) Acts (the PTAs)[153]

As indicated in the previous chapter on the scrutiny of primary legislation, the process by which the Prevention of Terrorism (Temporary Provisions) Acts have been kept in force is by annual renewal through a Continuance Order – that is, by Statutory Instrument. In view, therefore, of the challenges mounted against these Acts before the adjudicative authorities of the European Convention detailed in that chapter, not only must the system for scrutinizing primary legislation in this area be questioned, but so also must the way in which the scrutiny of relevant delegated legislation is conducted. The poignancy of this charge is magnified when it is recognized that the apparent reason why the annual renewal of successive PTAs by Statutory Instrument was considered necessary in the first place was to ensure that regular parliamentary scrutiny was exercised throughout the duration of this legislation which so seriously curtails certain basic civil rights.

Yet, as in the debating stages of all four Prevention of Terrorism (Temporary Provisions) Bills (1974, 1976, 1984 and 1989), during the 26 renewal debates that have taken place since 1974,[154] little account has been taken of the possible conflict between the provisions of the Acts and Articles of the European Convention. Indeed, the solitary direct reference to the issue made in debate attracted negligible attention from the Government.[155] In the renewal debates, as with those on the primary legislation, concern was regularly expressed over the infringements of civil liberties permitted by the provisions of the PTAs. However, with equal consistency these restrictions were held by the Government to be justified in the face of the continuing terrorist campaign in Northern Ireland, which occasionally spilled over into Britain, and which threatened to escalate in the absence of legislative controls. On no occasion was there a serious possibility that a PTA would not be renewed.

In this section (as in that dealing with the PTA as primary legislation in the previous chapter), attention will be focused exclusively on the two issues under the Acts which have attracted adverse rulings from the European Commission and Court, namely extended periods of detention, and access to friends, relatives or lawyers during detention. It was not until 1979 that any specific reference was made in the renewal debates to the relevance of the European Convention to the extraordinary powers that governed these matters. Ms Joan Maynard MP brought to the attention of the House of Commons the fact that the National Council for Civil Liberties was then taking six cases to the European Court, claiming that the provisions allowing detention for up to seven days were in violation of the Convention.[156] Yet far

---

153 See also the discussion of the PTAs and the EPAs in Chapter 3, *supra*, pp 54–63.
154 There was one debate in each House in every year between 1975 and 1988, except in 1975 when there were two in each House (six-monthly renewals were required by the 1974 Act), and none in 1976 and 1984 when new Acts were passed.
155 This attitude was manifested in the fact that successive British Governments consistently did not consider it necessary to invoke the derogation provision of Article 15 of the Convention with respect to the Prevention of Terrorism Acts, until 1989, whereas this was considered necessary in regard to the Northern Ireland (Emergency Powers) Acts of 1973, 1975 and 1978. On this question of derogation see Chapter 3, *supra*, n.118, and accompanying text.
156 HC Deb. Vol.964, col.1607 (21 March 1979).

from this being recognized as a forewarning of the adverse judgment subsequently to be given by the European Court in a case concerning precisely this issue[157] the point was completely ignored by the Rt Hon. Merlyn Rees (then the Home Secretary) in his concluding speech in the same debate.[158] It is not untypical for little attention to be given to such warnings of cases being brought before the European authorities, or to the more general voicing of reservations over the compliance of certain elements of anti-terrorist legislation with the provisions of the European Convention. Further examples include specific caveats offered by Martin Flannery MP (claiming that the "fair trial" requirements of Article 6 of the Convention would take precedence over the ill-conceived notion that it is necessary to deny such rights in the interests of combating terrorism);[159] and by David Alton MP when (prompted by the *Brogan* case before the European Commission), he made clear his anxiety over possible infringements of the Convention by the PTA.[160] Perhaps the most perceptive assessment, however, of the impact that the detention provisions of the Act might have on the rights protected under the Convention came from Mr Sam Silkin, a former Law Officer, during the 1981 renewal debate. Mr Silkin's argument deserves to be quoted in full, not only because of its forcefulness but also because of its rarity as a parliamentary speech recognizing the relevance of the European convention to any United Kingdom legislation:

> I have the gravest doubts whether these provisions [detention under s.12] are consistent with our obligations under Article 5 of the European Convention on Human Rights except when war or public emergency threatens the life of the nation. Such circumstances existed when the measure was passed. I have grave doubt whether such circumstances still exist. The effect of the provisions, however humanely and sympathetically the Home Secretary administers them, is that people may be detained not merely for 48 hours or 72 hours – which could be justified in the context of trying to discover whether a person entering the country is known as a terrorist – but for seven days. Such a period must be justified before one can argue that it should continue. The longer the period involved the greater risk of infringing Article 5.[161]

There are two points in particular in this passage which are worthy of expansion. Irrespective of its accuracy, Mr Silkin's reference to the change in the circumstances of terrorism over the years demonstrates the value, or at least the potential value, of an annual debate on the continuance of this so-called temporary legislation. Contentious issues such as the prevention of terrorism through legislative means involving significant curtailment of civil liberties must be made subject to frequent, if not continuous assessment. Not to ensure this is to abdicate responsibility for upholding not only the traditional values of a free democratic society, but also the rights guaranteed by the European Convention.[162]

The second point arises from Mr Silkin's insistence that for the extended detention provisions to continue in force, their professed necessity must be

---

157 *Brogan et al v United Kingdom*, ECHR Series 'A', No.145 (29 Nov. 1988); see also, Chapter 3, *supra*, pp 59–60.
158 HC Deb. Vol.964, cols 1620–24 (21 March 1979).
159 HC Deb. Vol.980, col.432 (4 March 1980).
160 HC Deb. Vol.1, col.368 (18 March 1981).
161 *Ibid*, cols 347–8.
162 Article 15(1).

justified. With respect to the role that the legislature must play in the enactment, supervision and re-enactment of "emergency" legislation, much the same can be said in support of this point as of the first point. "Justification" within the terms of the parliamentary system requires the addressing of doubts and criticisms raised by the Members of either, or both, houses. This requirement is itself inherently weak as it relies not only on sufficient awareness amongst Members of an issue that needs to be justified, but also on the often unpredictable system of exchange and compromise in which the party Whips engage when time-tabling the topics for debate that are to be included in the Order Papers. Even the fact that some sort of justification would appear necessary, therefore, is not a guarantee that it will be forthcoming or that the necessity will even be recognized. With regard to the relatively conspicuous nature of the prevention of terrorism legislation, one would not have thought that Members of Parliament and their Lordships would be unaware of the issues involved. The impact that these legislative provisions for extended detention was to have on the rights protected by the European Convention, however, was neither appreciated nor anticipated in the relevant parliamentary debates. It is of particular concern that the Government was not willing to offer any explanations as to how these provisions complied with the Convention, and equally, that opposition members did not press the Government into doing so. Often, it would appear, little more than lip-service is paid to the Convention. Indeed, even the onset of directly relevant proceedings against the United Kingdom before the European Commission passed almost unnoticed. The Commission's initial ruling that the *Brogan* application was admissible,[163] despite being noted in that year's special annual review of the PTA by Viscount Colville, was not so much as mentioned during either the 1986 or the 1987 renewal debates in Parliament.[164]

A partial explanation for this apparent obduracy is the hamstrung Statutory Instrument procedure to which the renewal of this most important Act falls prey.[165] Under the House of Commons Standing Orders, debates on Statutory Instruments are limited to one and a half hours.[166] As has often been remarked upon,[167] such a meagre length of time, and the fact that the debate is usually held late at night, is plainly not conducive to the thorough and reasoned discussion warranted by the grave issue of legislating against terrorism.[168] The fact that Statutory Instruments have to be accepted *in toto* or not at all is also an issue of some concern for the annual renewal of the PTAs. Clearly, the various elements of the terrorist legislation do not meet

---

163 On 11 July 1986. See *Brogan et al v United Kingdom*, Report of the Commission (14 May 1987).

164 HC Deb. Vol.92, cols 415–437 (19 Feb. 1986), and HL Deb. Vol.471, cols 728–56 (20 Feb. 1986); and HC Deb. Vol.110, cols 262–86 (10 Feb, 1987) and HL Deb. Vol.484, cols 1236–51 (19 Feb. 1987) respectively.

165 What Mr Alex Carlile has dubbed, "about the most inept form of scrutiny as one could imagine", HC Deb. Vol.52, col.940 (25 Jan. 1984).

166 HC S.O.No.14(1)b.

167 For example, see comments of Mr Alan Beith (HC Deb. Vol.927, col.1497 (9 March 1977)) and Lord Shakleton (HL Deb. Vol.493, col.575 (16 Feb. 1988)). See also, *The Review of the Prevention of Terrorism (Temporary Provisions) Act 1976* (the "Jellicoe Report"), Cmnd 8803 (1983), para.14.

168 For further discussion of the process for making secondary legislation, see Chapter 2, Part II, *supra*, pp 33–6.

with an equal response from MPs, and, of course, some are strongly opposed. It can be extremely frustrating, therefore, for the members of both Houses who may find an instrument broadly acceptable, but are strongly opposed to one or two aspects of it.[169]

It is nevertheless within these constraints that the issue of renewal of the PTAs has to be considered. Throughout the parliamentary debates, the two matters of detention and access have attracted a certain degree of concerned attention. In 1977 Alan Beith MP considered it "an extremely worrying feature" that 90% of those detained under the Act are released without charge, and of the remaining 10% nearly all are charged with non-terrorist-related offences[170] – a trend which appears to be continuing.[171] The Secretary of State's discretion to extend the detention period was often remarked upon as an infringement of civil rights.[172] Yet invariably it has been declared to be necessary in the face of the terrorist threat without any detailed reference to supporting statistics.[173] Discussion of the extent to which those detained had access to relatives and solicitors formally centred on the vagueness of the Judges' Rules under which access was regulated. From the very first renewal debate in 1975, concern was expressed over the apparent loophole in the Rules which might permit a detainee to be held incommunicado for the full seven-day period.[174] Typically, however, these fears were allayed with assurances that this power, if it existed at all, would not be utilized, and that in any case the matter was under review.[175] The Judges' Rules were superseded, in 1986, by the Code of Practice for the Detention, Treatment and Questioning of Persons by the Police (established under the Police and Criminal Evidence Act 1984), which limited the maximum length of time that access can be delayed to 48 hours.[176] Yet this is a blatant contradiction of the European Commission's opinion in the *McVeigh* case[177] – a point that was not recognized in either House's subsequent renewal debates. It is hardly credible for the Government to claim (as it does)[178] that all legislative proposals are always considered in the context of the relevant provisions of the European Convention, when it appears capable of such a conspicuous infringement.

It is quite conceivable that with appropriate alterations in the renewal

---

169 For example, Lord Mischon, in common with many other members, deplored the fact that the PTA could not be renewed without the controversial s.11 offence of "withholding information", HL Deb. Vol.493, col.571 (16 Feb. 1988).

170 HC Deb. Vol.927, col.1500 (9 March 1977).

171 *Review of the Operation of the Prevention of Terrorism Act 1984* (the Colville Report) Cm.264 (1987), p.69, Table 3. Although recently a higher proportion of non-terrorist-related charges are being made, the number of charges under the Act is negligible; see further, Chapter 3, *supra*, n.88 and accompanying text.

172 Mr Kevin MacNamara, HC Deb. Vol.892, col.1125 (19 May 1975); Mr Tom Litterick, HC Deb. Vol.964, col.1598 (21 March 1979).

173 For example, the Rt Hon. Merlyn Rees (when Secretary of State for Northern Ireland), HC Deb. Vol.927, col.1484 (9 March 1977).

174 HC Deb. Vol.892, col.1106 (19 May 1975); and a specific case cited by Mr Sidney Irving, HC Deb. Vol.946, col.586 (15 March 1978); and another example from Lord Longford, HL Deb. Vol.440, col.491 (14 March 1983).

175 For example, the then Secretary of State (Merlyn Rees), HC Deb. Vol.927, col.1479 (9 March 1977).

176 See Chapter 3, *supra*, n.112 and accompanying text.

177 *Ibid.*

178 See Chapter 1 and Chapter 6, *supra*, pp 12–13 and pp 130–2 respectively.

debate procedure,[179] these matters would not receive such inadequate consideration. Indeed, provisions might be made for greater opportunities for the European Convention to enter more fully into the debate. It is suggested that a pre-legislative scrutinizing scheme for checking the compliance of delegated legislation with the Convention would better ensure a more enlightened attitude within Parliament towards the relevance of the Convention to prevention of terrorism legislation. In apparent recognition of the benefits of such preventive scrutiny and the inadequacies of the Statutory Instrument procedure, a system of additional reviews of the operation of the Act was established when the PTA 1984 was enacted. Originally, it had been suggested that a Scrutiny Commission should be set up to "monitor the operation of this Act [the PTA 1984] and to report annually to both Houses of Parliament upon its working and effect".[180] Although this proposal was based largely on the arguments of Lord Jellicoe in his 1983 Report,[181] it was ultimately decisively rejected as being too elaborate a construction of what was finally recommended in the Report.[182]

What resulted instead was an undertaking by the Government[183] that until the new (1984) Act lapsed in 1989, there would be an annual survey conducted by an independent monitor who "would look at the use made of the powers under the Act and would consider whether changes were emerging in the pattern of their use",[184] and whose report was "intended to assist Parliament when considering any order laid before them by the Government for the continuation of the Act".[185] Though in Parliament much praise was lavished upon the two men chosen to conduct the inquiries (Sir Cyril Philips: 1984 and 1985; and Viscount Colville: 1986 and 1987), their resulting reports suffered from two major drawbacks. First, in their terms of reference there was no special direction given to assess the Act's impact on the United Kingdom's obligations under the European Convention. As a consequence, only the barest acknowledgement of the European Commission's ruling on the admissibility of the applications of the *Brogan* case was made in the annual report of 1986,[186] and no reference at all was made in the following year to the Commission's subsequent ruling despite its publication on 14 May 1987. No assessment of the potential problems that such a case might pose was ever attempted. Second, the undoubtedly worthy efforts made by both monitors in bringing to the attention of Parliament independently annotated statistics on the use of the Act's powers lost much of their effect due to the continuance of restrictions on the time allocated for the debate of the renewal motion.[187] The additional information provided for

---

179 Such as longer debates, to be held at an earlier time in the day, and the laying of a number of instruments allowing parts of the Act to be renewed separately, HC Deb. Vol.52, cols 934–5 (25 Jan. 1984).
180 Moved by Mr Alex Carlile, HC Deb. Vol.52, col.932 (25 Jan. 1984).
181 *Supra*, n.167, in particular paras 8, 14, and 17.
182 HC Deb. Vol.932, col.939 (25 Jan. 1984).
183 HL Deb. Vol.449, col.405 (18 March 1984) (Lord Elton).
184 *Report on the Operation in 1985 of the Prevention of Terrorism (Temporary Provisions) Act 1984* (1986), Home Office Paper, para.2.
185 *Report on the Operation in 1986 of the Prevention of Terrorism (Temporary Provisions) Act 1984* (1987), Home Office Paper, letter of Introduction.
186 *Ibid*, para.2.4.8.
187 This problem was exacerbated at times by the unforgivable failure to have the annual reports ready in sufficient time for the renewal debate; see, for example, HL Deb.

Members, therefore, did little more than put further pressure on the single limited opportunity which was annually set aside to address the issues raised by the Act. Consequently, with regard to the negligible consideration accorded to the Act's adherence to the Articles of the European Convention, it is not altogether surprising that this issue attained an even lower profile over the four years between 1984–88 just when, as the *Brogan* case demonstrates, an understanding of its implications was perhaps most needed.

The position is unlikely to change given that the present PTA 1989 reverted to the pre–1984 position where, contrary to Lord Jellicoe's recommendation,[188] the Act is to remain in force indefinitely, subject only to the familiar annual renewal procedure. With the future of the PTA thus defined, together with the Government's Notice of Derogation in respect of the seven–day detention provision following the European Court's judgment in the *Brogan* case,[189] it appears that particular vigilance against further encroachment on the Convention in this area remains a necessity.

Conclusion

There can be little doubt that the three legislative examples which are examined in this chapter concern conspicuously contentious issues. The rights that the legislation in question has sought to limit or deny are some of the most basic of the rights guaranteed by the European Convention. It has been said of the law governing the rights of prisoners that "imprisonment and human rights are naturally in conflict and there are many dilemmas in resolving the conflict";[190] a like conflict arises from immigration and anti-terrorism law. It is not an easy equation to balance, but it is perhaps surprising, in the light of the "natural" tendency for legislation on these issues to encroach on rights such as those protected by the Convention, to find so little appreciation of the relevance of the Convention in the making of this legislation. It was, of course, not always ignored – indeed, sometimes it was specifically addressed to Parliament, as the Immigration Rules example demonstrates – but the impact that any such consideration has had on the final form of the legislation (particularly secondary legislation, with its restricted opportunities for parliamentary scrutiny) has invariably been marginal. Governments – both Labour and Conservative – appear indifferent or at best, very occasionally, grudgingly deferential to the demands of the Convention. The inclination of governments to yield no more than is strictly necessary, even in the face of an adverse judgment of the European Court (as best illustrated by the prison regulations) is, of course, to be condemned, but it is not the whole problem. If machinery existed whereby an assessment could be made as to the compatibility of potential legislation with the Convention and that the results of such scrutiny were relayed to Parliament – and thereby indirectly the Government – then the latter in particular would be unable to maintain an attitude of indifference. There would remain, naturally, the authority knowingly to enact provisions that infringe the

---

Vol.493, col.568 (16 Feb. 1988); also, HC Deb. Vol.73, col.1300 (21 Feb. 1985).
188 Jellicoe Report, *supra*, n.167, para.14.
189 See Chapter 3, *supra*, p.60.
190 Sir James Fawcett, "Applications of the European Convention on Human Rights" in M Maguire, J Vagg and R Morgan (eds), *Accountability and Prisons* (1985), p.77.

Convention, or which had the potential to do so (as, for instance, with the PTAs), but at least an explicit recognition of this fact would have to be made and the political pressure that would accompany such action successfully countered.

It is proposed that the scrutiny system for secondary legislation suggested in this book (and detailed in Chapter Eight, below) could provide such a preventive effect.

5 EXAMPLES OF PRE-LEGISLATIVE SCRUTINY IN OTHER COUNTRIES

Little comparative analysis has been conducted of the various methods by which other countries approach the question of ensuring the constitutionality or human rights observance of legislative proposals.[1] From what little research there is, it is possible to identify a number of ideas relevant to the question of how a system of pre-legislative scrutiny might be incorporated into the United Kingdom's legislative process. Certain qualifications, however, have to be made. First, there are characteristics of many of the jurisdictions examined in this chapter which are not shared by the United Kingdom's form of government, but the systems examined are illustrative both of the scope of this form of scrutiny and the different methods by which it can be implemented. Perhaps the most distinctly unfamiliar element is that of federalism. The existence of regional legislatures, endowed with varying degrees of legislative competency, clearly imposes structural conditions on the corresponding processes of pre-legislative scrutiny that would not suit the present unitary government of the United Kingdom. Any variations or additions to federal scrutiny systems designed to ensure the constitutional compliance of regional legislatures, therefore, are not considered in this chapter.

A second, related factor, concerns the provisions made for the scrutiny of

---

[1] The only directly relevant studies which I have come across are: J Jaconelli, *Enacting a Bill of Rights* (1980), Chapter 2; Inter-Parliamentary Union, a Constitutional and Parliamentary Information Booklet: *Control of the Constitutionality of Laws*, 3rd series, 2nd quarter, 1982, No.130; a discussion paper presented by Mr Karl Czernetz to the Fourth Conference of Presidents of European Parliamentary Assemblies in June 1977, entitled *The European Convention on Human Rights as European Law* (see especially the Appendix).

delegated legislation. Though, as we have seen, at a general level,[2] secondary legislation is increasingly pervasive in modern democratic government, the provisions made for its scrutiny are, in most countries, "less well defined".[3] More often than not such scrutiny is not specially provided for and is simply incorporated in the process for examining primary legislation. There is a part of the Australian federal model, however, which has been designed specifically to vet statutory instruments and regulations issued under delegated powers. As we shall see, it is an example that is most pertinent to the United Kingdom, for its *modus operandi* is through a parliamentary select committee which is, of course, an institution familiar to the United Kingdom's system of government.

Forms of pre-legislative scrutiny

There are a number of widely differing processes which are intended to exert some degree of control over the constitutionality of legislation at the pre-enactment stage. In this chapter, however, their differences will be simplified so that those examined fall into one or other of three broad categories. The categorization is according to structure (that is, the position of the scheme *vis-à-vis* the law-making process), as opposed to powers (i.e. whether involving authority to censure or just advise). The principal reason for preferring a structural division is that in the systems considered, with the notable exception of the French system, it is the design or structure of the scheme which effectively determines the level of power to be wielded by the body or bodies charged with the duty of pre-legislative scrutiny. For similar reasons any pre-legislative scrutiny system for the United Kingdom is likely to exhibit the same relationship of powers to structure.

The systems examined are classified as follows: first, methods of constitutional control which are based within the legislature – that is, those which constitute a stage in the legislative process (termed "Parliamentary"); second, those based wholly within offices of the Government (termed "Executive"); and third, those based outside both the legislature and the Executive (termed "Independent").

1   Parliamentary systems

In addition to the installation of special institutional machinery for the pre-legislative scrutiny of legislation (which is the primary concern of this section), it might also be considered that the requirement in some countries for a legislature to abide by certain general fundamental principles (typically referred to as "directive principles") provides some form of preventive effect.[4] The existence of "directive principles" *per se* would not amount to a system of pre-legislative scrutiny, but the recognition commonly afforded to them by the courts may effectively necessitate some form of assessment of their relevance to legislation prior to enactment.[5]

---

[2]   Chapter 3, *supra*, pp 28 & 33.
[3]   Inter-Parliamentary Union, *supra*, n.1.
[4]   States which possess this type of provisions include Eire (Art. 45 of the Constitution) and India (Part 4, Arts 36–51 of the Constitution); for both these examples *infra*, n.5. For further details see Sir W Dale, *The Modern Commonwealth* (1983), pp 190–1.
[5]   For examples of judicial interpretation of "directive principles", see, in Eire, *Murtagh Properties v Cleary* [1972] IR 330, at 335 & 336 (and further considered in JM Kelly, *The*

The principal means of intra-parliamentary pre-legislative scrutiny, however, is by way of a specially equipped body established specifically to operate the examination system. In fact there exists only one example of a specialized and truly parliamentary scheme of pre-legislative scrutiny, that is, in the Parliament of the Australian Commonwealth.

Two Senate committees – one designed for primary and the other for secondary legislative proposals – are responsible for the examination. The Standing Committee on Regulations and Ordinances (that is, secondary legislation) was appointed in 1932 and under its (now revised) Standing Order, its seven members are charged with the duty of scrutinizing, and if necessary reporting on, "all regulations, ordinances and other instruments, made under authority of the Parliament, which are subject to ... disapproval by the Senate".[6] In order to appreciate the true breadth of this provision it has to be recognized that there exists *only* a disapproval procedure for Commonwealth delegated legislation (there is no affirmative procedure equivalent to that pertaining in the United Kingdom), and all such legislative instruments may be disallowed by disapproval of *either* house.[7] Whilst the Committee is concerned not to pronounce on the merits of the legislative proposals it scrutinizes, it strives "to achieve a balance between necessary executive functions on the one hand, and the rights and liberties of citizens on the other".[8] To this end it has developed a set of four specific criteria, against which it measures all putative delegated legislation. These are: (i) to be in accordance with the parent Act; (ii) not to affect adversely rights and liberties; (iii) not to oust the jurisdiction of the courts on administrative decisions; (iv) and not to concern a matter better dealt with by primary legislation.[9] These have certainly expedited a preventive influence both on those responsible for formulating policy and those who draft the regulations, as they publicize the grounds upon which the Committee will report.[10] Indeed, the impact of the Committee on the process of legislative formulation is such that Ministers, in an effort to avoid the disapprobation of the Committee, and possibly later, Parliament, not infrequently refer their draft proposals for delegated legislation to the Committee for preliminary examination.[11] In 1989 the Senate Procedure Office issued an advisory publication entitled *Legislative Scrutiny Manual* which was distributed to all government departments. The manual provides resumés of the history, powers and achievements of the Regulations and Ordinances Committee (as well as the Scrutiny of Bills Committee – on which, see below) and a set of guidelines on the Committee's application of its four principles of scrutiny. There is little doubt, what is more, that this informative exercise is having a

---

Irish Constitution (1984, 2nd edn), p.682); and, in India, *Mumbai Kamgar Sabha v Abdulbhai* AIR 1976 SC 1455 (para.29); and *Sanjeev Coke Mfg Co. v Bharat Coking Coal Ltd.* AIR 1983 SC 239 (para.23); see also, M Hidayatullah, *A Judge's Miscellany*, 3rd series (1979), p.72.

6   Senate of Australia, S.O.23 (formally S.O.36 A).

7   Acts Interpretation Act 1901 (Cth), s.48(5).

8   A Lynch, "50th Anniversary of the Australian Senate Standing Committee on Regulations and Ordinances" (1982) 50 The Table, p.71.

9   See further, (the late) Senator Allen Missen, "Human Rights Protection, Can Parliament do the Job?" in L Spender (ed), *Human Rights, The Australian Debate* (1987), pp 162–4.

10   *83rd Report of the Senate Standing Committee on Regulations and Ordinances* (April 1988), para.1.7.

11   A Lynch, *supra*, n.8, p.72.

salutary effect on the processes of departmental policy-making.[12]

The Committee, upon the advice of its independent Legal Adviser,[13] examines about 800 regulations each year, of which (it has been recently calculated) 10% require the Committee to correspond with the Minister responsible for the purpose of clarification or to seek amendments to the regulation.[14] Almost invariably the appropriate amendments are made. This is unsurprising in the light not only of the long history of the Committee and the recognized quality of its work,[15] but also, more directly, of the extremely effective and bipartisan performance of the duties required of it, as backed by a considerable power of sanction (see below). The determination of the Committee is well illustrated by the words of a recent former chairman of the Committee:

> It [the Committee] seeks the co-operation and advice of Ministers. However, though it endeavours to proceed to reasonable resolutions of its concerns, it is not for the Committee to make compromises if to do so would leave people prejudiced by or unprotected by legislative provisions in any dispute they might have with the powers of Government.[16]

If an appropriate response to queries raised by the Committee is not forthcoming from the relevant department, a Notice of Disallowance may be moved in the Senate by the Chairman of the Committee on its behalf[17] which effectively requires the Government to address the Committee's objections within 15 days of the Notice being laid, otherwise the regulation is disallowed automatically.[18] Though the device is seldom followed through to actual disallowance,[19] the threat of such an outcome is usually sufficient to elicit from Ministers not only specific amendments to regulations,[20] but also more general undertakings with respect to the procedure for making regulations and the nature of the terminology in which they are couched.[21] As a former member of the Committee put it, the laying of a Notice of Disallowance "is done as a procedural warning to Ministers who make law outside Parliament but under Parliament's authority that Parliament retains the same ultimate right of veto over subordinate law as it had over the parent legislation in the first place".[22]

---

12   For an account of some of the areas in which this consequence has been detected see DJ Whalan, "Scrutiny of Delegated Legislation by the Australian Senate" [1991] 12 Stat.LR 87, pp 102-3.

13   On whose role, see Whalan (the present encumbent of the position), *ibid*, pp 99-100.

14   Personal Statement of Senator Barney Cooney, then Chairman of the Committee, to the Senate on 4 June 1987 (Sen. Deb. Vol.121, 3524), reproduced in the *83rd Report of the Committee, supra,* n.10, p.9.

15   The high standard of its work and the regard in which it is held in the Senate have long been universally appreciated. See, for example, Senator Ian Wood's comments, Sen. Deb. Vol.77 (7.6.78), 2475.

16   Senator Cooney, *supra,* n.14, para.2.9.

17   The Senate has never refused to accept such a motion.

18   Acts Interpretation Act 1901 (Cth), s.48(5); see further, Senator Missen, *supra,* n.9, p.163.

19   Typically, only two regulations were disallowed in this way between February 1985 and June 1987 – Senator Cooney, *supra,* n.14, para.2.2.

20   *83rd Report of the Committee, supra,* n.10, para.1.7.

21   For example, *ibid*, para.1.8; see also, Whalan, *supra,* n.12.

22   Senator Austin Lewis, "Legislative Scrutiny – A Last Hope for Australian Parliamentarianism?", paper presented to the Second Conference of Australian Delegated Legislation Committees, Canberra, 26 April 1989, Senate Procedure Office, p.113.

The scrutiny of primary legislation in Australia is performed by the Senate Standing Committee for the Scrutiny of Bills. The Committee, despite being modelled on that responsible for secondary legislation, came into being (in the face of government opposition) almost 50 years later, in 1981.[23] The purpose of its terms of reference have been described as "assist[ing] the Senate in its function as a House of review with respect to legislation by drawing attention to provisions which might otherwise go unnoticed in the passage of bills through the Chamber",[24] and also to bring "to the attention of the Government oversights in the Government Bills which [equally] might otherwise have gone undetected".[25] In so doing, the Committee is required to report on any provisions in a bill which affect one or more of the following basic principles: to protect personal rights and liberties against violation; undue dependency on ill-defined administrative powers, or non-reviewable administrative decisions; inappropriately delegated legislative powers, or removal of parliamentary scrutiny of such powers. It must be emphasized that the Committee provides nothing more than information and assistance to the Senate. And although the Committee's comments are considered by Senators to be a valuable means by which they are alerted to the issues at stake,[26] the Committee itself "expresses no concluded view on whether the clauses on which it comments do in fact constitute infringements of rights and liberties or the erosion of the legislative power of Parliament. That judgment is left to Parliament."[27]

This point notwithstanding, the Committee's influence is brought to bear at two distinct points in the legislative process. The first is almost immediately after a bill has been introduced for the first time into *either* chamber, when initial comments are made by the Committee's Legal Adviser who assesses all of the bills introduced each week; these remarks are conveyed to the Senate (when it is sitting) by way of the weekly publication of an "Alert Digest". This scheme forms the basis for the Committee to seek an early response from Ministers to its concerns, and thereby to open dialogue between the Government and the Committee.[28] Government responses, whether written or oral, are given in practice to about three-quarters of the Committee's comments;[29] evidence suggests, furthermore, that a significant

---

23 It was established on the recommendation of the Standing Committee on Constitutional Affairs; *Report on the Scrutiny of Bills*, Paper No. 329/1978.

24 Senator Michael Tate (a former Chairman), "The Operation of the Australian Senate Standing Committee for the Scrutiny of Bills", Paper presented to the Conference on Australasian Study of Parliament Group on *The Legislative Process: How Relevant?*, Adelaide, August 1985, p.2.

25 *Annual Report of the Committee*, 1986-7, Parliamentary Paper, 443/1987, p.3.

26 See the observations of Mr Chaney (a former Senator), *Ten Years of Scrutiny*, proceedings of a seminar to mark the tenth anniversary of the Committee, Senate Procedure Office (Nov. 1991), p.28.

27 Tate, *supra*, n.24, pp 2 & 57.

28 To this end the Committee's terms of reference provide that "the Committee, for the purpose of reporting upon the clauses of a bill when the bill has been introduced into the Senate, may consider any proposed law or other document or information available to it, notwithstanding that such proposed law, document or information has not been presented in the Senate" (S.O.24(b)); see further, the *Ninth Report of the Committee* (May 1982), para.15.
The Government's awareness of the Committee's views is further assured by the practice of Parliamentary Counsel indicating to departments relevant comments made in the "Alert Digest", see *infra*, nn 32 & 33 and accompanying text.

29 *Ibid.*

number of these lead to formal amendments being made, either in the form of ministerial amendments or those successfully moved by non-ministerial Senators (or Members of the House of Representatives).[30] It is worth noting that although the evidence referred to indicates that the number of amendments in the non-ministerial category is less than half that in the former, the fact that many non-ministerial (that is, effectively, Opposition) amendments are nevertheless being moved and some are successful,[31] illustrates the impact of the Committee's work on parliamentarians in general as well as the Executive. It remains the case, however, that the Committee's most important influence, and potential influence, is on the Government. This is made evident not only through the above measured responses, but also, crucially, by the less tangible effect of the assimilation of the Committee's observations by government departments into their drafting practices. It is impossible to measure accurately the extent to which the reactions of the Committee are anticipated by those responsible for the content and design of legislation. It is understood, however, that the possibility of an adverse comment from the Committee is taken sufficiently seriously to warrant the informal issue of caveats by Parliamentary Counsel to departmental lawyers, specifying the types of clauses on which the Committee has had cause to remark,[32] and urging them to take appropriate preventive action.[33] In addition, of course, the 1989 *Legislative Scrutiny Manual* mentioned above has also had some pre-legislative impact as the manual's guidelines have been integrated into departmental policy-making systems.

The second point of impact by the Committee is during the main debating stages of a bill's passage through Parliament. Should the Government not respond to the Committee's initial comment, or do so unsatisfactorily, the Committee may lay before the Senate a detailed report of its objections (together with, if available, any response made by the Government) before the bill reaches its Committee stage. However, although approximately the same number of amendments are successfully made during the parliamentary passage of bills as modifications are made to bills before their introduction in response to Scrutiny Committee reports, many more amendments are moved but not carried after a bill's introduction.[34] The Committee's influence, it appears, is at its most effective *before* any proposal reaches the parliamentary stage of the legislative process.[35]

The successful establishment of the scrutiny committee on bills has brought symmetry to the Australian Commonwealth's system of prior examination of all legislation.[36] Its particular interest in relation to the scheme proposed in this book is twofold: first, the esteem in which the committees are held in both houses is based largely on their invariably

---

[30] Tate, *supra*, n.24, pp 63 & 72–5.
[31] *Ibid*, p.73.
[32] Senator Tate, *supra*, n.24, pp 64–6.
[33] Ian Turnbull, the current First Parliamentary Counsel, *Ten Years of Scrutiny, supra*, n.26, pp 59–62.
[34] Senator Tate, *supra*, n.24, pp 73–5.
[35] *Ibid*, p.75.
[36] But only at the Commonwealth level; though there exist current proposals (namely in Queensland and Victoria) there are no established scrutiny of bills procedures in any state or territory.

bipartisan reports and opinions, and the existence of legal counsel to advise each committee;[37] and second, the Committees' operation demonstrates the potential for the protection of broad principles of rights and liberties through scrutiny of legislation by parliamentary committees.[38]

2   Executive systems

Apposite developments in this area of pre-legislative scrutiny have occurred in New Zealand and Canada with the establishment in both countries of scrutiny schemes for bills as part of their respective Bills and Charters of Rights packages. In terms of the categorization of this chapter, these schemes are truly hybrids. For whilst in both cases the actual scrutiny is undertaken by the Minister of Justice (or officers from the Department of Justice), any finding of *prima facie* infringement of the rights legislation must be conveyed to Parliament.

The Canadian model, in common with that in New Zealand, lacks the degree of independence that is a beneficial feature of those systems which operate beyond the direct control of the Executive. The weakness of the Canadian scheme – in which the Department of Justice is responsible for the examination process – it is claimed, is that it "entrusts the Government itself with the responsibility of testing its own proposals against a Bill of Rights".[39] The author of this statement was referring only to the 1960 Canadian Bill of Rights. However, today the Department of Justice has also to ensure legislative compliance with the provisions of the Canadian Charter on Human Rights and Fundamental Freedoms.[40] Except in one respect, both enactments are furnished with very similar processes of scrutiny, and thereby the above statement applies equally to both. The exception would apply in the unlikely event of the legislature wishing to ignore, amend, or override the restrictions imposed on the Government either by the Bill of Rights or the Charter; in this case the constitutional hurdles (both legal and conventional) presented respectively by the two Acts are markedly different. The Bill of Rights, though considered "not a statute like any other",[41] is not an entrenched constitutional enactment.[42] In which case, regardless of the political furore that might result, there would be no constitutional restriction to prevent Parliament from tampering with the Bill of Rights in whatever way it chose or to enact legislation that contravened its provisions.[43] The

---

37   See, for example, GS Reid & Martyn Forrest, *Australia's Commonwealth Parliament 1901-1988* (1989), pp 215-8; see further DW Kinley, "The Parliamentary Scrutiny of Human Rights: A Duty Neglected?" in P Alston (ed), *International Human Rights In Comparative Perspective* (forthcoming, 1993), nn 104-5 and accompanying text.

38   For a fuller discussion of this potential and how it might be developed, particularly in the Australian context, see Kinley, *ibid*.

39   PH Russell, "Democratic Approach to Civil Liberties" (1969), 19 University of Toronto LJ, 109 at 125.

40   Enacted as s.1 of the Canada Act 1982.

41   PW Hogg, *Constitutional Law of Canada* (1985, 2nd edn), p.642.

42   Indeed, Hogg notes that in *Hogan v The Queen* [1975] 2 SCR, 574, 579, Laskin J described the Bill of Rights as "a half-way house between a purely common law regime and a constitutional one; it may aptly be described as a quasi-constitutional instrument," *ibid*, pp 642-3.

43   The singular and notorious case of *R v Drybones* [1970] SCR 282 can be discounted on the grounds that it concerned pre-existing legislation. It is unclear from the judgment in this case whether an Act passed after the Bill of Rights would be bound by it; see further AW Bradley, "The Sovereignty of Parliament" in J Jowell & D Oliver (eds), *The Changing Constitution* (1985), p.37.

Charter, on the other hand, is a constitutional statute (by virtue of its formal enactment by the United Kingdom Parliament as part of the Canada Act 1982), and can be altered only according to the special procedures laid down by it, and overridden by legislation only if accompanied by an explicit recognition of the fact – that is, by way of a *non obstante* clause.[44]

Section 3[45] of the Bill of Rights Act 1960 established a system of pre-legislative scrutiny of bills and regulations, pursuant to which in 1978 the Governor-General in Council made the Canadian Bill of Rights Examination Regulations.[46] In contrast, there is no section in the Charter which relates to the setting up of an examination system; rather, this is catered for by s.4(1) of the Department of Justice Act 1970;[47] but this fact aside, the two schemes differ not at all with respect to procedure. Indeed, the examination regulations issued by the Governor-General in Council (under the Department of Justice Act) for the Charter[48] are modelled on those issued for the Bill of Rights and they are implemented concurrently. Both require the Minister of Justice to examine "every bill introduced in or presented to the House of Commons by a Minister of the Crown ... in order to determine whether any of the provisions thereof are inconsistent with the purposes and provisions of [either statute]".[49] In both cases, also, a like examination is to be undertaken by the Clerk of the Privy Council in consultation with the Minister of Justice of all regulations, upon their being lodged with the former for registration.[50] A certificate, signed by the Deputy Minister of Justice, has to be attached to every bill and every regulation stating that it has been examined. In cases where any inconsistency is found, the Minister is obliged to make a report and submit it to the House of Commons "at the earliest convenient opportunity".[51] However, there has only ever been one such report made (in 1975) in respect of the Bill of Rights,[52] and there is yet to be one in respect of the Charter – a fact which appears to lend much credence to the above aired concern that the Executive might be naturally reluctant to question its own legislative proposals.

It is, nevertheless, possible for Parliament to pass a bill containing provisions contrary to the conditions of the Bill of Rights or the Charter, but in order to do so a bill must contain an explicit statement that the prospective Act is to operate notwithstanding these instruments.[53] No such facility exists for contraventions in regulations. Not suprisingly, the decision

---

44 *Constitution* (1985), p.37.
44 See s.33 of the Charter
45 As amended by the Statute Law (Canada Charter of Rights and Fundamental Freedoms) Amendment Act 1985, s.105.
46 Apart from reiterating the requirement contained in s.3 that the Ministry of Justice is to ensure that bills or regulations are not inconsistent with the Bill of Rights, these regulations relate mostly to technical and procedural matters.
47 RSC 1970, CJ-2, as amended by the Statute Law (CCHR & FF) Amendment Act 1985, s.106.
48 Canadian Charter of Rights and Freedoms Examination Regulations, PC 1985-2561 (13 August 1985).
49 S.3a of both sets of regulations.
50 S.4a of both sets of regulations.
51 S.6 of both sets of regulations.
52 See *The Canadian Charter of Rights and Freedoms*, G-A Beaudoin & E Ratushuny (eds) (1989, 2nd edn), p.13, at n.39 and accompanying text.
53 See s.2 of the Bill of Rights Act 1960, though, of course, this subject to my earlier remarks, *supra*, n.43 and accompanying text; and also s.33 of the Charter.

to employ this method is made only in extreme circumstances.[54] The potential of the use of *non obstante* clauses does not detract from the preventive effect of the scrutiny provisions. Indeed, if anything, the derogation provision actually strengthens this effect, in that the Government is aware that its reasons for using the exception must be sound, as they are sure to be stringently tested. To put it more prosaically, in the words of the late Elmer A Driedger – drafter of the Canadian Bill of Rights – "[n]o Government would be so stupid as to submit to Parliament a bill obviously in conflict with the Bill of Rights without this declaration";[55] though it has to be said that this does not preclude the possibility of a bill less obviously conflicting with rights legislation from submitted to, and being passed by, Parliament.

The preventive influence may also be effective with respect to those draft bills or regulations containing violations which have been overlooked by the department sponsoring them. If, after submission, the drafting officers of the Department of Justice consider a proposal to be in conflict with the Bill of Rights or the Charter, the Executive (through the department concerned) would be unlikely to insist that the impugned provision should remain unchanged, as it "could not politically afford to put itself in a position in which the Minister of Justice would resign over the issue".[56] It is claimed that the result of this two-tiered sieve is that "the chances that a statute patently in conflict with the Bill of Rights [or the Charter] could be enacted are virtually non-existent, unless that were deliberate Government policy, in which case the declaration [the derogation clause] would go in and the Government would have to face the music in the House of Commons".[57]

Despite these remarks, doubts nevertheless linger over the effectiveness of such a system in detecting and preventing those less evidently suspect provisions which, on the grounds of political convenience, a government may allow to pass through the scrutiny process unchecked. After all, without a representation of extra-governmental opinions at this scrutiny stage, there is likely to be little pressure on the Department of Justice to do otherwise than endorse any government-sponsored legislative provision coming before it.

The form of pre-legislative scrutiny in New Zealand under this heading differs from that pertaining in Canada in a number of respects. The principal distinction is the fact that in addition to scrutiny for compliance with the newly established New Zealand Bill of Rights (which is similar to the Canadian model in this regard) there has existed in New Zealand since 1986 a collateral system of more general pre-legislative scrutiny based on the

---

54 In respect of the Bill of Rights this facility has been used only once: see Beaudoin & Ratushny, *supra*, n.52, p.10, at n.32 and accompanying text. There has been sparing use of the s.33 override clause in respect of the Charter, though until 1987 Quebec had established a general *non obstante* clause for all legislation passed by its legislature (both prior and subsequent to the Charter); in addition to Quebec's further use of s.33 in a number specific instances, the only other occasion on which the override clause has been invoked has been by Saskatchewan in respect of a particular Act, see Beaudoin & Ratushny, *supra*, n.52, p.107, and Hogg, *supra*, n.41, pp 690-2.

55 "The Meaning and Effect of the Canadian Bill of Rights: A Draftsman's Viewpoint" (1977) 9 Ottawa LRev., p.311.

56 *Ibid.*

57 *Ibid.*

Legislation Advisory Committee (LAC). Together, these two parts to pre-legislative scrutiny in New Zealand comprise a curious amalgam. For, whilst the purely Executive-based scrutiny scheme established by s.7 of the Bill of Rights Act 1990 clearly lacks independence (and is thereby weakened in the same way as the Canadian model),[58] the LAC is in some respects more independent (only three of the total of ten members of the Committee are Government-based),[59] but it is questionable how much impact it has on the policy-making processes of the Executive and the legislation-making processes of the legislature, *especially* in respect of ensuring compliance with New Zealand's human rights obligations as this is merely one aspect of its broad ("public law")[60] purview.

Turning first to the LAC: the Committee's terms of reference indicate that it has two principal functions:

(i)   to scrutinize and make submissions to the appropriate body or person upon aspects of Bills introduced into Parliament affecting public law or raising public law issues.

(ii)   to report to the Minister of Justice or the Legislation Committee of Cabinet on the foregoing aspects of legislative proposals which the Minister or that Committee refers to it.[61]

The greater independence of the LAC is, in reality, only in respect of its operation ((i) above); the *initiation* of its scrutinizing function, as (ii) above indicates, lies in the hands of the Executive. This limitation notwithstanding, the Committee has always sought to have a more general and prophylactic influence over legislative formulation. In the words of the first Chairman of the Committee:

> the Committee is concerned with form rather than policy, that is to say, whether the draft legislation adequately and properly implements the policy which it is intended to put into effect. In this context it looks at, for example, compatibility with other legislation, with New Zealand's international and treaty obligations and with important legal principles relating, among other things, to natural justice. It may raise questions as to the adequacy of the consultation which has taken place with interested parties and even whether legislation is necessary to achieve the stated policy objective.[62]

The Committee's influence at this stage has been enhanced by the formal adoption by the New Zealand Cabinet of a set of *Guidelines* compiled by the Committee aimed at improving the quality both of the process and the content of legislation.[63] The *Guidelines* were prepared at the request of the

---

58   Rhetorically, it has been asked whether "... a Cabinet member [would] ever say Cabinet's legislation is not demonstrably justified in a free and democratic society?" – which is the only permitted form of qualification to the rights protected under s.5 of the Bill of Rights Act 1990 – G Taylor, "That Bill of Rights" (1990) 13 TCL 33/1, as quoted by P Fitzgerald, "Section 7 of the New Zealand Bill of Rights Act 1990: A very practical power or a well-intentioned nonsense" (1992) 22 VUWLR 135, 148.

59   They are, at the time of writing, the Chief Parliamentary Counsel, the Deputy Solicitor-General and an official from the Department of Justice; none of these holds the chair; see Walter Iles, "The Responsibilities of the New Zealand Legislation Advisory Committee" (1992) 13 Stat. LR 11, 13.

60   See the Committee's terms of reference, *infra*, text at n.61.

61   The terms of reference are reproduced in *Legislative Change, Guidelines on Process and Content*, Report No.6 by the Legislation Advisory Committee (Dec. 1991), p.ii.

62   GR Laking, Correspondence with the author. See also, *Guidelines, supra*, n.61, para.11, and Iles, *supra*, n.59, p.12.

63   *Legislative Change, Guidelines on Process and Content*, was first published by the

Minister of Justice, and intended primarily for the attention of those within government departments responsible for the formulation of policy and the drafting of legislation.[64] Guidance is given on a range of issues, concerning both matters of general principle[65] and specific subjects.[66] There are two aspects of the former category which are of especial relevance – namely, whether the legislative proposal complies with the Bill of Rights (in which the LAC acts as a supplement to the scrutiny scheme specifically established for this purpose by s.7 of the Bill of Rights Act)[67] and with New Zealand's international obligations and standards, including the International Covenant on Civil and Political Rights (ICCPR) to which New Zealand is a party.[68] The last mentioned point is of particular interest to my thesis as a strong analogy may be drawn between New Zealand's relationship to the ICCPR and that of the United Kingdom to the European Convention on Human Rights – particularly since the right to individual petition under the Covenant was granted in New Zealand in 1989.[69]

Some idea of the status of the *Guidelines* can be gauged from the fact that the Government now insists that in submitting any legislative proposal to the Cabinet's Legislation Committee for its approval the responsible Minister is required to answer a questionnaire affirming that the *Guidelines*, international obligations, the Bill of Rights and the principles of the Treaty of Waitangi have all been observed or, if not, providing an explanation as to why not.[70] It is, of course, difficult to say with any degree of certainty what impact these demands are having on the actual substantive process of legislative formulation. However, it is clear not only that the practice of prior departmental consultation with the Committee on these issues is not as frequent and widespread as it ought to be, but also (and perhaps most damagingly) that "political considerations" are "too often ... advanced as a justification for poorly thought out legislation when reasonable foresight and greater attention to the guidelines which Cabinet has adopted would have greatly improved the quality of the legislative product".[71]

In respect of the specific scheme of pre-legislative scrutiny under s.7 of New Zealand's Bill of Rights Act (1990) it is probably still a little early to evaluate its impact. But for the already mentioned reason of conflicting interest,[72] it would be unwise to suppose that it would ever be much more than a formality. Though the Attorney-General has reported to the House in respect of three, relatively minor, bills[73] – and that is three more than have

---

Department of Justice in August 1987; a revised and updated edition has since been published, see *supra*, n.61.
64   See *Guidelines, supra*, n.61, para.7.
65   *Supra*, n.61, paras 32–47.
66   For example, the establishing of new tribunals; the choice of criminal or civil sanctions and the boundaries of subordinate law-making, *supra*, n.61, paras 48–167.
67   *Supra*, n.61, paras 38–9; for discussion of the s.7 scrutiny process see below.
68   New Zealand ratified the Covenant in 1978, though it did not condone the right of individual petition under the Covenant until it ratified the First Optional Protocol on 26 May 1989.
69   *Ibid*.
70   See *Cabinet Office Manual* (1991), Chapter 5, Appendices 1 & 2, as reproduced in Appendix A of the *Guidelines, supra*, n.61, pp 57–59.
71   *Report No.5 of the Legislation Advisory Committee* (March 1990), para.14.
72   *Supra*, n.58 and accompanying text.
73   Fitzgerald, *supra*, n.58, p.141, n.24 and accompanying text, and Kinley, *supra*, nn 37 & 38 and accompanying text,

been reported under the comparable Canadian Charter scheme which has been operating for more than ten years – the fact remains that responsibility is entrusted to a member of the Executive. As, under s.7 of the Act, this responsibility is discretionary: "the Attorney-General shall ... bring to the attention of the House of Representatives any provision in the Bill *that appears* to be inconsistent with any of the rights and freedoms contained in this Bill of Rights",[74] the likelihood that after the still current embryonic period of the scheme's existence an equilibrium will be reached whereby political convenience will be preferred to concerns (where any are determined, which is a problem in itself)[75] over compliance with the Bill of Rights, is further advanced. It has been argued by Paul Fitzgerald, what is more, that

> ... the decision not to report a possible inconsistency will rarely be clearcut, for the high threshold test [see footnote 77] involves determining whether s.5 [justifiable limitations][76] applies. Consequently, many cases will involve a balancing of factors including normative assumptions. Where officials resolve such compliance questions in favour of not reporting, the House is deprived of any indication that the decision involved a balancing of factors ultimately favouring not reporting. The result is an information gap surrounding the scrutiny process leaving Members of Parliament literally in ignorance of substantive human rights issues in legislation before them.[77]

3   Independent pre-legislative scrutinizing bodies

The third form of scrutiny of statutes is that performed by bodies independent of both the legislature and the Executive. Examples of this type possess some significant individual features as well as some common characteristics. Of the three schemes reviewed, two are of particular relevance: the Human Rights Commissions of Australia and New Zealand. Both are variations of a single familiar model (the United Kingdom's Commissions for Racial Equality and Equal Opportunities are designed along similar lines). The other system (of France), however, is quite different from the antipodean designs, and, also, divorced from anything within the British system. Yet the analysis of this model serves to illustrate the variety of possible institutional designs devised to tackle this problem.[78] I shall deal with the French model first.

The French body responsible for pre-legislative scrutiny of both primary and secondary legislation for constitutional compliance – the *Conseil Constitutionnel* – is distinctive due largely to the singularly powerful position

---

74   Emphasis supplied.
75   See Fitzgerald, *supra*, n.58, pp 141–3.
76   See *supra*, n.58.
77   *Supra*, n.58, p.143. Fitzgerald uses the term "high threshold test" to mean that "a provision is inconsistent only where it is incompatible with any of the rights and freedoms contained in the Bill of Rights 1990 *and* is not a reasonable limit which can be demonstrably justified in a free and democratic society", *ibid*, p.137. He maintains that this is the test adopted in practice by the Attorney-General when implementing s.7.
78   I have deliberately excluded any consideration of the reviewing powers of certain "constitutional courts" (for example, the German *Bundesgerichtshof*), as the processes associated with such powers provide no systematic review of all legislative proposals, and in any case as the review is undertaken by the judiciary one of the principal distinguishing and beneficial features of the type of scrutiny procedure advocated in this book (that those who make legislation ought to ensure its compliance with human rights obligations) in the face of the standard Bill of Rights alternative is annulled.

it occupies within the Constitution.[79] Given the emphasis placed on basic principles in French law, it is hardly surprising that France has such a reputable and authoritative body to perform this function. Under the 1958 Constitution of the Fifth Republic, the *Conseil Constitutionnel* is charged *inter alia* with three important duties. First, it is required to examine all *lois organiques* (that is, laws which are concerned with the powers of the constitutional institutions, *viz*: the President of the Republic, Parliament, the *Conseil Constitutionnel* itself and the judiciary) prior to their promulgation to ensure that they are constitutionally valid.[80] Secondly, it examines, again prior to promulgation, those ordinary laws submitted to it by certain high officers of state (i.e. President of the Republic, the Presidents of the National Assembly or the Senate and the Prime Minister),[81] or, more commonly, any group of 60 Deputies or 60 Senators, also to ensure constitutional validity. Whilst scrutiny of *lois organiques*, therefore, is automatic, that of ordinary laws is conditional.[82] And thirdly, the *Conseil* is required to ensure that both Parliament and government do not exceed their respective legislative powers bestowed on them by Articles of the constitution. In all three instances the review of constitutionality includes consideration of compliance with the *Déclaration des Droits de l'Homme* (which is contained in the Preamble to the Constitution),[83] though interestingly *not* also the rights protected by the European Convention.[84] Usually the *Conseil* is required to give its decision on the constitutionality of a bill within a month, and should it rule against part or all of the bill, invariably the bill will be dropped or amended as is appropriate. This is so despite the fact that formally the decision of the *Conseil Constitutionnel* is not binding, although in practice it is invariably observed.[85]

In regard to its scrutiny of "executive legislation" (the *pouvoir règlementaire*), the *Conseil* is empowered, under Article 37(2) of the Constitution, to express a view on the constitutionality of a *règlement*, or decree, proposed by government – that is, whether in promulgating it the Government has remained within its legal boundaries and has not trespassed upon the legislative domain reserved for Parliament. In effect this exercise in delineation amounts to "a technique for confining and controlling

---

79   It is not strictly correct to say that there is only the one body responsible for this function. The *Conseil D'État*, though in a less formal manner, "not exceptionally ... expresses reservations about a draft law for reasons based on the Constitution". These reservations, despite being made privately to the Government (and not to be heard by Parliament except in the rare event of the Government disclosing them), carry, like all advice tendered by the *Conseil*, considerable weight. The Government, therefore, will be "disposed to follow the advice of the *Conseil*, primarily of course because of its general desire to respect the Constitution; a desire that will clearly be strengthened if there is a risk of seeing the law referred to the Constitutional Council by the Opposition." B DuCamin, "The Role of the *Conseil D'État* in Drafting Legislation" (1981) 30 ICLQ 833, 899.

80   Article 61(1).

81   Article 61(2).

82   See LN Brown and JF Garner, *French Administrative Law* (1983, 3rd edn), pp 9–14.

83   J Rivero, *Le Conseil Constitutionnel et les Libertés* (1984), p.129, and L Richer, *Les Droits de l'Homme et du Citoyen* (1982), p.28. I am indebted to Chantal Crozet for her assistance with these texts.

84   See Rivero, *ibid*, pp 136–7.

85   For an account of the strength of the *Conseil's* decisions, which effectively bind the Executive and the legislature, see Rivero, *supra*, n.83, pp 134–5.

the power to legislate by *règlement*".[86] The views of the *Conseil* carry considerable influence, and for government to persist with a *règlement* declared to be unconstitutional by the *Conseil* would be to "imagine the unimaginable".[87] An indication as to the weight carried by these assertions can be obtained from the fact that should the advice of the *Conseil Constitutionnel* be ignored, any interested party is able to challenge the *règlement* before the *Conseil D'État* on the grounds that it is *ultra vires*. In this event the *Conseil D'État* regards itself "as bound by the decision of the Constitutional Council, on the issue of constitutionality, under the doctrine of *res iudicata*" (that is despite the fact that the latter is not a court), and would duly annul the decree.[88]

Without doubt, one of the most important factors contributing to the authority enjoyed by the *Conseil Constitutionnel* is that its composition reflects a degree of independence from both the legislature and the Government. The Council's membership totals nine, all of whom are nominated: three are appointed by the President of the Republic, the President of the National Assembly and the President of the Senate respectively, who, although being themselves party to the legislative process, usually appoint those who are not so connected. Hence "the members tend to be judges, jurists and private practitioners".[89] In any case, the wording of the Constitution sets the tone of the quasi-judicial and objective nature of the Council by stating unequivocally that "the functions of a member of the *Conseil Constitutionnel* are incompatible with those of a Minister or member of Parliament".[90] As a leading authority on French constitutional law puts it, "its members are recruited according to a political criterion, that is a matter of personal qualities ... and not 'socio-professional', as with the Supreme Courts of the United States of America and ... Germany".[91] Clearly, the relative independence of the *Conseil Constitutionnel* can be asserted to great effect in restraining an over-zealous legislature,[92] and in performing such a vital role the position it occupies has been referred to as the "*conscience de la Constitution*".[93]

The alternative model of a Human Rights Commission playing largely an advisory role exists in both Australia and New Zealand. It is crucial to recognize that both Commissions were clearly established for reasons other than legislative review.[94] And indeed of that small part of the Commissions'

86   MM Favoreu and Philip, *Le Conseil Constitutionnel* (1980, 2nd edn), p.101, quoted in Brown and Garner, *supra*, n.82, p.11.
87   *Ibid*, p.11.
88   *Ibid*, pp 11-2.
89   J Jaconelli, *Enacting a Bill of Rights* (1980), p.31. For the regulations governing membership, see Article 56 of the Constitution.
90   Article 57.
91   J Gicquel & A Hauriou, *Droit Constitutionnel et Institutions Politiques* (1985, 8th edn), pp 291-2 [translation by the author].
92   See a decision of 30.7.82, CCF p.276, in which the widely drafted Articles 34 and 37 of the constitution on the powers of the legislature received a somewhat restrictive interpretation. Such treatment is hardly surprising given the expressed intent behind the Council's creation in 1958 - that it should be a weapon against the violations by Parliament ("... *une arme contre la déviation du régime Parliamentaire*"), *ibid*, p.292.
93   *Ibid*.
94   The principal duties of the Commissions for both countries have been complaint-handling; educative and research. In respect of Australia, see PH Bailey (who is the former Deputy Chairman of the Australian Human Rights Commission), *Human Rights*,

functions devoted to such review the scrutiny of legislative *proposals* (as distinct from the existing legislation) for compliance with human rights standards forms only a minor part.

The Australian model has existed in two forms, though in respect of those aspects relevant to this present study their formal powers and duties differed not at all. Both the original Human Rights Commission which was in existence between 1981 and 1986[95] and the Human Rights and Equal Opportunities Commission (HREOC) which immediately succeeded it,[96] were empowered, *inter alia*, to examine proposed enactments for the purpose of ascertaining whether they were inconsistent with the provisions of (amongst other United Nations' Covenants) the ICCPR, but *only* when requested to do so by the Attorney-General.[97] Clearly this qualification to the scope of the HREOC's discretion is especially significant to the potential impact that the Commission might have on those aspects of legislative proposals which affect human rights. In this specific respect it largely negates the independence of the Commission, for despite the membership of the HREOC (and its predecessor) being wholly non-governmental, the resultant independence of opinion is compromised if it can be expressed only in respect of matters referred to it by the Executive. It is true that HREOC inherited from the 1981 Commission the broad power to "make an examination or hold an inquiry in such manner as it thinks fit".[98] Indeed, it was recognized (if seldom acted upon) from the outset that this provision could include examination of a legislative proposal that the Commission considered *of its own volition* warranting such treatment. But on the sole occasion that the 1981 Commission seriously considered using this provision – to review a proposed Mental Health Ordinance – it ultimately decided that in terms of achieving its goal of influencing the Executive's attitude towards the ordinance, it would be best served if, rather than relying on this facility for unilateral action, the Commission sought an appropriate referral from the Attorney-General. The referral was forthcoming,[99] and the Commission duly submitted its report recommending alterations to the proposed measure,[100] almost all of which were incorporated in its final form. Clearly, the continuing importance of the political reality that lay behind the actions of the Commission in the above example can hardly be underestimated. Despite the broad discretion granted to the two Commissions to examine as they see fit, their role *vis-à-vis* the Executive has been one of subordination – the most that HREOC can do is to advise, ultimately the Executive may ignore or reject the opinion of the Commission. It would be difficult to construct a more poignant illustration of this fact than the consequences following the HREOC's unilateral decision[101] – as

Australia in an International Context (1990), pp 113, 123-8 & 143-7. For New Zealand, see *Annual Report of the Human Rights Commission (1991)*, p.5.

95   The Commission was established by s.6 of the Human Rights Commission Act 1981 (Cth) and discontinued in accordance with the "sunset clause" in s.36.

96   The new Commission was established by s.7 of the Human Rights and Equal Opportunities Commission Act 1986 (Cth).

97   See s.9(1)(a) of the 1981 Act, *supra*, n.95, and s.11(1)(e) of the 1986 Act, *supra*, n.96.

98   S.12 of the 1981 Act and s.14(1) of the 1986 Act.

99   See Human Rights Commission, *Proposed Mental Health Ordinance 1981*, Report No.2 (1982), p.16.

100 *Ibid*, pp 1-14.

101 Under s.14(1) of the 1986 Act.

opposed to seeking a referral from the Attorney-General (principally because such a request would have been unlikely to succeed) – to comment on the human rights implications of the proposed 1991 legislation to limit party political advertising on television and radio.[102] A series of communications between the Human Rights Commissioner and responsible Ministers detailing the likely infringements of the ICCPR of the proposed legislation (principally in relation to freedom of expression) were ignored by the Government which preferred instead to rely on contrary opinion supplied by the Attorney-General's Department. This episode – which resulted in the relevant provisions of the subsequent Act being declared invalid by the High Court[103] – demonstrates clearly the relative powerlessness of the HREOC's use of this provision for proactive and independent scrutiny, even in respect of a singularly conspicuous legislative proposal.[104]

In New Zealand the provisions for pre-legislative scrutiny by the Human Rights Commission for compliance with human rights standards (including the ICCPR) are even more insubstantial than those of its Australian counterpart. Though s.6 of the Human Rights Commission Act 1977 provides for the independent examination of proposed legislation, the Commission's reports must be submitted to the Prime Minister.[105] What is more, s.6(3) expressly prohibits the publication by the Commission of any report based on the results of an examination of proposed legislation, although its comments on any other matter may be published. As the acid test of the Commission's influence must surely be whether or not it can bring any effective pressure to bear on an apparently unwilling Government to conform to human rights provisions, it would appear, therefore, that the Commission, like its Australian counterpart, fails to pass. A former counsel for the New Zealand Human Rights Commission has candidly observed that, although "occasionally of course [the Commission's] comments have provoked some not always favourable responses from the Prime Minister of the day (which would not of course deter [the Commission])", she conceded that the Commission's "influence depends on the willingness of those in power to listen and sometimes it has not been great!".[106] The Commission's role as a "watchdog" of proposed legislation, what is more, is likely to be curbed in light of the development of alternative, more specialized means of scrutiny in the guises of the Legislation Advisory Committee[107] and the Department of Justice in its role under s.7 of the Bill of Rights Act 1990.[108]

Conclusion

Having conducted this international comparison of types of pre-legislative

---

[102] The Political Broadcasts and Political Disclosures Bill 1991 (Cth).

[103] *Australian Capital Television v the Commonwealth* (1992) 11 ALJR 695. The principal ground for the decision was that the impugned sections violated freedom of expression guarantees that lay implicit in the Commonwealth constitution.

[104] For an examination of the detail and ramifications of this saga, see Kinley, *supra*, n.37 and nn 66–80 and accompanying text.

[105] The Commission is not, however, precluded from making submissions to appropriate parliamentary committees on proposed legislation; see, for example, an account of such submissions made in 1990–1 in the Commission's *Annual Report (1991)*, *supra*, n.94, pp 26–7.

[106] Deidre Milne, correspondence with the author.

[107] See *supra*, pp 105–7.

[108] See *supra*, pp 107–8.

examination schemes, it must now be asked how relevant are the examples from all three categories to the unique structure of the United Kingdom Constitution. The Parliament of the United Kingdom stands alone amongst those legislatures which are founded upon a model of parliamentary democracy in respect of the power it possesses. In theory, if not wholly so in practice, it occupies a position of omnipotence. This and other singular features referred to in the following chapter make it difficult to draw close analogies with the legislative system of the United Kingdom. Still, the foregoing analysis of how other countries attempt to exert some control over the constitutionality or human rights compatibility of draft legislation will serve at least as an indication of what options are available and which it might benefit us to study further.

A glance at the examples described under the above three categories of pre-legislative scrutiny will tell us that the variety in the third group (independent systems) is greater than in the first two. This is not altogether surprising as the wholly independent systems are not restricted to the same extent as are the parliamentary and the executive ones, which, necessarily, have to conform to inherent structural limitations – that is, the generally unbending procedures and processes of their respective modes of operation. However, it is also the case that the independent models, almost by necessity, have least influence on the shaping of legislation, and as such do little to compel the legislature to consider fully the human rights issues in the legislation passing through its hands. The French Constitutional Council, however, is a notable exception. This form of judicial review, however, is rooted in the civil law traditions of European jurisdictions, and the idea of a constitutional council (or court) has always been inimical to the common law precepts of the English legal system. Even should the dissonance have been reduced since 1972 with increasing (if fitful) European integration, the idea is a shibboleth still strongly supported. There are few other issues that would so surely defeat the argument for pre-legislative scrutiny than if the task was to be entrusted to a (truly) independent body to settle. Since both the constitutional compatibility and the political acceptability of the chosen scheme are at least as important as its efficacy, we are forced not to pursue this line.

The executive-based systems of Canada and New Zealand, though by all accounts successful within the constraints placed upon them, are fundamentally flawed (at least in respect of the concern of this book) by the very positions they occupy. Ultimately, their location within the governmental machine places political pressures on them which allow the Government to have its way. As the discussions in the following chapter will demonstrate, that qualification alone would serve to negate much of the effect that a pre-legislative scrutiny system might have in the United Kingdom.[109] The most pertinent lesson to be learnt from the Canadian and

---

109 Since it is claimed that a system of internal scrutiny (albeit an informal one) is currently in operation throughout the drafting of government legislation in the United Kingdom (see Chapter 1, *supra*, nn 66 & 69, and Chapter 6, *infra*, nn 80 & 86 and accompanying text), the fact that so many legislative provisions have slipped through the net is indeed damning (see Chapters 3 & 4, *supra*). Formalizing such a process of intra-governmental restraint, even along the elaborate lines of the Canadian model, is, therefore, likely to do little to ensure better legislative compliance with the Convention in the United Kingdom.

New Zealand experiences is the amorphous, though nonetheless discernible, prophylactic effect that the installation of a scrutiny process can have. The mere fact, it would appear, that such a process is in operation, even if ultimately controlled by the Executive, has been enough to make Canadian and New Zealand policy-makers and legislators at least consider human rights implications before introducing a certain provision into the public arena. With time this factor may prove to be the single most valuable instrument of prevention possessed by *any* scrutiny system.

The most effective example of a scrutiny system, however, is that in the "parliamentary" group. To be operating within the legislature gives any such scheme system credibility, not only by way of its more representative committee membership, but also the level of influence that can be brought to bear through their place as part of the legislative process. There can be no clearer demonstration of these worthy features than the committee-based system of Australia. For despite the fact that in this jurisdiction there also exists an apparently independent human rights commission (HREOC) whose functions have the potential to involve *some* preliminary examination of legislative proposals, the efficacy with which this potential is borne out in action is negligible. The scrutiny committees in Australia, on the other hand – having been led boldly by the Senate's Regulations and Ordinances Committee and more recently supplemented by the Senate's Scrutiny of Bills Committee – have now established a respected and, what is more, increasingly influential position within the Commonwealth legislative process. It is argued in the following chapter that the basis for this relative success could be borrowed and enhanced to establish a scheme within the United Kingdom's legislative system whereby legislative compliance with the human rights provisions of the European Convention might be more surely obtained.

6 A PRE-LEGISLATIVE SCRUTINY SCHEME FOR THE UNITED KINGDOM: PROPOSALS AND POSSIBILITIES

The purpose of this chapter is to provide an assessment, in the light, where appropriate, of the international schemes discussed in the preceding chapter, of the proposals and possibilities for the establishment in the United Kingdom of a system of pre-legislative scrutiny of legislation for compliance with the European Convention. In continuity with the last chapter, the discussion here is divided into the same three categories, viz: independent scrutiny; intra-governmental (or executive) scrutiny; and intra-parliamentary scrutiny. For reasons that have been foreshadowed, the conclusion is reached that a system within the intra-parliamentary group would be the most appropriate for the United Kingdom given the context within which the United Kingdom's legislative process operates, and would be most likely to fulfil effectively the demands of such scrutiny.

Possible independent schemes

In considering the possibilities for an independent scrutiny scheme, it is clear that there is a particular limitation peculiar to this class. No body, truly independent of Parliament, could ever be granted a formal role within the legislative process. As a matter of orthodox constitutional theory, Parliament has the ultimate authority over the enactment of legislation – though in practice it has limited control over primary legislation, and only minimal control over secondary legislation.[1] Furthermore, the doctrine of

---

1   Quasi-legislation, what is more, remains beyond any form of parliamentary control, save through the outmoded and ineffective doctrine of ministerial responsibility; see Chapter 2, Part II, *supra*, p.38.

parliamentary privilege, which, *inter alia*, insists that each House has sole authority to regulate its own affairs, effectively obstructs any proposal that might require a scrutiny stage in the legislative process external to Parliament.[2] In which case it seems that the most that might be expected of a scrutiny scheme independent of Parliament (and government) is that it would have the authority only to advise Parliament how best to ensure that legislation conforms with the strictures of the European Convention. In this respect, however, such a scrutiny body operating from outside Parliament would be no more influential than any other well organized lobby group. It might be argued that even a purely advisory body dealing with issues of such gravity would not be completely without influence. The preventive effect, after all, of highlighting possible human rights deficiencies in prospective legislation cannot easily be brushed aside, and it is not unreasonable to assume that government sponsors of a bill so identified would be put under pressure to adjust their proposals accordingly.[3] But if the record of the advisory functions of the two antipodean Human Rights Commissions are anything to go by, such a sanguine outlook is short of reality.[4]

It seems probable, therefore, that if we are to adopt any form of pre-legislative scrutiny to be executed by an extra-parliamentary and extra-governmental body, its powers will be strictly limited – possibly even to the extent that the system would be worse than useless in that the impuissance of such a "watchdog" body may be overlooked and the mere establishment of a scheme might itself be considered sufficient protection against human rights violations by legislation. We might, in other words, be lulled into a false sense of security.

The true efficacy of such an independent scrutinizing body is, nevertheless, to a certain extent a matter of some conjecture and therefore we cannot in this study summarily ignore the arguments made in its favour. Briefly, there are four examples of schemes – three "pure" and one "hybrid" – that can be identified within this category of independent.

First, it has been suggested that a scrutiny system be operated from the office of the Parliamentary Commissioner for Administration by way of a considerable broadening of its terms of reference. The origins of the idea can be traced back to a Bill of Rights Bill introduced by the Earl of Arran in 1970.[5] Clause 3 of the draft Bill stipulated that "the Parliamentary Commissioner shall examine every Bill introduced in or statutory instrument laid before either House of Parliament, in order to ascertain whether any of the provisions thereof are inconsistent with the purposes and provisions of this part of this Act, and shall report any such inconsistency to both Houses

---

2   The arcane but not necessarily impotent Article 9 of the Bill of Rights 1689 which declares "that the freedome (sic) of speech and *debates or proceedings* in Parlyement (sic) ought not to be impeached or questioned in any court or place *out of Parlyement (sic)*" [emphasis supplied].

3   The Standing Advisory Commission on Human Rights has had some success in influencing Government legislation after it has been passed – notably in relation to the various emergency provisions applied to Northern Ireland during the seventies, culminating in Parliament's acceptance of the Commission's recommendation in its fifth report (1978-9, para.10) to abandon the detention without trial provisions then prevailing in the province (HC Deb. Vol.989, cols 434-5 (22 July 1980)).

4   See Chapter 5, *supra*, pp 110-2.

5   HL Bill No.19, (1970-1).

at the first convenient opportunity". Now although all that this demands is that an advisory service is to be provided by the Parliamentary Commissioner, the idea is effectively vitiated by those who are sceptical of the practicalities of the proposal. It has been pointed out, correctly I think, that such a proposal would precipitate "an inordinate increase in the burden of work of the Parliamentary Commissioner, extending it from an area of maladministration to that of legislation in general",6 and it is that additional burden which makes the whole proposition untenable. During the debate on the Bill's second reading, the Lord Chancellor (then Lord Hailsham) pointed out that as the intended function of the Parliamentary Commissioner was, of course, to detect *ex post facto* maladministration and that as the Commissioner has no legal staff, "clause 3 entrusts him with a task for which I would say ... he is unsuited".7 Indeed, it is surely the case that to alter the agenda of the Parliamentary Commissioner so drastically is to take it beyond an adaptation of the original office to the creation of an entirely new entity.

The second type yields possibly the most conspicuous and the most advanced examples of independent scrutiny. Both the late Sam Silkin, in his (Private Members') Protection of Human Rights Bill in 1971,8 and the Standing Advisory Commission on Human Rights in its 1977 Report,9 made proposals for the creation of an entirely new human rights body with the responsibility, *inter alia*, for ensuring legislative compliance with the European Convention. The purpose of Mr Silkin's bill was to establish a United Kingdom Commission of Human Rights charged with the duties "to investigate, report and recommend" courses of action in human rights matters.10 It was, like the Parliamentary Commissioner, to have no power of enforcement, it being left to "Parliament to give effect to its recommendations".11 There was to be no explicit authority to examine pre-legislative proposals, but rather it was to operate "not unlike the Race Relations Board [the predecessor of the Commission for Racial Equality] or the Equal Opportunities Commission ... [in] fostering the protection of human rights and monitoring the working of the domestic charter".12 It is quite plausible, however, that a power to examine at least some bills might have been construed as implicit in the presence of such words as "fostering the protection of", and similar provisions in the empowering statutes of the other bodies mentioned. But whether this role was intended or not (and in the case of the Silkin Bill, no recognition of this point was made before the Bill lapsed during its second reading),13 the fact of the matter is that neither the Commission for Racial Equality nor the Equal Opportunities Commission currently possesses any formal machinery through which they

---

6   J Jaconelli, *Enacting A Bill Of Rights* (1980), p.28.
7   HL Deb. Vol.313, col.267 (26 Nov. 1970)
8   HC Bill No.52 (1970-1)
9   *"The Protection of Human Rights in Northern Ireland"*, Cmnd 7009 (1977).
     Sir Douglas Wass has made a suggestion for a Standing Commission with special responsibility for constitutional matters which might conceivably incorporate pre-legislative scrutiny as well; "Checks and Balances in Public Policy-Making" [1987] PL, pp 195-8.
10   HC Deb. Vol.814, col.1858 (2 April 1971); clauses 11 and 12 of the Bill.
11   *Ibid.*
12   *Ibid.*
13   HC Deb. Vol.320, col.538 (23 June 1971).

can examine prospective legislation. Typically, it seems, the most that can be expected, in the words of a former solicitor to the Commission for Racial Equality, is that the "Legal Section [of the Commission] keeps an eye on new legislation".[14] In any event, there is nothing to prevent an explicit provision for pre-legislative scrutiny being included in any new bill if the political conviction is there. The legitimacy of such (admittedly limited) scrutiny, therefore, would not have to rely on inference drawn from such an ambiguously worded statutory provision.

The recommendations of the Standing Advisory Commission on Human Rights, in its report on human rights in Northern Ireland,[15] in which it considered at greater length the question of scrutiny of Bills for compatibility with the European Convention on Human Rights, also fell well short of developing a comprehensive system of pre-legislative assessment.[16] Despite the fact that the members of the Commission declared that "in principle we would welcome the introduction of some suitable mechanism for scrutinizing the potential effect of pending legislation upon fundamental human rights and freedoms",[17] they dismissed the idea of executing this function from within Parliament as impractical and putting the Parliamentary machine under "undue strain". Rather they believed that "a more practical approach might be to create a process of independent scrutiny ... of draft Bills and subordinate legislation before they entered the Parliamentary process",[18] but when it came to the nature of the powers and functions of the Human Rights Commission to which this duty of scrutiny was to be given, the Commission's reasoning was abstruse. On the one hand it took the bold step of recommending that the new Human Rights Commission should perform a function similar to that exercised by the Canadian Ministry of Justice,[19] whilst on the other it was content with bestowing on the new Commission "analogous functions and powers to those of the Equal Opportunities Commission and the Commission for Racial Equality in acting in the public interest to promote the protection of human rights".[20] This is confusing. Quite apart from the fact that scrutiny by the Minister of Justice is strictly an intra-governmental scheme, neither the Equal Opportunities Commission nor the Commission for Racial Equality (as is demonstrated above) performs anything like the pre-legislative functions developed in the Canadian model. It is possible, of course, that rather than taking these two aspects as being mutually exclusive, the Commission meant them to be complementary – that is, the new Commission was, in addition to the exercise of powers analogous to those of the Equal Opportunities Commission and the Commission for Racial Equality, to be able to go further than either by having the capacity to implement a process of formal pre-

---

14   Francis Deutsch, correspondence with the author. But as Mr Deutsch added, even this perfunctory "examination" is restricted by a "reliance on parliamentary agents who automatically supply copies of Bills in specified areas: police, nationality, immigration, education, housing etc".
15   *Supra*, n.9.
16   Neither was this specific aspect developed in the Commission's "*Second Report on Religious and Political Discrimination and Equality of Opportunity in Northern Ireland*", Cm.1107 (1990).
17   *Ibid*, para.7.17.
18   *Ibid*.
19   On which see Chapter 5, *supra*, pp 103–5.
20   Cmnd 7009, *supra*, n.9, para.7.22.

legislative scrutiny. If this is the case, however, the Report casts no light on how this proposed additional faculty is to operate within a governmental structure so different from that of the model which provided the inspiration for it. In view of this fact, and the likely pressure for severe limitation of the influence on the legislative process of any externally based body, a Human Rights Commission (whatever its configuration), if established, would at most "possess only an advisory (and possibly conciliatory) role, remedial rather than preventive in the protection of human rights".[21]

The third, so-called "pure", independent option is that of establishing a Constitutional Council. The idea was first raised in 1968 by Anthony Lester in a Fabian Tract entitled *Democracy and the Individual*. Details of the proposal went no further than an indication that it was "to make recommendations to Parliament about the compatibility of legislation or Executive action with the provisions of the [proposed] Bill of Rights".[22] Indeed, it is not clear whether it was intended that there be any *pre-legislative* scrutiny role for the Council. More recently, Simon Lee has expanded and adapted this notion by suggesting that a Constitutional Committee of the Privy Council be created "consisting of not only senior judges but also senior statesmen and perhaps augmented by the kind of people who head Royal Commissions and Committees of Inquiry",[23] and other constitutional cognoscenti. He believes that, "such a body could be modelled on the French *Conseil Constitutionnel*", and that it should have "the opportunity to consider matters [including, presumably, legislative proposals] in advance".[24] Still, in respect of the present concern, he goes no further than simply to declare that some degree of pre-legislative scrutiny is contemplated (in particular, no indication as to the authority of the Council's recommendations is given).

The fourth example in this category, although ostensibly independent, is nevertheless truly hybrid as it possesses an element which properly belongs to the intra-government type. It has been suggested that extended use be made of the power to refer legal matters to the Judicial Committee of the Privy Council.[25] Under the terms of s.4 of the Judicial Committee Act 1833, however, such power is to be exercised by the Crown, so although any opinion consequent to a referral would be that of the (independent) Judicial Committee, the process depends on the discretion of the Executive to refer the legislative proposal in the first place. Although the terms of the Act would appear to be broad enough to accommodate the scrutiny of draft legislation, the procedure has thus far never been used for such a purpose. It is worth noting, however, that a scheme for *ex post facto* scrutiny by the Privy Council was to have been established by the suspended Scotland Act 1978.[26] The idea was not endorsed by the House of Lords Committee on a

---

21   Jaconelli, *supra*, n.6, p.32.

22   P.15.

23   Simon Lee, "Against a Bill of Rights?", *Freedom of Information*, a booklet in the Days of Decision series, Julia Neuberger (ed) (1987) p.81; see also Simon Lee, "Who shall defend our rights?", *The Times* (6 Feb. 1987).

24   *Ibid*; for an account of the *Conseil Constitutionnel*, see Chapter 5, *supra*, pp 108–10.

25   See the written submission of Professor Owen Hood-Phillips to the House of Lords Select Committee on a Bill of Rights, *Minutes of Evidence*, HL 81 (1977–8) p.273; see also Jaconelli, *supra*, n.6, p.29.

26   Under s.19(1) of the Act every bill passed by the Scottish Assembly is to be considered by

Bill of Rights (to which it had been submitted), as there was some concern over the enormity of the practical difficulties in the adaptation of the Judicial Committee of the Privy Council for use in this way.[27] The quantity of legislation to be scrutinized (both primary and secondary), together with the argument over the supposed inherent unsuitability of the judiciary in this country to perform such a task,[28] ensured that the proposition was overturned.

Possible intra-governmental schemes

Within this category there are a number of possibilities for the United Kingdom that might be considered viable. The adaptation of existing offices within government has attracted some attention as a means by which internal scrutiny might be achieved. The offices primarily considered are those of the Lord Chancellor, the Attorney-General and the Parliamentary Counsel. However, in addition to the not inconsiderable indictment that all these offices lack independence to perform effectively the task of pre-legislative scrutiny (the bulk of legislation being introduced by the Government), the particular problem associated with the modification of current institutions is that the extraordinary demands of objective scrutiny sit very uneasily alongside the original structures, functions and purposes of these bodies.

That much having been said, the Institute for Public Policy Research (IPPR) has recently suggested that a *new* executive-based body be created called (not unfamiliarly) the Human Rights Commission.[29] The Commission's members are to be appointed by the Secretary of State, though only on the recommendation of the Public Service Commission – a device "intended to ensure that [the Commissioners] are appointed because of their expertise or other qualification for the post rather than because of any political views they may hold".[30] Amongst its powers it is suggested that the Commission "may examine legislation for the purpose of ascertaining whether it is inconsistent with any of the provisions of the Bill of Rights [as detailed by the IPPR] and shall report any inconsistency to Parliament".[31] Beyond this statement no details as to the Commission's execution of this duty are provided. In particular it is unclear, first, whether the Commission would be a reactive or proactive body (that is whether it would scrutinize only those legislative proposals referred to it, either by the Government or Parliament,

---

the Secretary of State for Scotland, and referred to the Judicial Committee of the Privy Council, should he or she doubt that its provisions are within the legislative competence of the Assembly.

27 *Minutes of Evidence, supra*, n.25, p.116, (Lord Jellicoe).
28 The United Kingdom's judiciary has some limited experience with such matters in respect of cases referred to it under s.51(1) of the Government of Ireland Act 1920, which involved challenges as to the *vires* of legislation passed by the former Northern Ireland Parliament – for example, *Re: Section 3 of the Finance Act (NI) 1934* [1936] AC 352. The validity of another Northern Irish Act (The Milk Act 1936) was also challenged, although not through a reference to the Judicial Committee, but rather by means of an ordinary action in *Gallagher v Lynn* [1937] AC 863. In both cases the Northern Ireland Parliament was held not to have acted *ultra vires*.
29 *The Constitution of the United Kingdom* (1991), Article 26 (pp 24-5) & pp 19-20 of the "Commentary" attached thereto.
30 *Ibid*, p.19 of the "Commentary".
31 *Ibid*, Article 26.7 (p.25).

or would initiate its own assessment of proposed legislation), and second, what procedures would exist to ensure that the advice tendered to Parliament by the Commission would be effective. In any case, and in spite of the input of the Public Service Commission in the selection procedure, it is surely fair to question the ability of the Human Rights Commission to perform this advisory task with unsullied objectivity.

Let me turn now to those proposals based on the adaptation of existing bodies. The only serious proposal for the Lord Chancellor to be considered for this legislative vetting role was made by the late Owen Hood-Phillips in his submission to the House of Lords Select Committee on a Bill of Rights.[32] He did not develop his idea, and it was ignored by the Committee when he was later examined. It is not hard to see why this is so, for it would surely be asking too much of the Lord Chancellor, who is not only a member of the Cabinet but also sits on the Cabinet's Legislation Committee and is therefore party to the formulation of policy initiatives, to be responsible for the objective examination of what will be, in effect, his or her own Government's legislative proposals. The much maligned "schizophrenia" that is already so much a characteristic of the office of the Lord Chancellorship would become untenable if such a task was entrusted to the holder. Such are the existing functions of the office that recourse to the objectivity, which might lie in the judicial element of the Lord Chancellor's office in an effort to exercise some control over compliance of legislative proposals with the European Convention, is effectively prevented by its counterpart – the executive aspect of the office.

The Attorney-General, on the other hand, has no judicial capacity and is not a member of the Cabinet. Furthermore, the Attorney-General is not generally subject to the same functional restrictions and contradictions which harness the Lord Chancellor. Nonetheless, the encumbent is a member of the Government and his or her duties are hardly less diverse than those of the Lord Chancellor; in fact, as John Edwards points out in his comprehensive study of the office of Attorney-General, "an elaboration of its exact parameters has never been the subject of public debate in Parliament or elsewhere".[33] In so far as the different roles played by the Attorney-General can be delineated, the holders both of this office and that of Solicitor-General must act as "first the Government's chief legal advisers, secondly, as ministerial colleagues assisting in piloting measures through the House of Commons, and thirdly, as servants of the House in their capacity as legal advisers to Parliament". Edwards adds, ominously, that this "is apt to confuse parliamentarians and non-parliamentarians alike, to say nothing of the ability of the Law Officers themselves to maintain the essential qualities attached to their respective roles".[34] For much the same reasons as those which disqualify the Lord Chancellor, therefore, the office of Attorney-General might not, after all, be suitable to perform the task of pre-legislative scrutiny. Such a proposed new responsibility would place an additional strain upon an office already requiring the most delicate judgement in reconciling collective ministerial responsibility and the wider

---

32 *Supra*, n.25, p.273.
33 JLI.J Edwards, *The Attorney-General, Politics and the Public Interest*, (1984), p.217.
34 *Ibid*, p.215. For further comment on the dual and sometimes conflicting duties of the Attorney-General, see Lord Hailsham, *The Child Lecture, 1978*.

public interest.

Nevertheless, the characterization of the office as occupying a "somewhat odd position" has not prevented some countries where there exists an office of Attorney-General similar to the United Kingdom model[35] from bestowing on it this very task. In Canada, for example, the Attorney-General invariably also holds the post of Minister of Justice, under whom the Canadian system of pre-legislative review is carried out.[36] Indeed, within the United Kingdom, it was common practice in the parliamentary process in Northern Ireland, before the dissolution of Stormont in 1972, for all bills to be submitted to the Attorney-General for his certification as to their validity (under the devolution powers of the Government of Ireland Act 1920) before they were presented for Royal Assent.[37] The Northern Ireland Attorney-General, of course, differed in a crucial aspect from the British counterpart in not holding a ministerial office.[38] Consequently, it can be argued, the former possessed greater independence, allowing execution of the duty of arbitrating on the constitutionality of the bills of the Northern Ireland Parliament with superior legitimacy. The proposal for a United Kingdom Attorney-General to adopt a like role[39] is fundamentally flawed by this issue of partisanship. As long as the office possesses its current status, there will always be room for doubt as to "the Attorney-General's ability to demonstrate the independence and impartiality of his decisions whilst serving as a ministerial member of the Government".[40]

This same issue of the potential for executive bias also effectively precludes any suggestion that the office of Parliamentary Counsel might be a suitable body through which pre-legislative scrutiny could be effected. *Prima facie*, the work of the office might be considered especially appropriate, as its main duty is to draft all government bills. Whilst the office may, where appropriate, indicate to departments the requirements of the European Convention, so long as it remains essentially an office that acts upon instructions it will be ill-equipped to perform the type of scrutiny here proposed.[41]

The idea has also been mooted that an entirely new body be established, the duties of which might include the scrutiny of legislative proposals. Most often, suggestions of this kind have been associated with the much broader notion of the creation of a Ministry of Justice. The idea of establishing a

35 Lord Dilhorne, "Proceedings of the Canadian Bar Association", Vol.39 (1956), p.138.
36 Chapter 5, *supra*, pp 103-5.
37 H Calvert, *Constitutional Law in Northern Ireland*, (1968) p.288. This practice had no origin in statute; rather, it emanated from a case in which the Attorney-General of Northern Ireland had found it necessary to intervene in an effort to support the validity of an impugned Act – *Northern Irish Road Transport Board v Benson* [1940] NI 133 at 150, *per* Babington LJ.
38 *Ibid.*
39 As promulgated by Owen Hood-Phillips, *supra*, n.25, p.278. See also the submission of the Government Departments to House of Lords Select Committee on a Bill of Rights (1977), *ibid*, p.101.
40 Edwards, *supra*, n.33, p.vii. It is suggested that some developments in the right direction might result if the United Kingdom Attorney-General was to be made a non-political appointment, *ibid*, pp 62-6.
41 It has been suggested, however, that an entirely new drafting body be established to draft, where necessary, legislation "to bring United Kingdom law and remedies into line with its human rights obligations under ... the European Convention", PJ Duffy, "English Law and the European Convention on Human Rights" (1980) 29 ICLQ 585, 618.

Ministry of Justice has a long and detailed history,[42] but the idea that it could be involved in pre-legislative scrutiny is as yet purely speculative. Even the most recent proposals for a Ministry of Justice[43] have all concentrated largely on the benefits of a consolidation of functions – that is, whether the present structure of responsibility for legal matters being divided between the Lord Chancellor, the Home Secretary and the Attorney-General could not be improved by the appointment of a single Minister of Justice who would have undivided responsibility for these matters. Apart from a brief reference made by Hood-Phillips, the question of how a Ministry of Justice might operate a scheme of pre-legislative scrutiny has never received any attention in these discussions.[44]

Such a role for a Justice Minister is not inconceivable, as, this is precisely the form of pre-legislative examination applied in Canada.[45] However, the conflation of the duties of the two offices of Ministry of Justice and Attorney-General in the Canadian model would be untenable in the United Kingdom. This would be due in part to the reasons stated above in respect of the unsuitability of the United Kingdom's Attorney-General in taking on the task of scrutinizing all prospective legislation. But it must also be recognized that even if the Attorney-General were kept separate, the very essence of the Ministry of Justice idea is that it will be a new government department, and as such will be no more independent than the Law Officers. This lack of independence (and therefore the potential loss of objectivity) has provided the most telling argument against any suggestion of a newly established Ministry of Justice being invested with the responsibility of legislative scrutiny.

In this review of the possibilities for a scrutiny scheme within the two categories of independent and intra-governmental bodies, two principal defects are readily apparent. First, between the two categories there exists a dilemma – namely, that where a suggested scheme might possess the independence required in order to provide an objective scrutiny of proposals, such independence necessarily distances the scrutinizing body from the legislative process; and where the proposed scrutiny body might occupy a position of potential authority within the nascent stages of the legislative process (that is, as part of the Executive's own scrutiny procedures), then it

---

42   In 1874 the Legal Departments Commission suggested that the Home Office might be reorganized to form a Ministry of Justice, see *Second Report of the Commissioners appointed to inquire into the administrative department of the Courts of Justice* (1874), p.105. For an account of the early history of the arguments for a Ministry of Justice and Bentham's views on the matter, see HJ Beynon, "Mighty Bentham" (1981) 2 Journal of Legal History, pp 62–76.
   More recently, Lord Gardiner consistently argued for the creation of a Ministry of Justice to help speed the necessary changes in the law and the legal system; see for example his letter to *The Times*, 21 March 1952, and "The Machinery of Law Reform in England", (1953) 70 LQR, pp 46–62. See further, RFV Heuston, *Lives of the Lord Chancellors 1940–70* (1987), pp 230–1.
43   See, for example, a recent proposal from the IPPR, *supra*, n.29, Article 43.1.3.2 (p.38), and also p.31 of the Commentary. Other suggestions include M Phillips, "The Need for a Department of Justice", *Guardian* (18 April 1984), p.13; L Lustgarten, *The Governance of the Police* (1986) p.179; and for general surveys: H Beynon, *Independent Advice on Legislation*, unpublished D.Phil. Thesis, Oxford 1982, pp 260–77, and G Drewry, "The Debate about Ministry of Justice – A Joad's-Eye View" [1987] PL pp 502–9.
44   *Supra*, n.25, p.273.
45   Chapter 5, *supra*, pp 103–5.

necessarily lacks independence. Secondly, the discussion of both categories has been marked by a conspicuous absence of any considered indications as to how the scrutiny of secondary legislation might operate. With a view to overcoming these problems, I turn now to the suggestions that the most appropriate placement of the any scrutiny procedure would be within Parliament's legislative process. It is suggested that the most effective mechanism for performance of such scrutiny would be that of a pair of joint committees of both houses – one each for primary and secondary legislation.

An intra-parliamentary scheme: the reasons for a joint committee model

The particular appeal of using a parliamentary committee is that it offers the opportunity to instil an element of parliamentary responsibility into the process of the scrutiny of all legislative proposals in addition to that supposedly operated by the Government. It also provides Parliament with the opportunity to exercise some control over the fundamental issue of compliance of all the legislation it enacts with the European Convention. These two aspects go some way towards justifying the creation of such a process in the first place.

It should be noted that an "ordinary" parliamentary committee is not the only intra-parliamentary option; use might be made either of an "extraordinary" parliamentary committee or of a non-member body. A suggestion within the first alternative category has been made by Liberty (as the National Council for Civil Liberties has now become) – that is, for the establishment of a Human Rights Scrutiny Committee, the membership of which would be *elected*, rather than *appointed*, from the House of Commons.[46] The apparent function of the Committee would be, broadly speaking, to scrutinize legislation for compliance with the proposed Bill of Rights of which it forms a part, though, crucially, not necessarily all legislation and not on its own volition. Whilst it is intended that the Committee would be empowered to "rule" on the compliance of *existing* legislation this process would be initiated *only* after a court had held the legislation to be in breach of the new Bill of Rights. The Committee's role in *pre*-legislative scrutiny for compliance with the Bill of Rights, on the other hand, would be restricted to those occasions when either the Executive or Parliament requested it so to act. In light of the observations made in the previous section of this chapter, the absence of any "self-initiating" power,[47] together with the loss of the opportunity to screen *all* draft legislation, surely significantly weakens the authority of this proposal.

What is contemplated in respect of the option of a non-member of Parliament body is, for example, the Speaker of the House of Commons or an entirely new parliamentary office. To be effective, however, this option would probably have to merge with a committee-based model (the task would likely be too large for one office alone, and in any case the need for an element of democratic participation in the scrutiny process must be accommodated). Indeed, it is suggested that the most satisfactory intra-parliamentary option

---

[46]   *A People's Charter: Liberty's Bill of Rights, A Consultation Document* (1991), Article 31 (pp 87-8) & pp 95-7.
[47]   *Ibid*, p.95.

would be a scheme which incorporated both these elements, so that one or more officers of the Houses would work in conjunction with the joint committees.

The requirement for the committees to be joint is, I think, beyond question. For although fewer bills originate in the Lords, the fact that the Upper House forms an integral part of the legislative process requires, on constitutional grounds, that it be represented;[48] in practical terms it also greatly enlarges the pool of expertise from which the Committee's membership can be drawn. It is further submitted that the case for two *separate* committees, one to be appointed by each House, is not viable. With such an arrangement there would always be the danger of confusing inconsistencies arising from their respective treatments of proposed legislation. It was, after all, with this very point in mind that in 1972 the Joint Committee on Delegated Legislation recommended that there be established a Joint Committee on Statutory Instruments, "since it was considered that the separate systems [for the technical scrutiny of statutory instruments] which had developed in both Houses had produced defects and anomalies in overall parliamentary control".[49] For much the same reasons the idea of single-house committees for the scrutiny of primary legislation is rejected.

The idea of using joint committees has some other positive advantages. Foremost amongst these is the fact that a joint committee can be endowed with all the beneficial features of a select committee,[50] and can thereby be freed from the limitations of standing committees. Structurally, select and standing committees differ in two crucial respects: the membership of the latter is arranged strictly according to party strengths, whereas that of the former need not be so;[51] and, secondly, whereas the basic line of inquiry in standing committees is adversarial, it is inquisitorial and investigative in select committees.[52] Thus, with respect to the first difference, one interlocutor has commented that "to entrust the function of review to the standing committee on each bill would be futile".[53] The usual absence of party political bias is one of the beneficial features of the deliberative process of select committees.[54] In respect of the second factor, it can be said that a

---

48 This point was put to the Canadian Special Committee on Human Rights and Fundamental Freedoms (1960), by the then Minister of Justice, the Rt Hon. ED Fulton, when addressing the question as to whether or not a pre-legislative scrutiny committee based purely on the House of Commons ought to be established; see *Minutes of Proceedings and Evidence of the Committee* (1960) - No.12, p.706.
Though the two scrutiny committees of the Australian Senate have operated with some considerable success, see (Chapter 5, *supra*, pp 99–103) it has been argued that their efficiency and efficacy could be enhanced if they were to become joint committees: DW Kinley, "The Parliamentary Scrutiny of Human Rights: A Duty Neglected" in P Alston (ed), *International Human Rights in International Perspective* (forthcoming 1993)
49 Erskine May, *Parliamentary Practice*, CJ Boulton (ed) (1989, 21st edn), p.551.
50 *Ibid*, p.665: "any of the powers which are given to select committees to enable them to discharge the duties of their appointment may be given to a joint committee".
51 Erskine May, *supra*, n.49, p.590 and pp 612–6, respectively.
52 See N Johnson, "An Academic's View" in D Englefield (ed), *The New Select Committees: A Study of the 1979 Reforms* (1984), pp 61 and 63.
53 Jaconelli, *supra*, n.6, p.29.
54 N Johnson, "Departmental Select Committees" in MT Ryle & PG Richards (eds), *The Commons Under Scrutiny* (1988), p.181. See also P Giddings, "What has been Achieved?" in G Drewry (ed) (1989, 2nd edn), p.372.

whole dimension of examination (and as a result of understanding also) would be lost if any scrutinizing body was restricted to adversarial inquiry. The relative merits of the two types of committee constituted the main concern throughout an experiment undertaken by the House of Commons in October 1980 in allowing three uncontentious (i.e. non-party political) bills to be placed before a select, as opposed to standing, committee at the committee stage of each bill's passage through the House.[55] The essence of the difficulty with the operation of standing committees was captured no more succinctly during debate than by George Cunningham MP in his vivid description of the atmosphere typically found in the committee rooms:

> [I]n the room there is an electrical force, which is the hunger for information of the members of the committee. In the corner of the room there is another electrical force, with I will not say all of the information, but an awful lot of the information. Between these two forces there is the narrow filament of the Minister's mind and that inevitably results in a fuse. What we are suggesting is that there should be some direct communication between these two corners, as it were, of the room.[56]

In further support of the House's experiment, the then Leader of the House declared that "many honourable Members find the present line-by-line scrutiny of legislation in Standing Committee an inadequate means of examining a Bill",[57] and that by changing the form of committee to the select type, a more thorough scrutiny might be achieved not only through an inquisitorial form of examination, but also in securing the assistance of the informed evidence of witnesses.

The power to call witnesses and to receive written submissions, as well as the less familiar but no less important facility to appoint specialist advisers to assist the members in deliberations, are perhaps the chief benefits to be derived from the special structural characteristics of the select committee model.[58] The last mentioned point is of particular relevance to any proposal for a pre-legislative vetting body, for the range of potential topics and issues which are likely to confront these committees would be enormous and, certainly during the initial years, the standing membership alone could not be expected to deal with them all with equal expertise. There would be considerable value, therefore, in choosing the select committee process in which there lies the authority to appoint specialist advisers and to send for persons, papers and records to be examined.[59] The powers in respect of examination are substantial. For in spite of the fact that the attendance of members from either House before a select committee is by invitation, not order,[60] refusals are very rarely made. As the Clerk of the House pointed out in his memorandum to the Select Committee on Procedure in 1978, "the

---

55 Acting on Recommendation 5 of the *First Report of the Select Committee on Procedure*, 1977-8, HC 588-I.
56 HC Deb. Vol.991, col.825 (30 Oct. 1980).
57 Norman St J Stevas, *ibid*, col.724.
58 For example, as provided for in the House of Commons Select Committees on European Legislation (S.O. No.127, s.4), and on the Parliamentary Commissioner for Administration (S.O. No.126, s.2(b)). See also JAG Griffith & MT Ryle, *Parliament* (1990), pp 422-3, for a concise account of such appointments.
59 *Ibid*, S.O. No.127, s.5, and S.O. No.126, s.2(a).
60 In exceptional circumstances an order of either house may be made to compel a member to appear, but such action is seldom taken.

overwhelming majority of select committees appear to find co-operation with the Government and state organizations satisfactory and seem to achieve good working relationships".[61] More recently the same general sentiment has been repeated – ironically during the Westland affair, when the Government attempted to protect civil servants involved in the scandal from the prying eyes of the Select Committee on Defence. The Liaison Committee in a report on the conduct and intentions of the Government throughout the affair, whilst registering its disapproval in respect particularly of the delayed appearance and subsequent reticence in the face of questioning of at least one Minister, nevertheless recognized that the "overall record of the present Government in encouraging the development of the Select Committee system has been good", and that its behaviour with respect to the Select Committee investigation into the Westland affair was, in truth, "an aberration".[62] In one recent assessment of the performance of the new select committee system, the earnest hope made of it when established that ministers would provide the fullest information to the new committees appears to have been met. "The quantity of evidence, oral and written," it is claimed, "remains impressive, and there is no doubt that departments – and this means officials at very senior levels – go to considerable trouble when preparing themselves for appearances before the select committees."[63] With respect to both the proposed joint committees for the scrutiny of legislative proposals this (informal) harmony, which normally exists between parliamentary committees and members and Ministers of the Government, is vital. The great variety of potentially complex issues likely to confront the two committees means that even with the authority to appoint specialist advisers, the committees, in order to understand fully the implications of the rights guaranteed by the European Convention for a bill, will depend, to some degree, on the co-operation of the Government department responsible for that bill.

The poignancy of this conclusion is sharpened when it is appreciated the extent to which the Government can control the information to be divulged about its actions and operation by regulating the part played by civil servants in responding to select committee inquiries. To understand the position held by civil servants in this respect, it is essential first to appreciate what is the nature of their relationship with their political superiors – the departmental Ministers. This association is based on a simple theoretical premise – namely, that the accountability of Whitehall staff is simply "absorbed by the responsibility of Ministers to Parliament".[64] Whilst in practice this line of responsibility might not be quite so clear, the theory is nonetheless of some use as an aid, for instance, to a better appreciation of the intention behind many of the directions given to civil servants in a particularly revealing in-house notice entitled *Memorandum of Guidance for Officials appearing before Select Committees*.[65] The directions

---

61   *First Report of the Select Committee on Procedure*, Appendix C (1978), para.49.
62   *First Report of the Liaison Committee*, HC 100 (1986-7), para.19. See also the Prime Minister's assurances of government co-operation with the Select Committee on Defence, HC Deb. Vol.90, cols 1091-2 (30 Jan. 1986).
63   N Johnson, in Ryle & Richards (eds), *supra*, n.54, pp 169-70.
64   CC Turpin, *British Government and the Constitution* (1990, 2nd edn), p.438.
65   Cabinet Office, March 1988 – this supersedes the Memorandum: General Notice, Gen.80/38 (16 May 1980).

contained in this document are commensurate with the general convention that it is to their Ministers (not Parliament) that servants of the Crown owe allegiance, and ultimately it is the Minister who decides what information a member of staff is permitted to reveal to a select committee. In the Memorandum civil servants who are called before a select committee to submit evidence are urged not to act independently of their Ministers; the general tenor of the instructions in the Directive is to impress upon civil servants that they are to reveal only as much as the Minister wishes to be made public. This notion is vividly illustrated by a sentence in the Memorandum's introductory paragraph concerning the submission of evidence: "Ministers' views should always be sought if any question arises of withholding information which committees are known to be seeking".[66] Indeed, in an effort to advance the efficacy of the Memorandum, a training programme for members of the Civil Service has been established to assist them in preparing evidence for any of the departmentally related select committees.[67]

It appears, therefore, from the point of view of a select committee, there exists a fundamental dilemma between remaining independent of government whilst still securing enough information from the Executive to enable it to do its scrutinizing job properly. The difficulty of the position is analogous to that faced by Members of Parliament when trying to prise information out of a government Minister – that is, "in order to extract information they must already know enough to ask the right question".[68] Whilst an understanding of this dilemma for select committees is essential, its dimensions should not be exaggerated, for in most cases where a select committee seeks information from Whitehall, the pressures of political prudence and the desire to preserve a state of amity between the Government and its parliamentary wardens is sufficient to allow the committees to perform their functions satisfactorily.[69]

The setting up of joint committees and the relevance of existing joint committees

The establishment of a joint committee, as befits its name, is a joint task. It involves a number of clearly defined steps: a proposal originates in one House, followed by a resolution by that House, should the proposal be supported; the informing of the other chamber of that resolution and the receipt of its sanction, equally by resolution; the setting up of a committee by each House, and finally their amalgamation. Generally speaking, the two Houses appoint the same numbers of members to their committees and give them identical powers. Examples of existing joint committees include one on consolidation bills, and, probably the most familiar, the Joint Committee on Statutory Instruments.[70] Both these committees deal with legislation concerning a broad range of topics and, therefore, in this respect at least, they provide a precedent for the similarly general nature of the task that

66 *Ibid*, para.21.
67 Second Report from the Select Committee on Procedure, *The Working of the Select Committee System*, HC 19-I (1989-90), para.340.
68 I Harden & N Lewis, *The Noble Lie* (1986), pp 90-1.
69 P Giddings, *supra*, n.54, pp 372-6.
70 S.O. Nos 123 and 124 respectively.

would face joint committees responsible for ensuring legislative compliance with the European Convention. This point is not without considerable significance, for in view of the joint committee model's dependence on the structure of select committees, there is a danger that in the heat of the metamorphosis undergone by the latter during 1979, certain qualities of the old order might have been lost. The main thrust of the 1979 changes was that all but a handful of select committees (including the two joint committees mentioned above)[71] became strictly associated with individual government departments. Fortunately, however, the tide of opinion that backed this new system was not so strong as to be blind to the singular quality of the work conducted by certain committees of the old style (the handful mentioned above) which, in contrast to the new models, cannot satisfactorily be tied to one government department. The same reasoning must prevail in the setting up of the proposed pre-legislative scrutiny committees as they would most certainly deal with topics associated with all aspects of government business. The type of task undertaken by some of the functionally orientated (as opposed to departmentally based) joint and select committees, therefore, provides further guidance as to how the proposed committees might work. The essential duty of the Joint Committees on Statutory Instruments, for instance, is to scrutinize legislation with a view to drawing to Parliament's attention any instrument that may be open to objection on a series of specified grounds, including whether it is within the powers of the original statute.[72]

Additional potential sources of guidance as to how the scrutiny committees suggested herein might operate are the two select committees (one from either House) established in 1974, which are concerned with the effects of draft European legislation. The House of Commons Select Committee on European Legislation is empowered, under Standing Order 127, to assess whether a proposal of the European Community raises issues of political or legal importance. It may also go on to report "on what matters of principle and policy may be affected thereby, and to what extent they may effect the law of the United Kingdom, and to make recommendations for the further consideration of such documents by the House".[73] If further consideration of any proposal is thought necessary, then both committees have the power to convey their opinions by way of a report to their respective Houses. Some reports are recommended for debate whilst others are provided simply for the information of the House. Both Houses are under an obligation to find time to debate those reports so recommended by the Committee before the draft legislative instruments in question are finally adopted by the European Council of Ministers. In the case of the Lords, however, this obligation takes the form only of an undertaking given by the Government during the debate

---

71   The others were the Select Committees on: European Legislation; Members' Interests; Public Accounts; Parliamentary Commissioner for Administration; Privileges; and House of Commons (Services).

72   See S.O. No.1241(B); and Erskine May, *supra*, n.49, pp 551-3.

73   Erskine May, *supra*, n.49, p.657. See further, Chapter 8, *infra*, n.8 and accompanying text.
      For the terms of reference of the complementary House of Lords Select Committee on the European Communities, see Resolution, HL Deb. Vol.351, cols 36-70 (7 May 1974). It is generally considered that the Lords' committee is the more influential on account, primarily, of its membership tending to be more expert, and its greater use of specialized sub-committees.

which gave birth to the committee, whereas in the Commons an identical government undertaking was superseded first by a resolution of the House in 1980, and more recently, with modifications, by a Resolution of 24 October 1990.[74]

A similar commitment would be desirable with respect to the reports of both proposed scrutiny committees, for with the sole exception of the House of Commons European Legislation Select Committee, select committee reports are not frequently debated in the Lower House, being granted what has been dubbed merely "cursory" attention.[75] In 1983, the Liaison Committee noted that despite the expressed intention of the Leader of the House at the time of the creation of the new select committee system that a "substantially increased priority" should be given to debates on select committee reports, "the number of reports from departmental committees that have been debated in the last three years is considerably lower than in equivalent periods in the 1970s. Moreover, the few days for such debates have often been at short notice, generally on a Friday, and in some cases long after the Report has been published."[76] The position has remained unchanged since 1983, with the Government continuing to stand by its original refusal in 1977[77] to allocate time specifically for the debating of select committee reports. As the product of their often intensive investigations seldom receives the kind of treatment it rightfully deserves, it is hard not to agree with the conclusion that the result is tantamount to "the exclusion of the committees from any institutional role in relation to legislative procedures" [emphasis supplied].[78] Despite the fact that the greatest impact of the departmentally related select committees has been at an informal, preventive level,[79] there is cause to view this exclusion as an opportunity squandered. For it cannot be forgotten that the usual bipartisan, consensual basis for the majority of select committee reports serves to heighten their level of objectivity, and therefore the authority of the reports, especially when they are critical of government policy or administration. Of course, the suggestion of a guaranteed minimum level of consideration by both Houses of the reports of the joint committees of the type I am advocating would be no panacea for these ills, but it would at least provide a definite opportunity for Members of Parliament, or interested pressure groups, to advance their ideas in respect of the important issue of legislative compliance with the European Convention in parliamentary debate.

Scrutiny of legislative proposals for compliance with the European Convention: the present position

It is claimed that in the formulation of all government legislative proposals due regard is paid to the demands of the Convention,[80] though the instances

---

74   HC Deb. Vol.178, cols 375–91 (24 Oct. 1990).
75   Nevil Johnson, *supra*, n.54, p.64.
76   *First Report of the Liaison Committee*, HC 92 (1982–3), para.4.
77   Mr William Hamilton's amendment to allocate eight days each session for the purpose of discussing select committee reports was defeated in a free vote, 99–145; HC Deb. Vol.969, cols 243–4 (25 June 1979).
78   Harden and Lewis, *supra*, n.68, p.110.
79   Select Committee on Procedure, *supra*, n.67, paras 353–69.
80   See Chapter 1, *supra*, nn 66 & 69; and *infra*, n.87 and accompanying text.

of legislative violation of the Convention detailed in Chapters Three and Four are clearly at variance with such a claim. This claim notwithstanding, it is apparent that there exists no permanent, formal Whitehall machinery designed to undertake this task. On only one occasion has anything like a formal body been set up to scrutinize a legislative proposal for conformity to the European Convention, and that was on a purely *ad hoc* basis. It will be recalled from Chapter Four[81] that in 1979 the Government, bowing to parliamentary pressure, invited the Home Affairs Committee, by way of its Sub-Committee on Race Relations and Immigration, to investigate the compatibility of proposed new Immigration Rules[82] with the terms of the Convention. Yet, despite the fact that in the resultant report[83] great emphasis was laid on the anxiety felt by many of the witnesses as to the vulnerability of some of the new rules in relation to Articles 8 and 14 of the Convention, and a reiteration of these fears in a consequent parliamentary debate,[84] the resulting new Immigration Rules were approved virtually unaltered.

What makes it so hard to determine the extent to which the relevance of the Convention is adequately recognized throughout the progress of a legislative proposal – from conception to the statute book – is the lack of any authoritative account of what the normal procedure is at the pre-parliamentary stage of a bill's life. In the United Kingdom, unlike most continental countries,[85] the influence of the European Convention on new legislation or administrative rules is not normally acknowledged in the one aspect of a bill that attempts to summarize the sponsor's basic intention for the measure – that is, the Explanatory Memorandum. This is so even when the new law is introduced as a direct result of the deliberations and judgments of the adjudicative organs of the Council of Europe in Strasbourg.[86] Nonetheless, in the view of one commentator the United Kingdom Government does consider the Convention when preparing legislation:

> [A]t least for the past ten years or so, lawyers experienced in human rights matters within relevant government departments (particularly the Home Office) are likely to be consulted on any potential legislation or administrative rules which conflict with the provisions of the Convention. The progressive build-up of individual petitions against the United Kingdom has seemingly made such legal consultation a political necessity to avoid subsequent publicity at Strasbourg.[87]

Even if allowance is given for the fact that this a very generalized opinion,

---

81 *Supra*, pp 85–6.
82 *Proposals for Revision of the Immigration Rules*, Cmnd 7750 (1979).
83 First Report of the Home Affairs Committee, *Proposed New Immigration Rules and the ECHR*, HC 434 (1979–80).
84 HC Deb. Vol.975, cols 312 and 329 (4 Dec. 1979).
85 See C Symmons, "The Effect of the European Convention of Human Rights on the Preparation and Amendment of Legislation, Delegated Legislation, and Administrative Rules in the United Kingdom" in MP Furmston, R Kerridge, and BE Smith (eds), *The Effect on English Domestic Law of Membership of the European Communities and of Ratification of the European Convention of Human Rights* (1983) p.390, n.25.
86 *Ibid.* See also the Government's refusal in a parliamentary debate on the Immigration Rules to state whether or not the Law Officers had been consulted on the question of compatibility with the Convention, HC Deb. Vol.975, col.256 (4 Dec. 1979).
87 Symmons, in Furmeston, Kerridge & Smith, *supra*, n.85, p.389.

the extent or efficacy of such consideration is manifestly inadequate.[88] We are unlikely to obtain a clearer picture, however, from those departmental lawyers referred to in the quotation, for the Civil Service memorandum on the submission of evidence to select committees expressly forbids the disclosure of "advice given to Ministers by their Departments", as well as "information about inter-departmental exchanges on policy issues, [or] about the level at which decisions were taken or the manner in which a Minister has consulted his colleagues".[89] The matter is further complicated by an indication from Clive Symmons (whose opinion is expressed in the quotation above) that not even the Government is consistent in its own statements as to whether or not it maintains a vigilant checking system to ensure that legislation conforms to the Convention.[90] It has been argued, furthermore, that even the Cabinet Legislation Committee (which is designed specifically for the purpose of the assessment and comparison of legislative proposals) "is not equipped to scrutinize government bills for compliance with the fundamental (if unwritten) principles of the constitution. Nor does it have the resources to scrutinize the mass of subordinate legislation drafted by the government departments themselves."[91] Yet, as has recently become apparent, the Cabinet is sufficiently aware of the significance of the European Convention at least to have issued a Memorandum to all government departments stressing the importance of taking due regard of the Convention when drawing up legislative proposals.[92]

The haphazard nature of this "system" of scrutiny and the uncertainty which accompanies it, through the absence of any guidance as to how departmental lawyers are to perform the task effectively, strengthens the case of those who wish to see instituted "some form of parliamentary watchdog committee to give systematic scrutiny to pending legislation in respect of its overall conformity with the Convention".[93] Anthony Lester, in his submission to the 1979–80 Home Affairs Sub-Committee on the proposed new Immigration Rules, was also strongly in favour of such a scheme.[94] Certainly, if nothing else, a fully integrated system would have the distinct advantage of allowing all questions of the relationship between both proposed primary and secondary legislation and the European Convention to be addressed by two specialist bodies rather than as, at present, through

---

[88] Yet note that the courts have always presumed that, in the absence of any words to the contrary, all Acts of Parliament are intended not to violate treaty obligations; see PJ Duffy, "English Law and ECHR", (1980) 29 ICLQ 585; and cases cited in Chapter 1, *supra*, n.2.

[89] *Supra*, n.65, para.30.

[90] Symmons, *supra*, n.85, p.390. On the one hand the silence with respect to the new immigration rules in 1979 (*supra*, n.82 and accompanying text), and on the other, the open declaration that legal advice had been sought in respect of the Contempt of Court Bill 1980 (though the latter was perhaps unsurprising in view of the fact that the legislation was instigated as a result of the European Court's judgment in *Sunday Times v United Kingdom*, ECHR Series 'A', No.30 (26 April 1979)), HL Deb. Vol.415, col.665 (9 Dec. 1980).

[91] A Lester, "The Constitution: Decline and Renewal" in J Jowell & D Oliver (eds), *The Changing Constitution* (1989, 2nd edn), p.366. For further discussion on the Cabinet's ability to scrutinize legislation generally, see D Miers & A Page, *Legislation* (1990, 2nd edn), pp 32–7, and I Burton and G Drewry, *Legislation and Public Policy* (1981), p.113.

[92] *Reducing the Risk of Legal Challenge*, Cabinet Office (6 July 1987); see Chapter 1, *supra*, n.69 and accompanying text.

[93] Symmons, *supra*, n.85, p.417.

[94] *Supra*, n.83, p.41.

each department's legal office, and thereby achieve some semblance of consistency of the legal opinion given.[95]

The idea of setting up a comprehensive system of scrutiny to replace the existing piecemeal method was in fact aired in a Lords debate in 1982 with respect to the extent to which the Mental Health Act (Amendment) Bill complied with the provisions of the Convention. In so far as it was seriously discussed at all, the idea of such a system was treated with a familiar degree of suspicion. Both Lord Renton and Lord Avebury were concerned about the "vast number of matters that we would have to take into consideration every time we brought a new bill before the House, to see whether it did not somehow affect the obligations we have assumed under the Convention",[96] should a special supervisory board be introduced. Although it might be unfair to upbraid their Lordships on this point, as they only mentioned it more or less in passing, it is suggested that if indeed there is a "vast number" of likely situations in which legislative proposals may be called into question on the grounds of possible infringement of the Convention, then some form of preventive machinery is precisely what is called for. If, on the other hand, their Lordships' fears are exaggerated, and in reality relatively few proposals are likely to occupy the time of the scrutiny committees, then it will not prove too great an impediment to the legislative process. Moreover, it is surely valid to argue that conformity to internationally protected rights is such a necessary and desirable aim that even should there be some delay in passing legislation, that is a small price to pay for achievement of the aim. In any event, the proposed scrutiny scheme is infinitely preferable, in terms both of time and political acceptability, to lengthy, expensive and conspicuous litigation before the European Court, which may in the end require amending legislation to be introduced. In any case, it is submitted that the present existence of analogous forms of parliamentary scrutiny machinery, together with a heightening awareness of the importance of conformity to the European Convention, provide sufficient precedent for the establishing of two new pre-legislative scrutiny committees not to be considered wholly exceptional.

As indicated earlier in this chapter,[97] the most effective scheme of pre-legislative scrutiny would involve an officer of Parliament working in conjunction with a joint committee. This view may draw support from the experience of the scrutiny committees of the Australian Senate,[98] which possess permanent independent advisers responsible for the initial scrutiny of all legislation to determine particular points that ought to be brought to the attention of a parliamentary committee for fuller consideration. A domestic precedent already exists for the *procedure* of such a scheme. The Speaker of the House of Commons is the ultimate authority to which are referred all questions as to the class of a bill - i.e. whether it is public, private or hybrid.[99] The Speaker is also responsible for deciding what is a

---

95   It appears that interpretational discrepancies between departments are not uncommon, see Symmons, *supra*, n.85, p.389, at n.18.
96   HL Deb. Vol.427, col.878 (23 Feb. 1982), *per* Lord Avebury.
97   *Supra*, pp 124–5.
98   See Chapter 5, *supra*, pp 99–103.
99   Initially, all draft Public Bills are laid before the Clerk of the Public Bill Office who examine them "to see whether they have been prepared in conformity with the rules of the House", Erskine May, *supra*, n.49, p.467. If the Clerk considers that certain

Money Bill under the terms of the Parliament Act 1911, and issues a certificate (the "Speaker's Certificate") if he or she finds a bill to be so.[100] Additionally, the Speaker's Counsel performs the preliminary vetting of all instruments that come before the Joint Committee on Statutory Instruments and advises the Committee where necessary.[101] With the office of Speaker already involved in the initial parliamentary stages of both primary and secondary legislation, it would seem logical to use its resources in a way that might assist the proposed joint committees. It would be possible for assistance in this task to be sought from within the Speaker's present office – that is, from the Speaker's Counsel and assistant (as suggested with respect to the scrutiny of secondary legislation in Chapter Eight below), or new appointments could be tailored for this job (as suggested for the scrutiny of primary legislation in Chapter Seven below).

Conclusion

It is clear that the present arrangements for ensuring that legislation complies with the European Convention are uncertain, unsatisfactory and ineffective. As the United Kingdom is already obliged (under Article 1 of the Convention) to secure the observance of the Convention, then for such an obligation to have any meaning there must be included an implied limitation on the Government not to propose, and Parliament not to pass, legislation that transgresses the Convention unless this is explicitly stated.[102] Yet as is evidenced in Chapters Three and Four, above, serious legislative breaches still occur, whether by mistake or design. It is submitted, however, that the establishment of machinery for pre-legislative scrutiny would significantly reduce the number of such instances.

The option of an intra-parliamentary scheme appears to offer the best prospect of rectifying this situation, through its combination of authority (that is, direct involvement within the legislative process) and legitimacy (that is, operating through the democratically elected members of the legislature), in contrast to the limitations in these respects of the independent and intra-government options. Indeed, the mere existence of even a moderately effective scrutinizing scheme would be sufficient to ensure that a constructive influence would be brought to bear not only on Parliament but also on the policy-makers within the Government. The Liaison Committee, in reviewing the work of the new select committee system, was of the opinion that as a consequence of a committee inquiry, "parliamentary interest focuses on a topic not chosen by the Government, the department has to reassess its position and defend it in public ... opposition members get access to Government departments, parties outside

---

Standing Orders relating to private business are applicable to the bill, then it may be declared by the Speaker to be hybrid. The Speaker, under S.O. No.59, may also declare a bill to be *prima facie* hybrid after the bill's first reading.

100 See Erskine May, *ibid*, pp 751–2. The Rt Hon. Herbert Asquith, who was Prime Minister during the passage of the Parliament Act, made certain comments about the competence of the office of Speaker and the opportunities open to him to seek expert advice during the debate on a bill; these comments are not without relevance to the current discussion, HC Deb. Vol.24, cols 297–8 (11 April 1911).

101 Under power of S.O. No.124 (4).

102 Indeed, under Article 15 of the Convention, member states are obliged to notify the Council of Europe of any "measures derogating from its obligations under the Convention".

the House – and Ministers – are given a parliamentary platform from which they can be heard, the House and country become better informed of the facts ... and a public debate on the matter is stimulated".[103] Sir Douglas Wass, a former senior civil servant, has had cause to remark that from his experiences at the Treasury "[o]ne question became commonplace: 'How do we explain this particular awkward fact to the select committee'".[104] In a recent assessment of the effectiveness of the select committee system, the Select Committee on Procedure concluded that one of the most important aspects of "the solid, unspectacular but undeniable achievements of the first decade of the new committees",[105] is "the intangible impact which the mere existence of the departmentally–related Committees has had on the conduct of the Departments because of the permanent possibility of an enquiry or a request for evidence".[106]

The same results might reasonably be expected of an intra–parliamentary scrutiny system for the specific purpose of legislative compliance with the European Convention.

---

103 *Supra*, n.76, para.12.
104 *Government and the Governed*, The Reith Lectures 1983 (1983) p.70; see also, p.69. An analysis of the impact of this attitude of anticipation is provided by P Giddings, *supra*, n.54, pp 374–6.
105 *Second Report*, *supra*, n.67, para.369.
106 *Ibid*, para.360.

7 A SUGGESTED SCRUTINY SCHEME FOR PRIMARY LEGISLATION

In the previous chapter it was suggested that legislative scrutiny for compliance with the European Convention on Human Rights in the United Kingdom would be most effective if it were to be based on an intra-parliamentary model. It was further suggested that a pair of joint committees (one for primary the other for secondary legislation) might suitably perform the task of scrutinizing legislative proposals. It remains, in the following chapters, to determine the means and manner of operation of such a scheme. This chapter is concerned with the machinery for the scrutiny of primary legislation, and the next chapter with that relating to secondary legislation. Before dividing the discussion in this way, however, it should be noted that the two sets of machinery are intended to be part of a complete scheme and as such are designed to complement each other. They share certain salient characteristics, of which three may be readily identified.

First, at the centre of both there is a joint committee charged with the duty of scrutinizing all draft legislation for compliance with the Convention. Second, in both cases the scrutiny is to be performed by way of a two-tier system. An initial examination is to be conducted by a specially appointed Examiner or Counsel to each committee, before the bills or statutory instruments reach the committees proper where, if necessary, they are considered more fully. Third, the reports of both joint committees, together with any comments made by the Examiner or Counsel, are to be submitted to both Houses of Parliament. It is then for Parliament to decide when it comes to consider the legislation what action, if any, should be taken in response to the committees' reports. The scrutiny undertaken by the joint committees, therefore, is intended primarily as an aid to Parliament in its consideration of the effect which that prospective legislation might have on the rights protected by the European Convention, and not a substitute for it. It is emphasized that whilst the joint committees might themselves express views as to whether a legislative proposal did in fact constitute a breach of Convention, the *conclusive* judgement is to be left to Parliament.[1]

The first problem to resolve in respect of the scrutiny of primary legislation is that of the point in the legislative process at which the scrutiny should be applied. Scrutiny of legislation at the pre-enactment stage might, of course, include a preventive influence on the Government's policy proposals for its legislative programme; that is, at a stage before the prospective legislation has even entered Parliament. It is considered, however, that whilst it would be desirable that the reactions of the scrutiny committee should be anticipated by those within government responsible for the formulation of legislative proposals, it would be unwarranted for direct parliamentary scrutiny to take place at this stage. It is certain that any government would view such a proposition as an invasion of its freedom to formulate whatever legislative programme it wished.[2] There can be little doubt that, as Sir Douglas Wass asserts, the last stage of policy review – that of deciding which policy to follow – "must always be made by the government ... the process of taking that decision – the business of making the essentially political choice from the available options – has to take place within the privacy of the government committee rooms".[3] Furthermore, it can be objected that scrutiny at the policy formulation stage may fail to detect those breaches of the Convention that may only become apparent when the policy is expressed in the detail of a bill. In any case, there is no precedent for such parliamentary involvement in governmental policy-making and any suggestions made along these lines have failed to gain any significant support. The mooted establishing of pre-legislative committees considered by the Select Committee on Procedure, for example, was rejected on the grounds not only that ultimate responsibility for government bills must lie with the Government, but also that previous use of pre-legislative select committees had not been uniformly successful (in particular it was found that the more controversial the bill, the more likely that party politics would dominate discussion), and the varying degrees of size, urgency and importance of bills obstructed the establishment of any standard procedure for the pre-legislative stage.[4] An equally decisive illustration of the antipathy directed against the idea of a parliamentary committee prejudging matters of policy is provided by the House of Commons Select Committee on European Legislation. That committee has the task – unique amongst permanent select committees – of scrutinizing what are in essence pre-legislative proposals (in this case draft European Community Regulations, Directives and other documents). However, the Committee's terms of reference

---

1   This is precisely the standpoint adopted to justify the operation of the Australian Senate Standing Committee for the Scrutiny of Bills; see "The Operation of the Senate Standing Committee for the Scrutiny of Bills 1981–85", a paper submitted to the Australasian Study of Parliament Group conference on *The Legislative Process: How Relevant?*, Adelaide, August 1985 by Senator Michael Tate, p.2. On the operation of the Australian committees see, Chapter 5, *supra*, pp 99–103.
2   DR Miers & AC Page, *Legislation* (1982), p.105.
3   "Checks and Balances in Public Policy Making" [1987] PL 182.
4   *First Report of the Select Committee on Procedure*, HC 588-1 (1977–8), para.2.4.

implicitly forbid its consideration of the *merits* of these documents.[5] Questions of merit, or policy, are seen as strictly for government initially, and Parliament ultimately, to determine.[6]

If the stages prior to a bill's introduction into Parliament – that is, of policy-making or drafting[7] – are not to host the proposed scrutiny scheme, then scrutiny at the point of a bill's introduction is to be preferred. Not only would scrutiny at this stage be the earliest viable point at which the task could be undertaken, but it has the added advantage of presenting no delay to the Government in initiating the bills in its legislative programme. The importance of having the scrutiny process begin as early as possible in a bill's passage through Parliament is principally to allow the scrutinizing organs the maximum amount of time in which to perform their duty. In this event, it is hoped, the scrutinizing committee would be able to submit its report to Parliament before a bill has finished its main debating stages but in time so as not to delay its passage.[8] The *raison d'être* of the scrutiny scheme, after all, is to provide information to Parliament in order that it may be better able to examine the legislative proposals before it in respect of the specific issue of compliance with the European Convention. The significance of this service is readily apparent when it is remembered that the Government department sponsoring a bill is likely to have an unmatched understanding of the possible implications of its draft legislation; Parliament, therefore, will need all the assistance it can get if it is to scrutinize effectively.

A model for scrutiny of primary legislation

The essential elements of a suggested scrutiny scheme are considered in this section in two stages: first, the actual machinery of scrutiny, and how it would operate; and second, the effect on the legislative process. The analysis takes the form, more or less, of general propositions as to what the model entails, which necessarily allows for some degree of variation in the exact terms of its implementation. Though it is proposed that the scheme be established by a combination of Standing Orders (in the Commons) and Resolutions (in the Lords), I have chosen, partly in order to preserve this degree of adaptability, not to present a detailed draft set of either.

Standing Orders, at least in the case of the House of Commons, are not the only means by which the scheme might be set up. Incorporation by statute might be considered. However, not only would this effectively entrench the scheme – itself an issue likely to be extremely controversial – it would also be an unprecedented, and therefore improbable, means by which

---

5   S.O. No.127. In contrast, the terms of reference of the House of Lords Select Committee on the European Communities (Resolution of the House of Lords, HL Deb. Vol.351, cols 369–70 (7 May 1974)), expressly provide for consideration of the merits of draft Community legislation.

6   The idea that a scrutiny scheme like the one here suggested might include the consideration of the *merits* of legislative proposals might be objected to on the ground not only that this is the proper province of Parliament, but also of the practical difficulty of obtaining cross-party agreement on this basis in committees.

7   Drafting, of course, must be viewed as a singularly governmental activity. Departmental solicitors *instruct* Parliamentary Counsel on the requirements of the legislation they are to draft; see DR Miers & AC Page, *Legislation*, (1990, 2nd edn), p.58.

8   Further details, *infra*, pp 149–53.

to establish a parliamentary committee.[9] A composite method – whereby some elements of the scheme would be established by statute, others by Standing Orders, might also be considered. But, like the purely statutory option, such an arrangement would not be viewed favourably as any degree of statutory *entrenchment* of a scrutiny system of the type here proposed is likely to be strongly resisted. It is as well to remember that it is the very idea of statutory entrenchment which so crucially impedes the proposal to incorporate the European Convention as a Bill of Rights; it would be most undesirable, therefore, to shackle the proposal for a scrutiny scheme in a similar way. The same reasoning applies to the setting up of committees in the Lords as, invariably, they are established by way of Resolutions (and infrequently Standing Orders), not by statute. In which case, there would be no reason why the Lords should not continue this practice in respect of the its responsibility to establish a committee (to join with one from the Commons) for the scheme here suggested.

The mechanics of the scheme

The principal element of the scrutiny scheme for primary legislation is the joint committee, which might be entitled the "Joint Committee on the European Convention on Human Rights".[10] It would be assisted in its duties by a specially appointed counsel, entitled, perhaps, "The Examiner for the European Convention on Human Rights". As indicated above, the scrutiny process would operate on two levels. An initial screening of all public bills introduced into either House – by Government or private members – for compliance with the Convention would be conducted by the Examiner, who would examine each bill on its publication. The Examiner would indicate in a brief report to the Joint Committee whether or not the bills he had examined contained any provisions that might *prima facie* infringe the European Convention. There would follow a through examination of all bills by the Joint Committee. In practice, the Committee would concentrate its attention on those bills marked by the Examiner as *prima facie* in breach of the Convention. Most if not all of the remaining bills would pass through the Committee without further comment. The purpose of the Examiner's check, after all, is precisely to separate those bills which pose no threat to the rights protected in the Convention from those which potentially do so. What is more, it is clear from observing the operation of two committees which are assisted in their scrutinizing task by a specialist counsel – the Joint Committee on Statutory Instruments in the United Kingdom and the Senate Standing Committee for the Scrutiny of Bills in Australia[11] – that the memberships of such committees relies heavily on the advice tendered to them by their respective counsel. That having been said, in respect of the two committees cited, it is clear that they are both capable of asserting independent views either by questioning a legislative proposal not identified by the assisting counsel or (more commonly) by overturning, or substantially

---

9   Invariably, committees of both Houses, whether joint, select or standing, are appointed
    by the individual Houses themselves in accordance with their Standing Orders.
10 Though, of course, in the Houses' respective Standing Orders and Resolutions the
    committee would not be referred to as "joint".
11 I am indebted to both the Joint Committee on Statutory Instruments and the Australian
    Senate Standing Committee for granting me permission to attend sittings of their
    respective committees as an observer.

altering, the reservations or comments indicated by counsel.

It is beyond doubt that an assisting counsel contributes enormously to the efficacy of these committees, if only in giving guidance to the committees as to how best to utilize the limited time available to them by indicating which legislative proposals are likely to require particular scrutiny. Such assistance would clearly be beneficial in respect of a Joint Committee on the European Convention on Human Rights, especially during its initial years of operation when the impact of the Convention on draft legislation will not be quite so clear.

With regard to the numbers and composition of the Committee, there is clearly some room for variation. On the one hand, like the Joint Committee on Statutory Instruments, the Committee here proposed might comprise seven members from each house, appointed *pro rata* to party strength in the Commons, and with a member of the Opposition in the chair. Alternatively, the membership might comprise equal numbers from the Government and non-Government with the chair alternating between the two groups. In either event it is presumed that the usual bipartisan relations between members of the select committees will prevail.

The sole duty of the new committee would be to investigate the terms and effect of those bills which could infringe the Convention and to indicate in a report to Parliament whether there is such danger, and if so, the grounds upon which their opinion is based. In so doing, in addition to availing itself of the expertise of the Examiner, the committee would be empowered to call upon specialists in areas relevant to the questionable provisions before it.

The operation of the scheme

It is instructive to consider at this point what the consequences might have been if a Joint Committee on the European Convention on Human Rights had been in existence when, for instance, the Prevention of Terrorism (Temporary Provisions) Bill 1984 was passing through Parliament. It would seem likely that the combination of the Examiner's initial screening and the Committee's examination – as assisted by the submission of evidence by expert witnesses and possibly the support of specialists appointed to advise the Committee – would have significantly aided Parliament's scrutiny of the bill. In particular, it might have helped to alert Parliament to the risk of conflict with Article 5 of the Convention (speedy access to the courts) of the provisions for the seven-day detention rule (subsequently s.12 of the Prevention of Terrorism (Temporary Provisions) Act (hereafter the PTA) 1984). As indicated earlier,[12] there exists a voluminous body of jurisprudence from the European Court on this issue of detention without trial, demonstrating a reluctance on the part of the Court to accept justifications argued by member Governments for such lengthy detention periods, even when used to combat terrorism. Yet no reference whatsoever was made to this corpus of decisions during the Bill's passage through Parliament. A subsequent ruling by the European Court against the United Kingdom with regard to the seven-day detention provision (for breach of Article 5(3) – the right to be brought promptly before a judicial authority[13] – obliged the Government to

---

12   Chapter 3, *supra*, n.105 and accompanying text.
13   *Brogan et al v United Kingdom*, ECHR Series 'A', No.145, para.62 (29 Nov. 1988).

register with the Council of Europe a Notice of Derogation[14] to enable the provision (now s.14 of the PTA 1989) to remain in force. Such an extreme measure involved considerable political embarrassment and attracted much criticism.[15]

With respect to another issue: guidance from the proposed scrutiny committee as to the compatibility of the notorious s.28 of the Local Government Act 1988 which prohibits the "promotion of homosexuality" by local authorities with Article 14 (right against discrimination on grounds, *inter alia*, of sexual orientation) would have contributed immensely to the discussion that surrounded this provision before its enactment. As it was, the impact of the European Convention on the legislation was never acknowledged during the Bill's passage. Indeed, the Convention was not mentioned throughout the Bill's examination in the Commons.[16]

Instrumental to the interpretation of this section is the meaning to be given to the word "promote" in the direction that "a local authority shall not intentionally promote homosexuality". It can be understood to extend to a merely tolerant attitude towards homosexuality on the part of the authority in the performance of its functions. It may cover the granting of financial support for lesbian or gay organizations (in particular, those which offer counselling services) of the kind extended to other minority sections of the community – for example, the elderly, the disabled, the homeless, or single parents. It may, on the other hand, be restricted to the advocacy of homosexuality. In a legal opinion prepared for the Association of London Authorities by Lord Gifford QC and Terry Munyard,[17] it is concluded that discrimination against homosexuals contrary to Article 14 of the Convention will be avoided *only* if the judiciary adopt the last mentioned meaning of "promote"[18] There is no guarantee, however, that this will be the view adopted by the courts.[19] In the meantime, and for as long as there continues to be "no satisfactory legal definition of promote", local authorities have been forced to "err on the side of caution and cease to implement policies which might well not be prohibited by the clause [sic]".[20] The lack of clarity over the position, therefore, might itself lead to a violation of Article 14. Yet Parliament, it would appear, was not aware of this possibility when examining the Bill. It is submitted that the Government might at least have been required to express its intention more clearly in this respect, had Parliament benefited from the information and guidance provided by a specialized scrutiny body.

The expertise available to the Joint Committee would also be of particular

---

14 Statement made by the Home Secretary (Rt Hon. Douglas Hurd), House of Commons Standing Committee B, sixth sitting, col.235 (22 Dec. 1988). See further, Chapter 3, *supra*, n.110 and accompanying text.
15 For example, the notice of derogation necessitated arguing that the whole of the United Kingdom was in a state of emergency. This was greeted by some in Parliament "with a mixture of disbelief and dismay": *ibid*, (Mr Sheerman MP).
16 See the second reading of the bill: HC Deb. Vol.119, cols 75–155 (6 July 1987), and its committee stage: HC Standing Committee 'A', cols 1199–1231, (8 Dec. 1987).
17 *Section 28, Local Government Act 1988: "Promotion" of Homosexuality Ban*, Public Document (22 June 1988)
18 *Ibid*, paras 9 & 16.
19 There has yet to be a case directly concerning s.28.
20 Keir Starmer, "The Scope of Clause 28", a legal opinion prepared for the Organization for Lesbian and Gay Action (23 May 1988).

benefit in those cases where legislation is being introduced as a direct consequence of European Court rulings against the United Kingdom. It might be thought that in this event a clear and comprehensive understanding of the demands of the Convention would be a necessary precondition to the successful formulation of the prospective legislation. Yet from the evidence provided by at least two instances where legislation has been precipitated by adverse judgments of the European Court, there is some doubt (and in one case, certainly, of inconsistency) as to the compliance of the new legislation with the requirements of the Convention as interpreted by the Court.

The Contempt of Court Act 1981 was introduced partly in response to the European Court's ruling in the case of *Sunday Times v United Kingdom*.[21] The Court held that certain aspects of the United Kingdom's common law of contempt – principally, the emphasis placed on the public interest in protecting the administration of justice at the expense of that invested in the freedom of expression[22] – infringed the right of freedom of expression as guaranteed by Article 10 of the Convention. It is true that the Article also states certain circumstances under which this protection might be qualified. But in this case the European Court decided that the grounds upon which the domestic courts held the *Sunday Times* in contempt[23] (and therefore effectively prevented it printing certain facts or opinions) did not sufficiently establish that the restriction was "necessary in a democratic society". It was in this case therefore, in the public interest for the newspaper to have its right to freedom of expression protected.[24]

Certain provisions of the Contempt of Court Act 1981 were designed specifically to comply with this definitive interpretation of the Convention. Section 2 of the Act imposes limits on the strict liability rule, so that now not only must the legal proceedings to which a publication refers be active (sub-s.(3) and Schedule 1), but also the publication must create a substantial risk of seriously prejudicing the course of justice in the proceedings in question (sub-s.(2)) for it to be held in contempt. This modification was probably sufficient to satisfy the demands of the European Court's ruling in respect of the pre-judgment test applied by the House of Lords in the *Sunday Times* case. However, the alteration made by s.5 of the Act, which was also prompted by the European Court's decision, less obviously conforms to that decision. This section provides an exception to the modified strict liability rule, where the risk of a publication prejudicing certain legal proceedings "*is merely incidental* to the discussion of matters of general public interest" [emphasis supplied]. The point of concern here is that the relevant newspaper articles in the *Sunday Times* case were concerned *wholly* with (and were not "merely incidental" to) the ensuing cases being brought against Distillers Plc by the families of children who had been disabled by a drug marketed by the company.[25] It is not improbable that the *Sunday*

---

21   ECHR Series 'A', No.30 (26 April 1979).
22   *Attorney-General v Times Newspapers Ltd* AC [1974] 273, 301 (*per* Lord Reid).
23   *Ibid*.
24   *Supra*, n.21, para.67.
25   See NV Lowe, "The English Law of Contempt of Court and Article 10 of the European Convention on Human Rights" in MP Furmston, *et al* (eds), *The Effect on English Domestic Law of Membership of the European Communities and of Ratification of the European Convention on Human Rights* (1983), p.344; and JAG Griffith, *The Politics of the*

Times would be no better protected today than it was prior to the 1981 Act. Implicit support for this claim comes from a statement made by Lord Diplock in *Attorney-General v English*,[26] when he declared that the risk of prejudice posed by the article in that case was "merely incidental" to the discussion, and referred to the article in the *Sunday Times* case as its "antithesis".[27] The inference here is that as the latter article was expressly devoted to the ensuing legal action, it would fail to qualify for the exception from strict liability for contempt under the terms of s.5 and thereby be held to be in contempt under the terms of s.2.

Furthermore, a separate provision in the Act concerning the obligations of secrecy on jurors (s.8) – which was not introduced to combat the detrimental decision of the European Court, rather it was intended to clarify the legal position in this matter – is also likely to infringe Article 10 of the Convention.[28] It is true that jurors in the United Kingdom appear to have been extremely reluctant to relay their curial experiences to the media so that *if* this attitude remains then s.8 alone may have little impact on freedom of expression. It is, however, of considerable concern that such a section with this potential could have been passed in the first place, especially within the particular context that the Contempt of Court Act was enacted.

Most recently, the compatibility of yet another section in the Act with the European Convention has been seriously questioned. Notwithstanding the apparent limitations to the so-called "strict liability rule" provided by ss 1 to 5 of the Contempt of Court Act, s.6(c) preserves the common law liability "for contempt of court in respect of conduct intended to impede or prejudice the administration of justice". In one of the many pieces of litigation spawned by Peter Wright's publication of his memoirs in *Spycatcher*, the Attorney-General sought to extend the effect of interlocutory injunctions previously obtained against the *Guardian* and *Observer* newspapers preventing their further publication of extracts from Mr Wright's book to cover other newspapers not named in the original injunctions. The Attorney-General sought to have the *Independent* and the *Sunday Times* (amongst others) held in criminal contempt under s.6(c) for their publication of that which by way of injunction had been expressly denied the *Guardian* and the *Observer*. The matter was referred from the High Court to the Court of Appeal on the preliminary point of law as to whether third parties could be bound by an injunction against another. The full bench of the Court of Appeal overturned the Vice-Chancellor's (Sir Nicolas Browne-Wilkinson) answer in the negative – adding, moreover, that publication in the public interest of the free flow of information is no defence to liability under s.6(c) – and the case was remitted to the High Court.[29] Thereupon, Morritt J found that the *Independent* and the *Sunday Times* had acted in contempt. He indicated that mere prior knowledge of the fact that others had been restrained from doing what these two papers did subsequently was sufficient to establish beyond all reasonable doubt that they had intended to prejudice the administration of

Judiciary (1991, 4th edn), pp 201-2.

26   [1983] 1 AC 116.
27   *Ibid*, 143.
28   J Jaconelli, "Some Thoughts on Jury Secrecy" (1990) 10 Legal Studies 92.
29   *Attorney-General v Newspaper Publishing Plc* [1988] Ch 333.

justice under s.6(c).[30] Crucially, the suggestion that such a result would likely violate Article 10 of the European Convention was summarily dismissed at this stage by Morritt J on the ground that he was bound by the House of Lords' earlier ruling on this point in the *Guardian* case which had determined that the public interest in the administration of justice (coupled with imprecise concerns over national security) outweighed that in preserving the right to freedom of expression.[31] The newspapers' subsequent appeals to the Court of Appeal and the House of Lords against this contempt ruling were dismissed.[32]

As a result, the *Sunday Times* (by way of the Commission) brought the case before the European Court of Human Rights claiming that the restriction imposed on its discretion to publish material from the Wright book was in violation of Article 10 of the Convention. The Court unanimously held that the continuation of the restriction after the confidentiality of the material in dispute had been effectively destroyed through its world-wide publication was such a violation as could *not* be justified, under Article 10(2), as a limitation to the freedom of expression "necessary in a democratic society".[33] It is true that the Court did not directly pronounce upon the compatibility of s.6(c) of the Contempt of Court Act with the Convention, though it recognized, of course, that it was as a consequence of this section alone that the injunctions obtained against other newspapers "were effectively binding on [the *Sunday Times*] too".[34] The section *per se* has not been impugned, but it is now clear that as a result of this ruling, where it is used to extend to others injunctions to which they are not privy, and which are found subsequently to conflict with Article 10[35] (or indeed any other Article) of the Convention, then such a use will, by necessity, violate the same Article. The potential for s.6(c) to be used in a manner which infringes the Convention remains manifest.

There has also been some doubt over the adequacy of the Interception of Communications Act 1985 in providing the legal framework for the protection of privacy identified as absent in this country by the European Court in *Malone v United Kingdom*.[36] Specifically, it is questioned whether the tribunal established by the Act to hear allegations of improperly authorized telephone tapping fulfils the requirement of Article 13 that in the event of a right protected by the Convention being violated (in this case privacy in Article 8), there must exist "an effective remedy before a national

---

30 *Attorney-General v Newspaper Publishing Plc* [1989] 1 FSR 457, 477.
31 *Attorney-General v Guardian Newspapers Ltd* [1987] 1 WLR 1248, 1297 (per Lord Templeman).
32 *Attorney-General v Times Newspapers Ltd & another* [1991] 2 WLR 994 (HL)
33 *Sunday Times v United Kingdom (no.2)*, ECHR Series 'A', No.217 (26 Nov. 1991), paras 54–56.
34 *Ibid*, para.48.
35 In a corresponding and contemporaneous case initiated jointly by the *Observer* and *Guardian* newspapers, against whom the original injunctions had been obtained, the European Court of Human Rights held unanimously that the injunctions had violated the rights of the applicants under Article 10 of the Convention: *Observer & Guardian v United Kingdom*, ECHR Series 'A', No.216 (26 Nov. 1991), paras 66–70.
36 ECHR Series 'A', No.82 (2 Aug. 1984). For an assessment of the extremely broad discretion allowed to the Executive in this regard in the absence of any legal regulation before 1985, see KD Ewing and CA Gearty, *Freedom under Thatcher: Civil Liberties in Modern Britain* (1990), pp 48–55.

authority notwithstanding that the violation has been committed by persons acting in an official capacity".37 As the domestic courts are expressly excluded from judicial review of the tribunal's decisions, or of its jurisdiction to make those decisions, the only "national authority" which is in a position to provide any remedy is the tribunal itself. This is of limited effectiveness as the tribunal's jurisdiction is narrowly restricted.38

The position is compounded by s.4(3) of the Official Secrets Act 1989 which prohibits *any* disclosure by a person who is or has been a crown servant of information concerning the issue of warrants for the interception of communications – no test of harm need be satisfied by the prosecution. The consequence, it is claimed, is to enable "a government to conceal any *unlawful* telephone tapping" [emphasis supplied].39 The Act, therefore, effectively exempts from legal sanction not only any surveillance activity which is unlawful by reason of exceeding the terms of an issued warrant but also all such activity that is undertaken without the authority of a warrant.40

The combination of the exclusion of the ordinary courts from review of authorized interceptions and this blanket prohibition on the release of any information by anyone employed by the Crown who might be aware of some such interceptions may amount to a denial of an *effective* remedy (under Article 13) for those seeking redress for interference with their mail or telephone communication. As indicated above, the initial breach of the Convention for which a remedy is sought is of the right of privacy protected under Article 8. The Article provides that this right may be qualified only in accordance with the law, which, as illustrated below, is an extremely complex notion. The fact that in the United Kingdom there exists no statutory or common law right to privacy ought to have emphasized the significance of any encroachments on this liberty as incorporated in the Convention. Yet even when passing an Act in direct response to a European Court ruling, Parliament failed to appreciate, let alone act upon, this position for potential violation of Article 13.41 Neither was any such consideration given to the relevant section of the Official Secrets Act 1989 during its passage.42

---

37 The relevance of the European Court's judgment in *Klass & Others v FRG*, ECHR Series 'A', No.28 (6 Sept. 1978), paras 39–75 was not appreciated. See also, Ian Leigh, "A Tappers' Charter" [1986] PL 8; and Ian Lloyd, "The Interception of Communications Act 1985", (1986) 49 MLR 86.

38 For example, under s.7(1) of the Act, the Tribunal may reach only one of two conclusions – either that there has, or there has not been, a contravention of the provisions laid down in ss 2 to 5 of the Act for the issue of warrants. In the case of the latter, the applicant is not told whether this is due to the fact that the issue of the warrant was (or continues to be) in order, or because no warrant had been issued in the first place (which, if revealed, would provide possible grounds for criminal investigation).

39 S Palmer, "In the Interests of the State: The Government's Proposals for Reforming Section 2 of the Official Secrets Act 1911" [1988] PL 528. See also JAG Griffith, "The Official Secrets Act" (1989) 16 Journal of Law and Society 273, 287.

40 In the latter event s.1(1) of the Act applies.

41 In respect of the Interception of Communications Bill, the matter of non-compliance with Article 13 was raised twice during the Bill's second reading in the House of Commons (HC Deb. Vol.75, cols 174 & 191 (12 March 1985)), but in both cases the Government offered no response.

42 In respect of the Official Secrets Bill, only general questions of the Bill's compliance with the right to freedom of expression guaranteed by Article 10 were raised during its second reading in the House of Commons (HC Deb. Vol.144, cols 489, 530 & 535 (21 Dec.

Another related example of recent legislation that might have benefited during its parliamentary debating stages from the expert scrutiny of the proposed joint committee is the Security Service Act 1989. For the first time the Security Service (that is, MI5) has been statutorily identified.[43] Now any complaints against the actions of its members are to be heard by a newly established tribunal. Section 5(4) of the Act, however, expressly excludes the courts from review of the tribunal's decisions or the limits of its jurisdiction. Moreover, only complaints concerning actions of the Security Service authorized by the Secretary of State under s.3 of the Act are to be settled by the tribunal. Actions that are not so authorized will remain formally subject to the general constraints of criminal law and the law of torts but informally will continue undetected and unchecked by the courts.[44]

It is ironic that in making the first legal identification of the Security Service, the Act has failed to make the Service effectively accountable for its actions. It is at least questionable whether a system of dispute settlement which expressly excludes the courts can be considered sufficient to comply with the requirements of access to an independent tribunal under Article 6(1),[45] and the provision of an effective remedy under Article 13 of the Convention.[46] Of course circumstances do exist where recourse to a specially established tribunal alone may adequately meet the demands of both Articles.[47] Indeed, this principle has been recognized by the European Court

---

1988)). The Government responded glibly by pointing to the qualification to Article 10 in respect of the protection of national security; see col.541.

[43] Indeed, until this Act, the typical response of the Government to allegations brought against the activities of the Security Services was simply to disclose no information whatsoever. See, for example, the Government's submission to the European Commission in the application of Harriet Harman and Patricia Hewitt, where this policy was openly used. In this case the Government chose "neither to accept or deny the facts on which the applicants rely", but instead answered the charges raised against the Security Services *in abstracto*; see Decision of the Commission as to the Admissibility of Application No.12175/86, *Patricia Hewitt and Harriet Harman against the United Kingdom*, (12 May 1988). Subsequently, the Committee of Ministers determined that there had been a violation of Articles 8 & 13; Dir (90)4, p.2.

[44] An indication of the difficulty that is to be encountered when seeking legal redress for the invasion of one's privacy through surveillance and electronic bugging, whether authorized or not, is provided by the *Hewitt and Harman* case (*ibid*). In view of this established practice of secrecy it is not difficult to understand how few members of the Security Services have proceedings brought against them, let alone be convicted or lose a civil action.

[45] See *Golder v United Kingdom*, ECHR Series 'A', No.18 (21 Feb. 1975), para.26; and *Silver & Others v United Kingdom*, ECHR Series 'A', No.61 (25 March 1983), para.82.

[46] See the *Silver* case, *ibid*,para.113; and *Campbell & Fell v United Kingdom*, ECHR Series 'A', No.80 (28 June 1984), para.124. The remedies available from the tribunal consist of discretionary compensation, termination of the Security Service's enquiries in question, and the quashing of warrants issued by the Secretary of State (see para.6 of Schedule 1 to the Act). Nothing like an injunction, that might be obtained under judicial review, is available.

This matter was raised during the Bill's second reading, but the Government failed even to acknowledge, let alone address it; see HC Deb. Vol.143, cols 1169-70 (Mr Randall) and cols 1177-1179 (Mr C Patten – summing up for the Government) (15 Dec. 1988). The Bill fared little better in its committee stage (which was taken on the floor of the House; HC Deb. Vol.145, cols 32-118 (16 Jan. 1989) and 178-256 (17 Jan. 1989)), where the single reference to the possibility of a breach of the Convention related to the ambiguous nature of the Bill's definition of "national security" as an exception to the general obligation to protect the right of privacy; see *ibid*, cols 184-5, (Mr R Shepherd).

[47] See *Ashingdane v United Kingdom*, ECHR Series 'A', No.93, (28 May 1985), para.57 (in reference to Article 6(1)); and *Lithgow v United Kingdom*, ECHR Series 'A', No.102 (8 July

in the Swedish *Leander* case in respect of tribunals with jurisdiction in cases concerning the activities of national security services.[48] In this case however, the adequacy of the effective non-curial remedy provided in Sweden was due largely to the fact that it was considered in the context of an aggregate of no fewer than four such remedies available to the complainant.[49] In the United Kingdom, under the 1989 Act, there is only the tribunal mentioned above.

It is submitted, on the strength of these examples, that the proposed Joint Committee's ability to call not only upon those with expertise in the application of the European Convention on Human Rights, but also those with specialist knowledge in any of the vast number of issues that are made the subject of legislative proposals, would significantly contribute to an appreciation of how the Convention might be affected by prospective legislation. Clearly, the most complete understanding of the likely effects of a bill will reside in those members of the Government department responsible for a bill's sponsorship. It is envisaged, therefore, that both through their formal appearances before the Joint Committee, and a more informal (preventive) liaison between the Committee and members of the Government, a relationship of mutual respect, similar to that sustained in the present select committee system, would be established. As indicated earlier, the benefits of such an association are particularly important in terms of promoting a sense of self-restraint within the Executive itself; it is that type of internal or self-reflective scrutiny (however prompted) which is likely to prove the most effective form of protection against possible future transgressions. Nonetheless, it is suggested that where the scrutiny committee intended to report to the House that, *prima facie*, a legislative proposal infringes the Convention, then, as with the current procedure operated by the Joint Committee on Statutory Instruments, the Government Department involved would be afforded the opportunity to comment on any such report prior to it being laid before Parliament.[50]

Having, where necessary, called witnesses and collected evidence, and liaised with the appropriate government department, the Joint Committee on the European Convention on Human Rights would be required under its terms of reference to submit a report (which would also be published) simultaneously to both Houses on each bill examined, before the beginning of the committee stage in the House into which it has been introduced.[51] It is timely at this stage to note that even during the initial years of the scheme's existence, few bills are likely to be subjected to intensive scrutiny of the kind

    1986), paras 193–5 (in reference to Article 6(1)) & 204–8 (in reference to Article 13).

[48]   *Leander v United Kingdom*, ECHR Series 'A', No.116 (26 March 1987), paras 76–84.

[49]   *Ibid*, para.84. No recognition of this extremely pertinent case was made in Parliament, or expressed by the Government; for the relevant Commons debates, see *supra*, n.46.

[50]   HC S.O. No.124(9), (HC 271 (1990)).

[51]   The only viable alternative to the committee stage as the deadline is second reading. On balance, however, the usual two-week interval between introduction and second reading would be unrealistically restrictive in those few but vital instances where a legislative proposal taxes the resources of the scrutiny committee. What is more, delaying the Committee's report until after the second reading should not be a disadvantage as it would be known at the second reading stage that the bill was under scrutiny thereby alerting the House to the effect on human rights of relevant provisions in the proposed legislation. In any event, if the scrutiny committee's report raised issues not earlier anticipated, there would still be the opportunity for amendments reflecting these points to be tabled at the bill's committee stage.

discussed thus far. The majority of bills will pose no threat to the rights protected by the Convention and, therefore, the Committee's examination and subsequent report will be largely perfunctory. It should be reiterated that in those cases where a more detailed examination is required, the task of the Examiner and the Committee together would be to identify those legislative provisions that *prima facie* contravene Convention-protected rights and to indicate the grounds upon which this belief is based.[52] As I have foreshadowed, it would not be for either to concern itself with the merits of such provisions, or even to seek to justify or criticize the policy objective behind them. These decisions would be taken by Parliament; the scrutiny process is intended merely to assist Parliament by providing necessary information to enable it to reach a conclusion as to the compatibility of draft legislation with the European Convention.

The effect on the enactment process

The principal concern under this heading is that the new scrutiny scheme is intended to form a part of the normal legislative process for Acts. If the scheme is to be effective this has to be so. An outline of what might be expected of the scrutiny system and how it might operate has been developed above; the question remains, therefore, how it might be integrated into the process of enactment. Earlier in this chapter it was suggested that the scrutiny should begin (with the Examiner's initial screening) at the point of a bill's introduction. Upon the conclusion of the scrutiny by both the Examiner and the Joint Committee, the resultant report would be laid before both Houses in advance of the bill's committee stage in the House into which it has been introduced. It is suggested that usually this process would require no delay in the progress of most bills – in particular, those bills considered as posing no threat to rights protected by the Convention. Under certain circumstances, however, the usual period between introduction and committee stage might not be sufficient even for the initial scrutiny to be completed. This might be the case with those bills which the Government wished to have rushed through their parliamentary stages, as well as those which provide the Examiner and the Joint Committee with a difficult and therefore lengthy task of ascertaining their compliance with the Convention.[53] It is hoped, of course, that few of the former would be considered necessary, but when this course is adopted the Joint Committee might take the requisite steps to expedite its examination of the bills in question. Should even this prove insufficient, then it would be possible for the Government to take the extreme action of suspending the Standing Order that covers the scrutiny process. In so doing, however, the Government would necessarily draw attention to the question of the draft legislation's compatibility with the Convention and so effectively submit its actions to the scrutiny not only of the relevant House, but also of a wider public audience. Short of this extreme measure, it is likely that, to preserve

52   HC S.O. No.127, requires the Select Committee on European Legislation to perform a very similar task with respect to the legal and political consequences of draft European Community legislation and other documents, see Chapter 6, *supra*, n.73.
53   There are no minimum or maximum intervals between the presentation and second reading, and second reading and the committee stage for bills introduced into either House, though it is usual for each to be two weeks; see JAG Griffith & Michael Ryle, *Parliament* (1989), pp 242 (for the Commons) and 481 (for the Lords).

the good working relations between government departments and the select committees in general, the Government would endeavour to give the new scrutiny committee some notice, however brief, of legislation which it wished to hurry through Parliament. This itself would at least demonstrate the Government's willingness to co-operate with the Joint Committee and thereby demonstrate its good intentions towards ensuring the legislation's compatibility with the Convention.

In respect of those bills over which the Committee had particular difficulty – due to the bill's length, complexity or significance for the protection of human rights – the position would be slightly different. It is less likely (but not impossible)[54] that these bills would "rushed" through their parliamentary stages. In which case there would be greater opportunity for the scrutiny committee (through the Examiner) to have been made aware of the issues raised by the bill. It is envisaged that this would be achieved by means of the informal liaison which, as has already been suggested, would develop between the Joint Committee and the government departments. Moreover, as, presumably, the Government would be anxious not to obtain an adverse report from the scrutiny committee, it is likely, in the case of legislative proposals directly affecting Convention rights, to seek the Committee's opinion (or, indeed, the Committee could offer its views unsolicited) in advance of the final draft of such bills. Much of the pre-legislative scrutiny in certain cases, therefore, might be completed before a bill formally reaches the Joint Committee, in consequence of which many potential violations may also have been identified and removed from draft legislation by this stage.

For those bills where no such advance scrutiny is possible, or where the Committee's examination had not been completed by the committee stage, once again the Government will be faced with a decision either to seek to suspend the Standing Orders (in the case of the Commons) or to have the bill delayed. Few governments will welcome having to make such a choice, but if the scrutiny scheme is to operate effectively, then it is precisely those bills which *potentially* pose the greatest threat to the rights guaranteed by the Convention that would require the most attention. Indeed, it is under these circumstances that the operation of a scrutiny scheme would be most relevant, for if it raises any question over a bill's compatibility with the Convention it is likely to be thoroughly investigated whichever the above options the Government chooses to adopt.

With the exception of rushed or emergency legislation, in the event of the scrutiny committee's report being delayed, causing a bill's committee stage to be postponed, it would be due to the efforts of the Examiner and the Committee to understand fully the impact of the European Convention for the bill. Such efforts are made so that Parliament may be properly alerted to any possible danger of infringements of the Convention. In other words, the delay should not be seen as a hindrance to Parliament (rather, it is more an inconvenience to the Government), but as a necessary element of the parliamentary process of legislative scrutiny. It is suggested that this element of sanction (by way of delay to the bill) of the scrutiny process might be made mandatory through a direction in the Standing Order (or

---

54   The original Prevention of Terrorism (Temporary Provisions) Act 1974 progressed from
        introduction to Royal Assent in only 48 hours.

Resolution) not to commence committee proceedings on the bill unless a report on the bill from the Joint Committee on the European Convention on Human Rights has been laid before both Houses.[55] It will be noted that it is the laying of the report that would be instrumental to the chairman of the committee proceedings in this situation, not whether or not the House has taken any notice of it. Of course, in most cases the report would indicate that there was no *prima facie* indication of violation of the Convention and, therefore, no notice of it need be taken. It is extremely unlikely, on the other hand, that where a report indicated grounds for a possible breach, it would be ignored. The relative inattention to select committee reports paid by the House of Commons that certain commentators presently discern[56] is not, it is submitted, to be taken as necessarily significant in this respect. Existing select committees (with the possible exception of the two committees on European legislation)[57] are distanced from the formal legislative process, whereas the Joint Committee here outlined would be an integral part of it. Moreover, as has been already pointed out, it would not really be the House from which a response is sought or expected, but from the government departments – it is they who are the true addressees of committee reports.[58] In regard to the new scrutiny committee, co-operation between the Joint Committee and Whitehall would be an essential component of the Committee's functioning, although ultimately it would be the decision of the relevant House that would determine the fate of the report.

Amendments to bills

Thus far we have considered the effect of the proposed scrutiny scheme on the basic process of enactment. There are, of course, irregular and variable aspects of the legislative process[59] that the new scheme would have to incorporate. The most important of these is the matter of amendments to the original bill that might be made in either or both Houses – although, of course, all amendments must be *approved* by both Houses.

It should be noted that, as with the formulation of bills, it is suggested that there will develop a (preventive) awareness of the demands of the European Convention amongst those, particularly in government, responsible for the drafting of amendments. Such an attitude would manifest itself through the informal channels existing between the departments and the new scrutiny committee. It may come to be that before moving amendments government departments would seek to "clear" them with the scrutiny committee (this would be especially likely in respect of those amendments made to a bill on which the committee had cause earlier

---

55   As a viable, though less attractive alternative to the mandatory laying of the Committee's report before the committee stage, a Resolution or undertaking so to do might be sought from the Government.

56   See the comments of I Harden & N Lewis, *The Noble Lie* (1986), p.110.

57   The House of Commons Select Committee on European Legislation, and the House of Lords Select Committee on the European Communities.

58   N Johnson, "Departmental Select Committees" in Michael Ryle & PG Richards (eds), *The Commons Under Scrutiny* (1988), p.180; and in this regard it is generally acknowledged that the new select committees have had some success, see Chapter 6, *supra*, n.79 and accompanying text.

59   For example, the opportunity for a member of the House of Lords to introduce a bill without notice (HL S.O. No.39 (3)); provision for the second reading of a bill to be debated in committee (HC S.O. No.90); and provision for re-committal of a bill (HC S.O. No.72).

to comment in its original report). Though a large proportion of amendments moved in committee are initiated by opposition members, the majority of successful amendments are moved by the Government.60 It is suggested that with the existence of the Joint Committee these amendments would not be conceived in disregard, or ignorance of, the European Convention.

In addition, the Joint Committee (by way of the Examiner) would be able to note nearly all tabled amendments in advance, "as it is usual", in the words of Erskine May, "to give notice of an amendment to a bill in committee".61 Most amendments are moved at a bill's committee stage, even if the impetus for them may have originated during second reading. It is also possible for new amendments to be tabled during the report stage; though usually this period is devoted to further consideration of matters first discussed in committee. As few of the total number of tabled amendments (apart from government amendments) are eventually adopted, a detailed examination of them all would be quite unnecessary. However, to allow the Committee some opportunity to assess their impact on the rights protected by the Convention it might be possible to provide, at least, a cursory examination of all amendments.

It may be considered that this account of how the scrutiny scheme would incorporate the examination of amendments could be faulted in that it lays too great an emphasis on informal liaison between the Government and the new scrutiny committee, and that what is required is a more formal and more stringent procedure. Perhaps, therefore, the above proposals might be supplemented by a requirement that both the Speaker of the House of Commons and the Lord Chancellor should ensure that the reports of the scrutiny committee on all agreed amendments should have been laid before the relevant House in advance of the third reading; otherwise the bill would not be given a third reading. If the Committee reported that, as a result of the amendments, the bill was in conflict with the requirements of the Convention, then it might be required that the bill be re-committed for further consideration of the amendments,62 or alternatively, that the Government (or whoever moved the amendments) be required formally to respond to the Committee's report. This procedure of sanction by delay (that is, a requirement either to re-commit or to respond) would complement that suggested for the scrutiny of the whole bill before the committee stage. Its justification, however, is less compelling. This, it must be stressed, is not because amendments are any less likely to pose a threat to the Convention; drafting amendments aside, alterations to the substantive provisions of a bill are just as capable of such possible infringements as the original policy provisions of the bill. Rather, in purely practical terms, the longer task of scrutinizing a complete bill might cause the use of the delaying procedure significantly more often than the task of scrutinizing amendments to a bill. Furthermore, in the event of a large number of amendments being tabled – whereby the matter of examining them is correspondingly inflated – there would exist the option of the committee delaying its scrutinizing function until after the completion of the bill's committee and report stages, when it

60   See JAG Griffith, *Parliamentary Scrutiny of Government Bills* (1974), pp 197–8; see also, Griffith & Ryle, *supra*, n.53, p.508.
61   Erskine May, *Parliamentary Practice*, CJ Boulton (ed) (1989, 21st edn), p.488.
62   I am indebted to Michael Ryle for this suggestion.

would be known what amendments the House has agreed to.[63] Clearly, it would be preferable for the committee to have examined these amendments before they would be approved by *either* House, but at least by this method not only would any delay be avoided, but also any report from the Joint Committee would still bear directly on the amendment, as it would yet have to be approved by the *other* House. It is important to note in this case that where a large number (possibly hundreds) of amendments have been tabled in the Commons, it is very likely that a significant proportion would not be considered – some might be declared inadmissible (on any one of the eleven possible grounds listed by Erskine May),[64] and others, though admissible, might fail to be selected to be moved either in the House by the Speaker, or in committee by the Chairman.[65] Finally, where further amendments to a bill have been tabled in the second House considering the bill (or indeed at any later stage in the bill's passage through Parliament), then the above cycle of scrutiny and report would be repeated in respect of those new amendments.

Conclusion

The principal objective of the proposed scheme of the pre-enactment scrutiny of primary legislation is to impress upon the Government the importance of legislative compliance with the European Convention, and thereby to instil in those responsible for the formulation of legislative proposals an awareness of the demands made by the Convention. The resulting preventive effect would benefit both the Government and the citizens of the United Kingdom. In practical terms, there would be a reduction in the flow of applications made to the European Commission (and thereby the number of cases before the European Court) concerning United Kingdom statutes. And, of course, the rights under the Convention would be better protected.

The incentive for the policy-makers within government to adopt a preventive attitude comes primarily from the knowledge of the forthcoming scrutiny of their proposals. Not only would they be critically appraised by a Joint Committee specifically designed for the task, but also, ultimately, by Parliament which would receive the committee's reports. If they do not take full account of the effect their proposals might have on the Convention throughout the policy-making process, then such consideration would very likely be forced on them subsequently.

The essence of this central role of the scrutiny committee is well described in the words of Nevil Johnson, when commenting on what he sees as the major achievement of the new departmental select committees:

> They ensure that a significant proportion of Members of Parliament are engaged

---

63 The exception would be those amendments moved in response to a report by the Joint Committee questioning the compliance with the Convention of a provision in the original bill.

64 *Supra*, n.61, pp 491–493.

65 HC S.O. No.31. For a detailed explanation of "selection", see Griffith & Ryle, *supra*, n.53, pp 233, 236–7; see also, Erskine May, *supra*, n.61, pp 404–405, and JAG Griffith, *supra*, n.60, pp 70–86.
    It is true, of course, that in respect of the Lords, all amendments must be considered by the House (even if that is to deem them inadmissible, which happens very rarely) as there exists no procedure by which the admissibility of an amendment can be determined in advance, see Erskine May, *supra*, n.61, p.453.

in a critical dialogue with the government and its agents. Governments respond to the views of select committees in part out of respect for the Commons, in part because they too recognise the benefits to be gained from such a critical explanatory dialogue ... . [T]he inquisitorial and informative functions performed by select committees ... [form] a vital element in the parliamentary control of the Executive ... [allowing a] kind of critical dialogue that is possible only in the interaction between the members of select committees and their witnesses.66

These qualities, it is submitted, would be characteristic of the Joint Committee on the European Convention on Human Rights.

---

66   *Supra*, n.58, p.184.

8 A SUGGESTED SCRUTINY SCHEME FOR SECONDARY LEGISLATION

The scrutiny scheme for secondary legislation outlined in this chapter is intended to complement that described for primary legislation in the last chapter. The constraints of the normal legislative procedure for secondary legislation within which the suggested scheme must operate are far less complex than those for the enactment of primary legislation. The machinery and operation of the scheme, therefore, are relatively simple. What is more, there already exists within Parliament apparatus designed for the scrutiny of the principal form of delegated legislation (that is, Statutory Instruments) for other purposes, and this might readily be adapted for the purpose of ensuring compliance with the European Convention. The relative simplicity of the scheme, however, has to be qualified by the quantity, diversity and often detailed nature of today's secondary legislation. As adverted to earlier,[1] the steady increase in all three of these variables since the war has presented parliament with considerable problems in terms, particularly, of the examination of the Statutory Instruments laid before it. All Statutory Instruments, however, are initially scrutinized either by the Joint Committee on Statutory Instruments, or the House of Commons Select Committee on Statutory Instruments, for those instruments required to be laid before the Commons alone, and it is through an adaptation of these two committees that scrutiny for conformity with the European Convention might be secured.

---

1   Chapter 2, Part II, *supra*, p.33.

Adaptation of the Joint and House of Commons Select Committees on Statutory Instruments

Strictly, these are two separate committees; the Commons membership of the Joint Committee, however, is the same as that for the Select Committee, and the same terms of reference which cover the two committees are incorporated in the one Standing Order of the House of Commons.[2] A more detailed assessment of the existing terms of reference and operation of the committees was made in an earlier chapter;[3] suffice it to say at this point that the general purpose of the committees is to scrutinize all Statutory Instruments laid before Parliament (as well as those few Statutory Instruments not required to be laid, and certain other instruments), "with a view to determining whether the special attention of the House should be drawn to [an instrument]" on any of a number of specific grounds, such as the *vires* of an instrument in respect of the enabling statute; and if it should seek to exclude challenge in the courts, or to have retrospective effect.[4] There is no specified form that the report must take (other than that reasons for its decision must be stated), nor, indeed, is there any requirement that it be submitted to Parliament before the instrument is made or becomes effective.[5]

It is here proposed that these terms and conditions should be altered, or added to, in two crucial respects: first, that there be included in the list of grounds upon which the committees might have cause to report, the new ground of *prima facie* infringement of the European Convention by an instrument; and, second, in order that Parliament would be able to utilize effectively the information yielded by any such report, it be stipulated (or at least formally agreed to), that there be established a procedure by which, save in exceptional circumstances, a committee report is laid before the House in advance of the provisions of any instrument coming into force.

In regard to the first suggestion, it should be noted that in addition to the specific grounds requiring the special attention of the House stated in the committees' terms of reference, there is a general provision for scrutiny "on any other ground which does not impinge on [the] merits or on the policy behind [the instrument]".[6] This itself might be considered capable of sustaining investigation on the basis of possible infringement of the European Convention, although no such use of this "catch-all" provision has ever been made. In any case, in view of the gravity of the suggested new ground, it would be necessary to direct the committees more specifically in their scrutiny. It may be argued, of course, that an additional ground concerning conformity to the European Convention might cause the Committee to become concerned with the *political* merits of an instrument. It

---

2   HC S.O. No.124. The corresponding terms of reference of the House of Lords for the Joint Committee, which are identical to those of the Commons, are stated in a Resolution of the House, HL Deb. Vol.346, col.246 (6 Nov. 1973).

3   Chapter 2, Part II, *supra*, p.35.

4   HC S.O. No.124(1)B.

5   There is, however, an informal time limit, known as the "21-day rule" for negative instruments which applies to both the Joint and Select Committees on Statutory Instruments. The Government has undertaken to endeavour to allow at least 21 days to elapse between an instrument being laid and its coming into effect. This does not guarantee that the appropriate committee's report will have been laid in that time, but it does provide a clear deadline against which the committee can work; see Erskine May *Parliamentary Practice*, CJ Boulton (ed) (1989, 21st edn), p.549.

6   HC S.O. No.124(1)B.

might be thought that any examination on this ground might necessarily entail inquiry into the "merits" of the instrument in respect of its compliance with the relevant Convention rights. This argument, I think, can be successfully countered. As with the proposed scrutiny committee for primary legislation described in Chapter Seven, the question to be answered here is principally a technical one. Indeed, there exists a strong precedent for this distinction. The Commons Select Committee on European Legislation was empowered initially to consider the "legal and political importance" of European Community legislative proposals, and despite the fact that its terms have been recently extended to include consideration of "any issue" arising upon a broad range of European Community documents,[7] a combination of deliberate self-restraint, the nature of much of what it considers and the sheer quantity of documents it considers in one year (800-900) effectively preclude the Committee from commenting on whether a particular Community proposal is agreeable or otherwise. It should be noted, also, that the European Legislation Committee's authority to assess the "legal or political importance" of the documents before it extends beyond what is being suggested as the necessary terms for the scrutiny of Statutory Instruments for conformity to the European Convention, specifically in respect of the consideration of how (in this case) Community proposals might affect "matters of principle or policy".[8] The existence of this provision is due primarily to the peculiarity of many Community proposals being in the form of draft policy suggestions; that is, they are at a relatively early stage in the legislative process. As Statutory Instruments are never laid before Parliament as policy suggestions, such a power in respect of their scrutiny would be unwarranted. The significance, therefore, of the operation of the European Legislation Committee is that it illustrates how it is possible for the meritorious consideration of matters of political substance to be separated from the more specific and restricted function of review on technical grounds.

The task of scrutiny for compliance with the European Convention is similar in substance to that of assessing whether a Statutory Instrument is *intra vires*. It is conceded that in terms of degree there may be a difference between determining the exact parameters of legitimate ministerial authority under a domestic Act and a delineation of the extent of the broadly drafted rights protected by the Convention, especially in the initial years of the scheme's operation. But that is a difficulty that could be eased with a small increase in the numbers in the office of Speaker's Counsel (which assists the Joint Committee).[9] What is more, as a better understanding of the demands of the Convention and its jurisprudence is obtained with time the task would become clearer. In addition it would be of particular assistance to adopt Hayhurst and Wallington's suggestion that the Joint Committee's current powers to examine witnesses and receive submissions ought to be extended to those enjoyed by other select committees to include evidence form non-

---

7   HC S.O. No.127(1)(c).
8   HC S.O. No.127(1)(a).
9   The current Speaker's Counsel (Mr Henry Knorpel) suggested in discussion with the author that an additional Assistant might be sufficient. Presently the office consists of The Speaker's Counsel, his Assistant and the Second Counsel; the Joint Committee is also assisted by the Counsel to Lord Chairman of Committees from the House of Lords.

governmental sources.[10] Needless to say, experts in the relationship between rights guaranteed by the European Convention and the subject-matter of domestic legislation reside outside, as well as inside, the offices of Whitehall.

The second indicated suggestion would require an agreement that no instrument would come into effect without Parliament having first received a report from the appropriate committee on Statutory Instruments indicating whether there is any *prima facie* case of infringement of rights protected by the Convention. More specifically, in the case of those instruments requiring affirmative action, none would be *made*, and, in the case of those subject to the negative procedure, none would be *made effective*, until Parliament had received a committee report on this matter. This distinction can be explained in that "affirmative instruments" require parliamentary consideration before they are made and actually become law, whereas, of course, almost all "negative instruments" obtain the status of law at the point when they are made. The only way, therefore, to provide a procedure where the *effect* of a "negative instrument" may be pre-empted is to require that there be a delay in the coming into force of the provisions it contains. The pre-existing "21-day rule" referred to above,[11] would suffice in this regard, though it may be considered necessary to re-establish the rule by way of Resolution rather than to persist with a mere informal agreement. It can be reasonably argued, furthermore, that even if this 21-day period proves inadequate for the appropriate committee to report in those exceptional instances where expeditious implementation of an instrument is necessary, it nonetheless remains possible later to withdraw the instrument in the event of an adverse report (on whatever grounds) from either committee being laid before the relevant House.

The initiative for this requirement comes from a concern to ensure that any doubts reported by the committees concerning the compatibility of Statutory Instruments with the European Convention are available to Parliament in advance, where possible, of the instrument's implementation impinging upon the rights of those whom it affects. As, however, the committees consider individual instruments in the light of all the stipulated grounds (including this mooted additional ground) at the same time a report on the matter of compliance with the Convention alone would not be easily separated from a report on all other grounds. In consequence, the requirement of the instrument's delayed implementation would apply equally in respect of *all* grounds within the committees' orders of reference. Such an effect, incidentally, might thereby meet the demands of those who see an increasing need for the Government to be procedurally obliged to delay the parliamentary consideration of an instrument until the relevant committee has reported.[12]

---

[10] JD Hayhurst and P Wallington, "Parliamentary Scrutiny of Delegated Legislation" [1988] PL 547. HC S.O. No.124(6) presently limits the sources to those within government departments.

[11] *Supra*, n.5.

[12] In their survey of the work of the Statutory Instrument committees in the period 1973–83, Hayhurst and Wallington noted that, in respect of the Commons, "[a] greatly increased proportion of debates in the Chamber and the standing committees occurred before the Committee reported the instrument concerned to the House", *ibid*, p.565; see also their recommendations as to the imposition of time limits in respect of the Committees' reports, *ibid*, p.575. The position appears not to be so bad in the House of

It is not possible, however, in respect of the Commons, to establish this process by way of an amendment to the relevant Standing Order. As Erskine May points out, the Standing Orders (of both houses) are the means by which "the House directs its committees, its Members, its officers, the order of its own proceedings and acts of all persons whom they concern".[13] As invariably it is not Parliament, but (usually) a Government Minister that is empowered to make secondary legislation under an enabling statute (the former being generally restricted to the exercise of a "veto"-power),[14] any limitation on the exercise of a Minister's statutory power both to make an instrument and to bring it into effect is beyond the scope of the Standing Orders. In regard to the House of Lords, this problem does not arise as the terms of reference for the Joint Committee as laid down by that House are in a Resolution.[15] Indeed, short of legislative change (which would place unacceptably rigid restrictions on the Executive's exercise of delegated authority),[16] the most appropriate alternative means of effecting the alteration here suggested in both Houses is by Resolution. "[B]y its Resolutions", states Erskine May, either House "declares its own opinions and purposes".[17] A Resolution similar to the one considered here already exists. Once again it can be found in the analogous situation of the Commons Select Committee on European Legislation. In this case a Commons Resolution declares that no Minister of the Crown should give agreement to a Community proposal until the House has both received the Committee's report and (should the report so recommend) has acted upon this recommendation and debated the matter.[18] Once more these requirements go further than is necessary for the purposes of the suggested scrutiny of delegated legislation by the Statutory Instrument committees for compliance with the European Convention. The present suggestion would insist only that the committees' reports be laid before Parliament before implementation of the instrument, and the decision to consider in debate any instrument marked for special attention by either committee would be left to the respective Houses.

Through the establishment of such a Resolution, any attempt by the Government to circumvent the declared opinion of the House that no instrument was to be made effective preceding the laying of a report of the relevant committee would necessarily have to be explicit. Inevitably the Government would be challenged should it ignore the Resolution, or seek to waive or alter its provisions. The decision to take such conspicuous action would not, therefore, be made lightly.[19] Nevertheless, it would be desirable to

---

Lords, ibid; and see n.18, infra.

13   Erskine May, supra, n.5, p.359.

14   See R v Her Majesty's Treasury, ex parte Smedley [1985] 1 QB 657, 666, 668 & 672.

15   Supra, n.3.

16   Chapter 7, supra, n.9 and accompanying text.

17   Supra, n.5, p.390.

18   For the terms of the original Resolution, see HC Deb. Vol.991, cols 843–4 (30 Oct. 1980). The House has recently agreed to replace this with a revised and more extensive Resolution: HC Deb. Vol.178, cols 375–91 (24 Oct. 1990). Note that in respect of the Lords no instrument (whether or not prompted by a European Community proposal) subject to the affirmative procedure may be approved unless the Joint Committee on Statutory Instruments has laid its report before the House (HL S.O. No.69).

19   Apparently, the derogation element of the Commons Resolution in respect of the European Legislation Committee (see ibid) – that where the Minister agrees to a

obtain, in addition, an "undertaking" from the Government not to take such action without, at the very least, a formal explanation to Parliament of the reasons for so doing.[20]

The effect on secondary legislation procedure

The proposed alterations would not affect the initial stages of the process of scrutinizing Statutory Instruments. Upon the laying of an instrument,[21] a copy is transmitted to the appropriate Statutory Instruments committee. Instruments for which the Joint Committee is responsible are examined first by either the Speaker's Counsel or the Counsel to the Lord Chairman of Committees, depending on the type of instrument. Though no formal division of labour is stipulated, it is the practice for the latter Counsel to take all affirmative instruments to be considered by both Houses (which are relatively few in number, but tend to concern the most important issues), and the Speaker's Counsel to take the rest (which comprise the vast majority of instruments, often involving more technical matters).[22] Naturally, all those instruments laid only before the Commons are examined by the Speaker's Counsel.

This initial screening is intended to ascertain those provisions which under the appropriate Committee's order of reference might especially require its attention when it comes formally to consider the instrument. In regard to those instruments vetted by the Speaker's Counsel, Counsel may take any of a number of courses of action. He or she may recommend that the Committee let the instrument continue on its way unreported; or recommend that the Committee requests clarification from the government department responsible, either in a memorandum or by way of oral evidence; or, finally, Counsel may of his or her own volition write to the department with comments or requesting information or elucidation.[23] There exists, in fact, a strong informal liaison between the government departments and Counsel, with those responsible for the drafting of Statutory Instruments in the departments frequently referring to Counsel for advice on the compatibility of particular proposals with the requirements stipulated in the

---

European proposal without (should the Committee so recommend) the House having debated it, he or she must provide reasons to the House for doing so at the earliest opportunity – is invariably used for practical reasons (for example, when agreement is required during the parliamentary recess), rather than to avoid political controversy.

20 A similar undertaking was originally made in respect of the Commons Select Committee on European Legislation (HC Deb. Vol.872, col.525 (w) (2 May 1974); subsequently this has been incorporated in the Commons Resolution concerning the Committee, *supra*, n.18.

21 The procedures for which are dictated by HC S.O. No.138, in respect of the Commons, and HL S.O. No.67, in respect of the Lords.

22 This information was provided by the Speaker's Counsel, Mr Henry Knorpel, in discussion with the author. On instruments which implement or supplement European Community law advice is given by a Speaker's second Counsel (who is also Adviser to the Commons Select Committee on European Legislation). Speaker's Counsel is helped by an Assistant specially appointed for the task.

23 This information was provided by the Speaker's Counsel, Mr Henry Knorpel, in discussion with the author. The first two of these options are provided for in HC S.O. No.124, the third is a purely informal but, according to Counsel, an extremely effective preventive adaptation; a similar and equally effective informal liaison also exists in respect of the Counsel to the Lord Chairman of Committees in the Lords.

The same process is used by the Australian Senate Standing Committee on Regulations and Ordinances, Chapter 5, *supra*, p.100.

Committee's terms of reference in Standing Order 124.[24] It is not an exaggeration to say that it is the use of these private channels (which provides the Speaker's Counsel, and the Counsel to the Lord Chairman of Committees, with an early opportunity to exert some preventive control) that accounts for the detection of the greater proportion of potential defects in Statutory Instruments.

This is a crucial part of the examination process, for in practice both Committees rely very largely on the advice tendered by Counsel when deciding what action to take over any impugned provision and whether it should report that the special attention of the House ought to be drawn to any particular instrument. This process would be no less important in respect of the examination of instruments for conformity to the European Convention, should such a requirement be incorporated in the committees' Standing Orders. In particular, it would provide both committees with the valuable opportunity to obtain informed opinion as to the compatibility of specific instruments with the Convention. In this context, either Counsel would operate in a manner similar to that of the Examiner suggested in the previous chapter on the scrutiny of primary legislation. The opportunities for a single (and legally trained) expert, with a small but permanent assisting office of appropriate expertise, to achieve a working relationship with those in government departments responsible for the formulation of delegated legislation are much greater than those available to an unwieldy committee comprising members with other interests and duties.[25] This would be favourable to the effectiveness of an additional requirement that the demands of the European Convention should also be made subject to preventive scrutiny; that is, to be examined first by Counsel and then by one or other Committee on Statutory Instruments, before any instrument reached either chamber.

The consequences of the second suggested alteration to the process of making delegated legislation – that an instrument not be made effective until the appropriate Statutory Instruments Committee has laid its report before Parliament – is likely to produce little or no change to present *procedure* other than to help reverse the current trend of increasing numbers of instruments being considered in advance of either committees' report. It is submitted, however, that substantively there is likely to be greater effect. It is reasonable to conclude that instruments marked for the special attention of the House on the ground of their *prima facie* infringement of a Convention-protected right will not be amongst that (substantial) proportion of instruments currently reported by either committee but not debated in Parliament.[26]

---

24   Knorpel, *ibid.* It appears that some departments use this facility more often than others, according to their level of confidence in drafting instruments for the proposals before them.
25   The achievement of this end would be greatly expedited if, as is presently the case, those assisting the Committee were themselves conversant with the demands made of departmental counsel – the current Speaker's Counsel, his Assistant and the Counsel to the Lord Chairman of Committees all possess considerable experience as departmental counsel.
26   Hayhurst and Wallington have calculated that proportion to be 85% in respect of the Commons and 88% in respect of the Lords, *supra*, n.10, p.564.

The operation of the scheme

An indication of the effect of these suggested changes might be obtained from examining specific examples of relatively recent secondary legislation. Within a period of three weeks between October and November 1988 the Government introduced two extremely controversial measures. The first was a direction from the Home Secretary restricting the broadcasting media in their coverage of certain terrorist organizations, and the second was an Order in Council modifying the so-called "right of silence" in criminal trials in Northern Ireland. The media ban may be considered to be an illustration of the use of quasi-legislation and strictly, therefore, falls outside the scope of either Statutory Instruments committee, whereas the evidential alterations have been implemented by means of an Order in Council, and with only one exception all such Orders are subject to the scrutiny of the Joint or Commons Select Committees on Statutory Instruments.[27] We shall examine first the right to silence changes.

The Criminal Evidence Order 1988

On 8 November 1988 the Commons was asked to approve The Criminal Evidence (Northern Ireland) Order 1988.[28] In the words of Mr Tom King, the then Secretary of State for Northern Ireland, when introducing the Order to the House, its purpose is "to allow the courts in certain carefully defined circumstances to draw such inferences as would be proper from an accused's silence".[29] No guidance as to what constitutes "proper" inferences was given save that failure or refusal to answer questions or to give evidence would not itself be sufficient to secure a conviction.[30] Subsequently, however, a Home Office Working Group established to investigate the possibility of extending the modifications to the right to silence to England and Wales has indicated that "the primary inference which may be drawn from a defendant's previous failure to answer questions or to mention a fact

---

27   The exception is those Orders in Council made under para.1 of Schedule 1 of the Northern Ireland Act 1974 (the very authority under which the Criminal Evidence Order was made – see *infra*, n.28). The principal reason for their exclusion is that Orders made pursuant to this Act, which effected the prorogation of the Northern Ireland Parliament and provided the legislative means by which direct rule is maintained, are, in effect, primary legislation for the Province. They replace, therefore, the Acts of the former Northern Irish Parliament. In this case, the Joint Committee's remit, tailored as it is to secondary legislation, is unsuited for the task of scrutiny. It is submitted, however, that for the sole purpose of scrutiny for compliance with the European Convention, the Joint Committee ought to be empowered to examine the relatively few Orders made each year (usually between 20–25) by this procedure.

28   S.I. 1987/1988 (N.I. Order 20). The Order was made under authority of para.1 of Schedule 1 to the Northern Ireland Act 1974, in reference to reserved matters under para.4 of Schedule 3 of the Northern Ireland Constitution Act 1973, which includes issues of general criminal law.

29   HC Deb. Vol.140, col.185 (8 Nov. 1988). The principal provisions of the Order are described in an Explanatory Note appended to it in the following way: "Article 3 specifies circumstances in which inferences may be drawn from an accused's failure to mention particular facts when questioned about or charged with an offence. Under Article 4, an accused person may be called upon by the court to give evidence at his trial, and certain inferences may be drawn if he refuses to do so. Article 5 authorizes inferences to be drawn from an accused person's failure to or refusal to account for objects, substances or marks in certain circumstances. Article 6 allows inferences to be drawn from an accused person's presence at a place about the time when the offence in respect of which he was arrested was committed, if specified conditions are satisfied."

30   HC Deb. Vol.140, col.188 (8 Nov. 1988), Mr King.

subsequently relied upon at his trial is that the subsequent line of defence is untrue".[31]

In respect of parliamentary procedure (quite apart from the substantive questions involved), it was a matter of some concern for many members in both Houses that an issue of such gravity and significance should be introduced by way of an Order and not in the form of a bill.[32] As it was, a maximum of 4½ hours debate on the Order was provided by the Government.[33] There was also considerable criticism over the great haste with which the measure had been drawn up and presented (in an unamendable and final form) to Parliament.[34] There was no period of consultation prior to its introduction, and indeed not even the Standing Advisory Commission on Human Rights in Belfast was consulted on the matter in advance.[35]

The Order applies to all criminal cases in Northern Ireland, although it is clearly directed towards those involving terrorist suspects. In this respect, therefore, it adds to the already peculiar position such cases occupy. Since 1973 suspected terrorists have been tried before a single judge and in the absence of a jury.[36] Since the first Prevention of Terrorism (Temporary Provisions) Act (PTA) in 1974, it has been possible to hold terrorist suspects in detention without charge for up to seven days (the current authority so to do is provided by s.14 of the PTA 1989).[37] In addition, a terrorist suspect in Northern Ireland may be deprived of legal assistance for up to 48 hours under section 58(13)(a) of the Police and Criminal Evidence Act 1984,[38] and (at the time of the making of the Order) did not have their interviews recorded on tape in the same way as in England and Wales.[39] Furthermore, it ought to be noted that part of the Order would appear to duplicate yet another provision peculiar to terrorist cases – that is, s.11 of the PTA 1984

---

31   *Report of the Home Office Working Group on the Right of Silence*, (13 July 1989), para.126(vii); see also the suggested (but unadopted) set of Guidelines to the Courts drawn up by the Working Group, *ibid*, Appendix D.

32   HC Deb. Vol.140, col.184 (Mr I Gow), and col.209 (Mr N Budgen) (8 Nov. 1988); and HL Deb. Vol.501, col.786 (10 Nov. 1988) (Lord Moran), and col.794 (Lord Harris).

33   HC Deb. Vol.140, col.188 (8 Nov. 1988).

34   HL Deb. Vol.501, col.782 (10 Nov. 1988), (Lord Hylton); and HC Deb. Vol.140, cols 190–1 (8 Nov. 1988), (Mr K McNamara). The final draft was published on 20 October 1988, it was debated in Parliament on 8 and 10 November, and made on 14 November, with Articles 2 & 4 coming into operation on 21 November, and the remaining Articles on 21 December.

35   HL Deb. Vol.501, col.782 (10 Nov. 1988), (Lord Hylton). The Commission was severely critical of this in its *Annual Report 1987-9*, HC 394 (1988-9), p. 9.

36   For an account of the operation of the "Diplock Courts", see Standing Advisory Commission on Human Rights, *Annual Report 1985-6*, HC 151 (1986-7), pp 57-63.

37   Though a Notice of Derogation in respect of this provision has had to be lodged with the Council of Europe following an adverse decision of the European Court of Human Rights; see Chapter 3, *supra*, n.110 and accompanying text.

38   That is in spite of the fact that the European Commission has ruled in a United Kingdom case that any period exceeding 45 hours is contrary to the European Convention; see comments on the case of *McVeigh, O'Neill & Evans v United Kingdom* in Chapter 3, *supra*, n.112 and accompanying text.

39   Though during the debate on the 1988 Order in the Lords, Lord Lyell, the then Parliamentary Under-Secretary of State for Northern Ireland, assured the House that the same procedure for recording interviews as exists in England and Wales would soon be introduced into Northern Ireland; HL Deb. Vol.501, cols 802-3 (10 Nov. 1988). The same interview provisions were indeed introduced by Article 60 of the Police and Criminal Evidence Act 1984 (Northern Ireland) Order 1989, S.I. 1989/1341.

(now s.11 of the PTA 1989 Act), which makes it a criminal offence to withhold evidence relating to terrorist activity.

During the parliamentary debates on the Order, further questions were raised concerning, amongst other things, the constitutional nature of the unadulterated right to silence, the contention that any limitations to the right are more likely to affect the innocent than the hardened criminal,[40] and the statistical evidence used by the Government to support its argument for the alterations to the right.[41] Significantly, however, no assessment whatsoever was made of the possible implications there might be for rights protected by the European Convention. Of principal concern in this context is Article 6(2) of the Convention which directs that "[e]veryone charged with a criminal offence shall be presumed innocent until proved guilty". This is not to suggest, of course, that the alterations to the right to silence themselves reverse this presumption – after all, many other countries who are signatories to the European Convention possess no such thing as a right to silence in their criminal law. However, it cannot be overlooked that the criminal legal traditions and procedures of the civil law jurisdictions are fundamentally different from those obtaining in the United Kingdom. The basically inquisitorial system of, say, France generally necessitates direct judicial involvement in the inquiries concerning a suspect once they have been charged by the arresting authority (that is, the police).[42] In the adversarial system of English criminal procedure the prosecution is conducted by the Crown Prosecution Service (the CPS). In almost every case it is the CPS's duty to conduct the prosecution in court based wholly on the information provided to it by the police who are solely responsible for the interrogation of a suspect.[43] It follows that in France the intensity of pre-trial investigation by the police (as opposed to the examining judge – the *juge d'instruction*) is necessarily less than that obtaining in England, Wales and Northern Ireland.

Moreover, in the French system should the *juge d'instruction*, after his or her examination, direct that the accused should be brought to trial in court, it is not the judge but a separate prosecuting body (*ministère public*) that then conducts the case. In the English system, on the other hand, whilst

---

[40]   See further J Wood and A Crawford, *The Right to Silence*, a Civil Liberties Trust publication (1989), pp 25 & 31.

[41]   Mr K McNamara claimed that the Government possessed no such statistics, HC Deb. Vol.140, col.194 (8 Nov. 1988). Mr Tom King, the then Secretary of State for Northern Ireland, however, stated, rather lamely, that statistics from the RUC indicated that almost 50% of terrorist suspects refused to answer any questions of substance, *ibid*, col.189. In response and in contradiction, Mr Seamus Mallon quoted statistics from the Northern Ireland Office showing that during the period 1980-7 the annual conviction rates had ranged between 90% and 95.4% in such cases, which appears to indicate that refusal to answer questions has had little effect on the outcome of cases, see col.214. It would appear from the results of a survey of 121 cases before the Belfast criminal courts in the year immediately after the making of the Order that the proportion of defendants giving or not giving evidence was unaltered by the new restrictions on the right to silence; see JD Jackson, "Curtailing the Right to Silence: lessons from Northern Ireland" [1991] Crim. LR 409.

[42]   Upon arrest of a suspect a public officer (a *procureur*)) takes control of the prosecution. In respect of cases involving more serious offences, an examining judge – *juge d'instruction* – is made responsible for the procedure of enquiry; see René David, *English Law and French Law* (1980), pp 64-69.

[43]   Prosecution of Offences Act 1985, s.3.

there is a nominal séparation between the police's pre-trial interrogation and the prosecution by the CPS, in practice (as indicated above) the latter relies totally on the information provided by the former. Consequently, to introduce even a marginal alteration to the means by which the police (in Northern Ireland) are able to obtain evidence at the pre-trial stage, in order to substantiate the prosecution's case so as to require it to do nothing more than point to the accused's silence in the face of questioning, will by necessity mitigate the demands of proving guilt during the trial.

It is the opinion of the Criminal Bar Association that the changes introduced by the Order may provide some disincentive to investigation by the police.[44] In this matter, we might learn from a leading American case concerning the right against self-incrimination in which it was concluded that "the process of custody interrogation of persons suspected or accused of crime contains inherently compelling pressures which work to undermine the individual's will to resist and to compel him to speak where he would not otherwise do so freely".[45] These pressures are undoubtedly increased by the possibility of adverse inferences being drawn from a suspect's silence. Indeed, it has been argued that the unfairness of the Order stems principally from the fact that cautions given by the arresting authorities to criminal suspects that if they remain silent then it is possible for certain inferences to be drawn from their remaining so induces them "to respond to questioning and have their answers used against them at a stage when a reliable record may not be able to be produced of what they have said and where there may be no case against them".[46] It might be added that as the Government has thus far omitted to provide, in a Code of Practice (or initiate in legislative form), any guidance as to what sort of matters may properly attract the inferences indicated in the Order,[47] the discretion allowed to the judiciary both in drawing inferences itself and in directing juries (where they exist)[48] how to do or how not to do so will remain unacceptably broad;[49] "silence", after all, "is equivocal".[50]

If the onus of proof of guilt beyond all reasonable doubt is to remain wholly with the prosecution - as is the claim of the Government[51] - then it must be recognized, as the Royal Commission on Criminal Procedure stated, that "[t]here is an inconsistency of principle in requiring th[is] onus ... to be discharged without any assistance from the defence and yet in enabling the

---

44   Stated by Mr K McNamara, HC Deb. Vol.140, col.199 (8 Nov. 1988).
45   *Miranda v Arizona* 86 SCt 1602 (1966), *per* Chief Justice Warren.
46   Jackson, *supra*, n.41, p.413.
47   *Supra*, n.29.
48   See *supra*, n.36 and accompanying text.
49   See JD Jackson, "Criminal Evidence (Northern Ireland) Order 1988 – Need for Statutory Guidance on Drawing Inferences from Silence?", paper for the Standing Advisory Commission on Human Rights, *Annual Report 1990-1*, HC 488 (1990-1), Annex H, especially pp 243-4.
     It remains unclear the manner and extent of the judiciary's use of this discretion is very seldom expressly relied upon, though for a (rare) example of an adverse inference apparently being drawn by a judge, see *Kane & others*, unreported judgment (30 March 1990), as discussed by Jackson, *supra*, n.41, p.412.
50   *Ibid*, p.239. Jackson argues that there ought to be some form of statutory guidance: "since Parliament has sought to change the law in this area, it is only appropriate that Parliament should state what the content of any guidance should be", *ibid*, p.237; see also, p.249.
51   HC Deb. Vol.140, col.222 (8 Nov. 1988), Sir Nicolas Lyell (Solicitor-General).

prosecution to use the accused's silence in the face of police questioning under caution as any part of their case against him at trial".[52] The Home Office's own Working Group, mentioned above, would appear to endorse this view as it stated unequivocally that "penalising the defendant for refusing to give evidence is tantamount to compelling him to do so and represent[s] an unacceptable shift in the burden of proof".[53]

It is conceded that these criticisms do not amount to a certain infringement of Article 6(2), but they are sufficient to indicate that such an infringement is a possibility.[54] This being so, a detailed consideration of the matter by the Joint Committee on Statutory Instruments as modified by the suggestions made earlier in this chapter would at least have ensured that Parliament was aware of this possibility.[55] Moreover, as it is the Government's intention eventually to extend these alterations in criminal evidence to England and Wales,[56] the need for recognition of the demands of the European Convention relevant to this issue at the pre-legislative stage remains significant.

Broadcasting restrictions

On 19 October 1988 the Secretary of State for the Home Department sent a letter to both the British Broadcasting Corporation (BBC) and the Independent Broadcasting Authority (IBA), prohibiting them from broadcasting words spoken by any person representing certain terrorist organizations where "the words support or solicit or invite support for such ... organization[s]".[57] The organizations concerned are those proscribed under the PTA 1984 (now PTA 1989),[58] and also Sinn Fein (both the Northern Irish party and that in Eire) and the Ulster Defence Association.[59] The only excepted circumstances to this general ban are where the words are spoken in Parliament or during parliamentary or local election periods.[60] The Home Secretary's authority emanates, in the case of the IBA, from s.29(3) of the Broadcasting Act 1981, which provides the Secretary of State with the

---

52   Report, Cmnd 8092 (1981), para.4.51.
53   Report, *supra*, n.31, para.113. As it is almost inconceivable that anything but an adverse inference would be made of a defendant's silence, defendants would effectively always be "penalized".
54   Indeed, this is precisely the position that Canadian law occupies in respect of the analogous s.11(c) of the Charter of Human Rights and Fundamental Freedoms, where it is yet to be determined whether it would be a breach of s.11(c) to draw inferences from an accused's failure to testify; see DC McDonald, *Legal Rights in the Canadian Charter of Rights and Freedoms* (1989, 2nd edn), p.463.
55   Subject, of course, to the necessary amendment to the current exclusion from the Joint Committee's terms of reference of certain Orders made under the Northern Ireland Act 1974. supra, n.27.
56   *Report of the Home Office Working Group on the Right of Silence, supra*, n.31, Terms of Reference, para.3. See also, HC Deb. Vol.138, cols 983–4 (*w*) (20 Oct. 1988).
57   Letter from the Rt Hon. Douglas Hurd to the IBA and the BBC, Home Office, 19 October 1989. para.1.
58   Principally the Provisional IRA, the Ulster Volunteer Force and the Ulster Freedom Fighters.
59   Letter of the Home Secretary, *supra*, n.57, para.2.
60   *Ibid*, para.3; the Ulster Defence Association has since been added to the list of proscribed organizations in Northern Ireland contained in Schedule 2 of the Northern Ireland (Emergency Provisions) Act 1991 by the Northern Ireland (Emergency Provisions) Act 1991 (Amendment) Order 1992, S.I. No.1992/1958, which came into force on 11 August 1992.

power to "require the Authority to refrain from broadcasting any matter or classes of matter", and in the case of the BBC, from clause 13(4) of its Licence and Agreement, which provides an almost identical power. Both the IBA and the BBC were already under certain obligations in regard to coverage of "terrorist material",[61] but clearly the Home Secretary considered these limitations, or their implementation, to be ineffective.[62]

Shortly after the ban's introduction, the Home Secretary invited the House of Commons to endorse his action upon a motion of approval.[63] Predictably, the debate centred on the fundamental right to freedom of speech, its nature, its purpose and its limits. Yet, despite the emphasis placed on these basic principles, there was no recognition of the requirements of the European Convention at any stage in the debate. Ironically, however, many of the arguments advanced both by those supporting the restrictions and those opposing them during the debate bore directly on these requirements and on the European Court's interpretation of them. It is unquestionable that an enhanced understanding of the Convention would have enabled better use of the facts and arguments relevant to this issue.

Article 10(1) of the Convention enshrines the basic right to freedom of expression. Article 10(2), however, determines that "the exercise of th[is] freedom ... may be subject to such formalities, conditions, restrictions or penalties *as are prescribed by law and are necessary in a democratic society*", in the interests *inter alia* "of national security ... public safety ... or for the prevention of disorder or crime" [emphasis supplied].[64] The United Kingdom had at the time of the introduction of the ban twice previously been brought before the European Court under this Article: first, in 1976, in *Handyside v United Kingdom*, and then again in 1979, in *The Sunday Times v United Kingdom*.[65] In both cases the Court investigated, in particular, the meaning of that crucial provision of Article 10 emphasized above, reaching the same conclusions on both occasions. It is evident that there are two components of the phrase in question. In respect of the first of these – "as prescribed by law" – the Court declared that one of its essential elements is that the "law" at issue must be "formulated with sufficient precision to enable the citizen to

---

61   The IBA, under s.4(1)(a) of the Broadcasting Act 1981 (the Authority must be satisfied that programmes are not "likely to encourage or incite to crime or lead to disorder or to be offensive to public feeling"); and the BBC, though under no duty according to its Charter or Licence and Agreement, has adopted exactly the same obligation in a resolution of its Board of Governors (8 Jan. 1981). Both institutions also issue detailed guidelines to all editors emphasizing and elaborating on these requirements; see, for example, "Extract from IBA Television Programme Guidelines relating to Coverage of Terrorism in Northern Ireland (s.8(1))" as appended to the IBA Press Statement on the Home Secretary's Direction, 20 October 1988.

62   It should be noted also that in Northern Ireland it was already an offence under s.21 of the Northern Ireland (Emergency Provisions) Act 1978 (now s.28 of the Northern Ireland (Emergency Provisions) Act 1991), to solicit or invite support for a proscribed organization.

63   HC Deb. Vol.139 cols 1075–1155 (2 Nov. 1988).

64   For an assessment of the importance of this Article for the media, see G Robertson and AGL Nicol, *Media Law* (1984), pp 3-6.

65   ECHR Series 'A', No.24 (7 Dec. 1976), and ECHR Series 'A', No.30 (26 April 1979), respectively. Since that time the European Court of Human Rights has had further cause to find that United Kingdom law – in this case injunctions prohibiting the publication of extracts form Peter Wright's book *Spycatcher* – violated Article 10 of the Convention: *Sunday Times v United Kingdom (no.2)*, ECHR Series 'A', No.29 (26 Nov. 1991); this case is discussed in Chapter 7, *supra*, p.145.

regulate his conduct".[66] The Home Secretary's edict, issued under the extremely broad authorities of the Broadcasting Act and the BBC Charter, has been held by domestic courts not to be contrary to domestic law.[67] However, for the ban to satisfy the European Court's interpretation of the phrase "as prescribed by law" as used in the Convention it must attain a certain degree of precision. Quite apart from the difficulty in understanding precisely what it is that the restrictions are intended to achieve – it is, after all, only the spoken words of those members and supporters of the proscribed organizations that are affected, and such words may be broadcast through a written caption or "voice over"[68] – the "meaning, scope and intention of the banning order issued by the [Home Secretary]" was not wholly apparent to the broadcasters themselves.[69] In an effort to clarify the position, the Home Office sent a letter privately to the IBA and the BBC expanding on the broad directions in the ministerial order.[70] The Home Office's interpretation appeared to be more liberal than that previously constructed by (for example) the BBC's lawyers. The latter, however, were adamant in their refusal to alter their opinions subsequent to the Home Office letter, adding percipiently that the correct interpretation was not necessarily that proffered by the Home Office but rather that decided by the courts.[71] It is far from certain, therefore, that the Home Secretary's directive will be sufficiently clear to satisfy the European Court.[72]

In respect of the second element of the phrase in question – that any limitation on the freedom of expression must be "necessary in a democratic society" – the Court has also stated some firm opinions. It has noted that "whilst the adjective 'necessary', within the meaning of Article 10(2), is not synonymous with 'indispensable', neither has it the flexibility of such phrases as 'admissible', 'ordinary', 'useful', 'reasonable', or 'desirable'".[73] Consequently, in determining what does constitute "necessary", the signatory states have a margin of appreciation within which to act, but its extent is subject always to the principles characterizing a "democratic society".[74] Furthermore, as the right to freedom of expression "constitutes one of the essential foundations of such a society", particular care must be taken to ensure that any restrictions imposed upon its exercise are "proportionate to the legitimate aim pursued".[75]

It can be argued that the current restrictions on the broadcasting media are neither "necessary", in the sense indicated above, nor "proportionate" to the achievement of the purported aim. The intention of the ban is, of course, to restrict the opportunities for members and supporters of certain Northern

---

66 ECHR Series 'A', No.30 (26 April 1979), para.49.
67 See infra, n.84, and accompanying text for an account of the domestic legal challenge to the ban.
68 This anomaly was emphasized by Ms Clare Short MP, HC Deb. Vol.139, col.1075 (2 Nov. 1988).
69 See The Independent (21 Oct. 1988), p.2. See also, John Birt (Deputy Director-General of the BBC), "Gagging the Messenger", The Independent (21 Nov. 1988).
70 Letter from CL Scoble, Home Office (24 Oct. 1988).
71 HC Deb. Vol.139, col.1087 (2 Nov. 1988). See also col.1105 (per Mr R Maclennan).
72 Brind & Others v United Kingdom is pending before the European Commission, Application No.187/14/91 (March 1991).
73 Handyside case, supra, n.65, para. 48.
74 Ibid, para. 49.
75 Ibid. Cf the first Sunday Times case, supra, n.65, para.62.

Irish terrorist organizations to voice their opinions on radio and television – "to deny them the oxygen of publicity".[76] Yet, according to information provided by Mr R Hattersley MP throughout the Commons debate, during the first ten months of Independent Television broadcasts in 1988, there were only "four minutes of interviews with supporters and associates of Sinn Fein. Some three minutes 59 seconds of those interviews were highly critical, in that the interviewer demanded to know of Sinn Fein how it could even attempt to justify the horrors and enormities for which the IRA were responsible".[77] Moreover, it was pointed out in a leading journal on media law that the United Kingdom Government may have difficulty in justifying the ban as strictly necessary when at the time it had "failed to proscribe [under the relevant anti-terrorist legislation] the organizations concerned [that is, Sinn Fein and the Ulster Defence Association], and has done nothing to stop their spokespersons from being quoted in the press".[78]

The Standing Advisory Commission on Human Rights has questioned the necessity of imposing conditions on the broadcasting authorities in preference to introducing a new criminal offence targeted at those who actually support or incite terrorist actions.[79] The Commission has also found it difficult to understand why the Government appeared to consider it acceptable for persons representing the affected organizations to be elected local councillors (there were at the time 59 Sinn Fein councillors in Northern Ireland) provided they signed a declaration against terrorism (now provided by s.3 and Schedule 2, part 1 of the Elected Authorities (Northern Ireland) Act 1989), but unacceptable for them or their supporters to be reported directly by the broadcasting media, even when commenting on non-terrorist issues.[80] "Article 19", the International Centre on Censorship, also considers the ban "unwarranted"; the United Kingdom Government, in its opinion, has failed to justify its actions as necessary in the sense determined by the European Court.[81] Perhaps the most unsatisfactory aspect of the imposition of the restrictions has been the resultant effect on the media coverage devoted, in particular, to Sinn Fein and the IRA. Following his claim concerning the total television coverage of the IRA before the ban, Mr Hattersley stated that during the two weeks subsequent to the ban's introduction, "three or four times as much broadcasting time on Independent Television News [was] devoted to discussing and describing the IRA and sometimes even defending it".[82] Moreover, there can be no doubt that despite the wane of the initial surge of interest in the ban's implications, whether to the detriment or benefit of the IRA specifically, the ban remains

---

76 A phrase adopted by the then Prime Minister, the Rt Hon. Mrs Margaret Thatcher, on which see HC Deb. Vol.139, col.1086 (2 Nov. 1988).

77 *Ibid*, col.1085. Indeed, a strong argument may be mounted to the effect that broadcasts of Sinn Fein spokespersons, especially after the repeated fatal "accidents" perpetrated by the IRA including, and subsequent to, the Enniskillen bombing on 8 November 1987, did more harm than good to the group's cause. See col.1092 (Mr S Mallon).

78 "Opinion" (1988) 12 International Media Law, p.90; note that the Ulster Defence Association was added to the list of proscribed organizations by Order in August 1992, see *supra*, n.60.

79 *Annual Report, 1987-9*, HC 394 (1988-9), p. 26.

80 *Ibid*.

81 "Statement of Support to National Union of Journalists and Broadcasters", 10 Nov. 1988.

82 HC Deb. Vol.139, cols 1085-6 (2 Nov. 1988). The ban was also considered to encourage international support for the IRA, see cols 1086 & 1111.

conspicuous. Indeed, as it has become the practice of broadcasters to indicate explicitly, in every relevant instance, that a programme has been compiled under, or amended according to, the ban, attention is automatically drawn to its existence.

In the light of this evidence, therefore, it is not unreasonable to question whether the media restrictions can be considered "necessary in a democratic society" as understood by the European Court. The Government, however, has made no attempt to answer this specific question, even when challenged to do so in a House of Lords debate on the issue.[83] The Government even avoided having to answer this question throughout the course of the challenge to the ban in the courts. For despite ruling that the wide powers bestowed on the Secretary of State by s.29(3) of the Broadcasting Act 1981 (the BBC was not dealt with) must be subject to the demands of Article 10 of the European Convention (on the ground that the courts will not construe any statutory provision to be inconsistent with the Convention unless that provision is incapable of bearing such a meaning), the Divisional Court, at first instance (relying on no submission of the Government to this effect) decided that there was *prima facie* evidence that the restrictions were permissible under the exceptional circumstances provided in Article 10(2).[84]

It is likely that a system of pre-legislative scrutiny of legislation with respect to conformity with the Convention would have alerted Parliament to the specific problems of the relationship of the broadcasting restrictions to Article 10 of the Convention and thereby have gone some way towards anticipating and correcting the potential conflict between the two.

Quasi-legislation

The media ban might be considered to be a quintessential example of the use of quasi-legislation (though, as was indicated earlier, the term yet remains ill-defined)[85] in all but one essential aspect. Unlike the overwhelming majority of instances of quasi-legislation, the media ban received considerable parliamentary attention – though no such consideration was required and any conclusions reached by Parliament did not affect the Minister's authority to make and implement the ban. Except for a very few notable examples (eg. the Immigration Rules), no quasi-legislation falls within the current terms of reference of either the Joint or the Commons Select Committees on Statutory Instruments. Without an appropriate enlargement of these terms, therefore, a large proportion of secondary legislation (including a plethora of administrative rules and regulations regulating government departments, "quangos", local authorities and the

---

83   HL Deb. Vol.502, col.712 (8 Dec. 1988), (Lord Prys-Davies).
84   *R v Secretary of State for the Home Dept. ex parte Brind & Others*, the *Times* Law Report, 30 May 1989, and also, Transcript of the unreported judgment of the court, 26 May 1989, p.12. Significantly, the Divisional Court in reaching this decision took no account of relevant European Court cases. In any case this line of reasoning was later expressly overturned by both the Court of Appeal and the House of Lords on the ground that use of the Convention as an aid to interpretation is inapplicable in respect of delegated legislation: [1990] 2 WLR 787 (CA), and [1991] 2 WLR 588 (HL) respectively. For a critical analysis of this reversal see DW Kinley, "Legislation, Discretionary Authority and the ECHR" (1992) 13 Stat. LR. 63.
85   For further consideration of the nature and scope of this type of legislation, see Chapter 2, Part II, *supra*, pp 36–9.

police)[86] would escape the committees' scrutiny for conformity to the European Convention as suggested in this chapter. There would be many difficulties, however, in making such a change. The sheer number and breadth of subject-matter is daunting, in addition to which there is the relevance and complexity of many regulations.[87] Furthermore, any such large-scale increase in the work-load of the Statutory Instruments committees would slow their scrutiny progress and thereby rob quasi-legislation of some of its most beneficial characteristics – brevity, speed and flexibility. As noted in Chapter Two, Part II, above, it has been suggested, in the context of enhancing the general parliamentary scrutiny of quasi-legislation, that the committees' terms of reference be extended "to all non-statutory instruments or ideally to all such instruments made under statutory powers".[88] The first of these, however, would cover very few additional instruments, whilst the second suggestion would possibly cover too many and simply invite the problems indicated above. For the purposes of the proposal of this chapter, perhaps the most helpful suggestion would be to establish a "code of practice regulating codes of practice".[89] Such a code might easily include a direction as to the necessity for all quasi-legislation to comply with the European Convention. A combination of reliance on this sort of documented guidance and the fostering of the relationship between the government departments and the suggested scrutiny organs for both primary and secondary legislation (indicated above), and, in particular, the former's respect for the task of the latter, would, it is submitted, go some way towards better ensuring compliance with the Convention of quasi-legislation.

Conclusion

As indicated both in this chapter and earlier in Chapter Two,[90] of those forms of delegated legislation which are required to be laid before Parliament (and are therefore formally open to parliamentary debate) few receive formal consideration beyond that conducted by the Joint or Select Committee on Statutory Instruments. To extend the terms of reference of these committees, therefore, in order to incorporate examination on the grounds of compliance with the European Convention (if not also to redefine and broaden the categories of delegated legislation to be scrutinized) would at least capture all those measures that have to be laid. Furthermore, by obliging the Executive not to make any instrument until Parliament has received a report from one or other of the Statutory Instruments committees, attention would not only be drawn to any *prima facie* case of infringement of the Convention, but also Parliament would be able to draw upon the specialized opinion of the relevant committee in determining whether to approve (or negate) the instrument. Yet, in spite of these formal requirements (or indeed, quite possibly because of them), the most effective preventive device in respect of legislative proposals that affect Convention-protected rights would be the further development of the private, informal channels of communication that

---

86   See Chapter 2, Part II, *supra*, p.36.
87   *Ibid.*
88   G Ganz, *Quasi-Legislation: Recent Developments in Secondary Legislation* (1987), p.107.
89   *Ibid.*
90   Part II, *supra*, pp 34–5.

already exist between the Government departments and offices of Counsel to the Statutory Instruments committees, through which passes so much advice and guidance.

It would be difficult to exaggerate the importance of parliamentary scrutiny of delegated legislation. For as the Australian Senate's Standing Committee on Regulations and Ordinances (which exercises a significant degree of control over delegated legislation) has observed, such a function is nothing less than "the oversight of the bureaucracy as a law-maker".[91] Furthermore, as the Committee argues,

> bureaucratic law-makers can wittingly and unwittingly overlook the problems and predicaments of individuals who may be affected more than marginally by the impersonal, mechanistic and discretionary methods of even the best-intentioned bureaucratic organisation ... . Administrative efficiency is a tarnished goal if to attain it individuals must be treated unjustly through the agency of unjust regulatory laws.[92]

In the United Kingdom a scheme to advance legislative conformity with the European Convention must be considered an essential element of the defence against such unjust laws.

---

[91]   *83rd Report* (1988) of the Senate Standing Committee on Regulations and Ordinances, p.14.
[92]   *Ibid.*

9   CONCLUSIONS

Under Article 1 of the European Convention on Human Rights, the United Kingdom is obliged "to secure to everyone within [its] jurisdiction the rights and freedoms defined in ... [the] Convention". The debate in the United Kingdom as to how best this demand is to be met has been dominated by repeated proposals for the Convention to be incorporated into law as a Bill of Rights.[1] Though the relative merits of these proposals have been assessed herein, the primary object of this book has been deliberately to shift the focus of debate away from this singular, and to a substantial degree intransigent preoccupation, towards the consideration of a particular aspect of the legal system, hitherto little discussed in this context but which has a profound effect on the United Kingdom's ability to fulfil its obligation. As stated in Chapter One, and as demonstrated in Chapters Three and Four, most of the total number of European Court decisions against the United Kingdom have concerned legislative provisions. The United Kingdom's legislative process, it would seem, is ill-equipped to prevent, or often even to detect, potential breaches of the Convention at the pre-enactment stage. A scheme, therefore, by which this impotence might be rectified would ensure that Convention-protected rights are better secured in the United Kingdom and that there would be less reason for recourse to the adjudicative organs of the Convention to be taken by aggrieved individuals seeking enforcement of their rights. To achieve so much would be valuable without more; however, such a reform, it is argued, provides a viable *alternative* to incorporation of the Convention into United Kingdom law as a means of meeting the requirement of Article 1 of the Convention. Though this is the preferred option for establishing the scrutiny scheme, it is not improbable

---

1   See Chapter 1, *supra*.

that *in addition* incorporation of the European Convention as a Bill of Rights will eventually occur; indeed, such an event might conceivably be expedited by the raising of the level of consciousness of the rights guaranteed by the Convention that the operation of the scheme would likely generate. However, if incorporation should eventuate the full force of the arguments for the creation of a pre-legislative scrutiny scheme would endure, as an *ex post facto*, judicially enforced Bill of Rights *alone* would fail to prevent, or even detect, those potential violations in legislative proposals. Should, then, a Bill of Rights Act be enacted the scrutiny scheme here proposed would be a necessary concomitant.

Within this context, let us review, collectively, the proposals made in this book. Broadly, my arguments have been constructed around the twin issues of the pressing need for an enhanced system of legislative scrutiny for compliance with the European Convention, and the means by which this might be most effectively achieved. The problem of infringement of the Convention by legislative provisions has been approached by way of a detailed examination of the occasions when this has occurred. In each case, particular attention has been paid to the opportunities for, and the resulting level of, parliamentary and governmental scrutiny of legislative proposals with regard to their conformity to the Convention. This has revealed an alarming degree of seeming ignorance, within both Parliament and the Government, of the requirements, or even relevance, of the Convention to the prospective legislation that they are considering. In one instance, it will be recalled, weighty opinion (that Parliament itself had sought) specifically warning against the introduction of the legislation for the reason that it was likely to violate rights protected by the Convention was disregarded by the Government and not pressed by Parliament; in predictable consequence of this action the legislation in question was held by the European Court to be in violation of the Convention.[2]

A variety of possible schemes of pre-legislative scrutiny of legislation have been considered, including a number of models operating in other countries, in an effort to devise a solution to this problem in the United Kingdom. It has been argued that the most suitable and the most effective type of scheme for the United Kingdom would be one which would function as part of the normal legislative process of Parliament.[3] In Chapters Seven and Eight, finally, a detailed suggestion as to the form that this scheme might take, together with an account of the mechanics involved in its establishment and operation, has been offered. Though the suggested scheme would be formally instituted as part of the machinery of Parliament's scrutiny of legislation, it is designed so as to encourage the development of informal liaison and understanding between the scrutiny committees and government departments which would have *at least* as powerful a prophylactic influence on the final legislative product.

A strong case for the adoption of the proposals detailed in this book has, it is hoped, been constructed in the foregoing chapters. Where appropriate, justification for the criticisms, statements and arguments that I have made have been offered throughout the book. Mindful of the error, therefore, of

---

2   The Immigration Rules, Chapter 4, *supra*, pp 85–7.
3   See Chapter 5, *supra*, p.114 and Chapter 6, *supra*, pp 115–24.

here cravenly repeating my reasoning, it is perhaps only necessary to emphasize two especially pertinent aspects of my general argument in this concluding chapter. Both of these issues lie at the heart of my thesis – one relates to the previously mentioned need for the design and institution of better scrutiny procedures to screen legislative proposals for potential breaches of the Convention, and the other concerns an integral component of the means by which the pursuit of this end might be greatly assisted.

The first matter largely reflects the significance of the Executive's control of the legislative process.[4] It is able virtually to dictate the content of the parliamentary legislative programme, and often also the outcome, when through party unity it is able to command a majority in the Commons. Furthermore, considerable discretion is increasingly allowed to modern governments by Acts of Parliament as to the implementation of the policies they outline. Such discretion may be exercised not only by direct executive action or through delegated legislation but also in the more informal and elusive modes of "quasi-legislation". Such authority in the hands of government does not *per se* violate the rights extended to the citizens of the United Kingdom under the European Convention, but it does provide a ready potential for their infringement.

It is of course today a not infrequent occurrence for actions of the Government to be held by the courts to be unlawful.[5] Moreover, the Government is not averse to seeking to avoid or minimize such curtailment of its authority by securing the passage of legislation which grants extremely wide powers to it.[6] In consequence, whilst the Government may not, therefore, be acting unlawfully in exercising these powers, they do provide it with sufficient discretion, as Graham Zellick has put it, to "allow the Government certain freedoms, immunities or protections which are ... incompatible with the rule of law and subvert the principle of legality upon which our Constitution is said to rest".[7] This bears directly on the extent of the United Kingdom's observance of the rights protected by the European Convention. The continuing extension of the legal boundaries of executive discretion, as the case studies in Chapters Four and Eight clearly illustrate, provides circumstances in which rights guaranteed by the Convention are increasingly threatened or infringed. The establishing of a pre-legislative scrutiny scheme for legislation to ensure conformity to the Convention may not arrest the growth of such statutorily provided discretion, but it would at

---

4   See Chapter 2, Part II, *supra*, especially pp 29–36.
5   For a catalogue of 12 noteworthy examples of an (apparently) casual approach to the use of governmental power, see P McAuslan & JF McEldowney, "Legitimacy and the Constitution: Dissonance between Theory and Practice" in P McAuslan & JF McEldowney (eds), *Law, Legitimacy and The Constitution* (1985), pp 28–33. To this list can be added *M v Home Office* [1992] 2 WLR 73, in which the Home Secretary was held in contempt by the Court of Appeal for disobeying a High Court injunction.
6   See for example s.1 of The Rates Act 1984, which provides the Secretary of State for the Environment with the unprecedented authority to "rate-cap" those local authorities that according to his calculations (under s.4 of the Act) have not levied an "adequate" rate. It should be noted that the Minister has refused to reveal to Parliament the details of how such calculations are made; HC Deb. Vol.55, cols 258–299 (29 Feb. 1984). See also, more generally, Chapter 2, Part II, *supra*, pp 33–6.
7   "Government Beyond Law", [1985] PL 283. The provisions in the Interception of Communications Act 1985 might be considered to provide just such protection for the Home Secretary, as his authority in this matter cannot be reviewed by the ordinary courts; see Chapter 7, *supra*, pp 145–6.

least require both Parliament and the Executive to be cognizant of relevant provisions of the Convention when granting, or seeking the grant of, further powers to the Executive.

The second issue concerns what is perhaps the single most important indicator of how the provisions of the Convention ought to be interpreted – that is, the jurisprudence of the European Commission and Court. The United Kingdom's record of appreciating the meaning and significance of decisions of both bodies in cases involving its own law has not been good. A succession of five adverse European Court judgments in cases involving essentially the same issue of prisoners' correspondence rights and rights of access to legal advice and to the courts was necessary before the Prison Rules were considered to be in conformity to the demands of Articles 6(1) and 8 of the Convention.[8] Also the European Commission's finding against the United Kingdom in the *East African Asians* case[9] concerned, *inter alia*, the sex discriminatory nature of immigration legislation which differentiated between the admission into this country of immigrants' husbands and wives; the Commission's finding was blatantly contradicted by the re-introduction of the same grounds for discrimination in the 1980 Immigration Rules.[10] Furthermore, the Commission's finding in the case of *McVeigh, O'Neill & Evans v The United Kingdom*,[11] that the authority (then under the Judges' Rules) to detain a suspect without access to his wife for 45 hours was contrary to Article 8 of the Convention, was subsequently manifestly contradicted by a provision of the Police and Criminal Evidence Act 1984 which permitted such detention for up to 48 hours.[12] And also there was a failure to appreciate the analogous nature of the European Court's determination in the 'X' case that Article 5 requires that there be periodic review by an independent body of the continued detention of mentally disordered persons, with the provisions under the Criminal Justice Act for the review of the continued detention of mentally disordered persons who had committed crimes. In consequence, the review procedures pertaining to the latter were thereafter held to be in violation of Article 5 in both the cases of *Weeks* and *Thynne et al.*[13]

In the light of this evidence, therefore, it is unsurprising that there has been a marked disregard in the United Kingdom for relevant decisions of either the European Commission or Court in cases brought against *other* member states. There have been a number of European Court judgments which, despite having been specifically pertinent either to pre-existing United Kingdom legislation, or to legislative proposals subsequently introduced into Parliament, were nevertheless totally overlooked by the Government and Parliament. As a result, for instance, of the failure to appreciate the significance of the *Winterwerp* case,[14] the Mental Health Act 1959 remained unaltered until the latter stages of a United Kingdom case (subsequently decided against the United Kingdom) involving issues similar

---

8   See Chapter 4 for details, *supra*, pp 67–82.
9   *East African Asians v United Kingdom* (1981) 3 EHRR 76.
10 See Chapter 3, *supra*, pp 46–7 and Chapter 4, *supra*, pp 83–7.
11 Report of the European Commission, 18 March 1981.
12 See Chapter 3, *supra*, pp 61–2.
13 ECHR Series 'A', No.114 (2 March 1987) and ECHR Series 'A', No.190 (25 October 1990). See further Chapter 3, *supra*, p.50.
14 *Winterwerp v The Netherlands*, ECHR Series 'A', No.33 (24 Oct. 1979).

to those considered in the Dutch case.[15] The catalogue of ten previous European Commission and Court rulings concerning the acceptable lengths of time under Article 5 of the Convention that terrorist suspects could be detained without trial[16] was not once considered during the long parliamentary history of the Prevention of Terrorism Acts.[17] And finally, in the judgment of the European Court in the *Klass* case, considerable emphasis was placed on the necessity of adequate procedures to control surveillance and the interception of communications, including provision for independent review of the authorization of such activities, if the compliance with the Convention was to be assured.[18] As a result of this judgment, the United Kingdom ought to have been alerted to the danger of the then total absence within its jurisdiction of any specific statutory provisions concerning the activities of the Security Service, and equally the lack of any form of redress for those whose privacy was violated by such activities.[19] However, it was not until the Court's adverse decision in a later United Kingdom case – *Malone v United Kingdom*[20] – that statutory provisions concerning the opportunity for independent review of authorized actions of, *inter alia*, the Security Service were introduced.[21] And it was not until the Security Service Act 1989 that the Security Service was placed within a statutory framework. In the latter instance, also, neither the *Klass* case nor the *Leander* case[22] (which had been decided in the intervening period) were considered at any stage of the parliamentary debates on the Bill.[23]

Clearly, there are lessons to be learnt from all these examples, and there can be little doubt that their significance would be more keenly appreciated by members of both Parliament and the Government if the scrutiny scheme here proposed were to be established. However, it is not only these decisions relating to specific issues which are relevant, but also, importantly, those pronouncements of the Commission or Court on certain key provisions of the Convention that are more generally applicable. For example, present in nearly all of the Convention's major rights are two particular exceptions to the otherwise unhindered exercise of these rights; both were defined relatively early in the jurisprudential history of the European Court, and have often been relied upon in subsequent cases. These are (i) that restrictions to the right in question must be "in accordance with the law" (Article 8), or "as prescribed by law" (Articles 5, 9, 10 and 11); and, (ii) that they must be "necessary in a democratic society" (Articles 6, 8, 9, 10 and 11). It has been determined that the former is not to be reduced simply to being

---

15 *'X' v United Kingdom*, ECHR Series 'A', No.46 (24 Oct. 1981). For further details, see Chapter 3, *supra*, pp 47–9.
16 Cited in *Brogan et al v United Kingdom*, Report of the Commission 14 May 1987, paras 102–104.
17 See Chapter 3, *supra*, pp 54–9 and Chapter 4, *supra*, pp 89–94.
18 *Klass & Others v Federal Republic of Germany*, ECHR Series 'A', No.28 (6 Sept. 1978), paras 39–75.
19 This point has been argued by Joseph Jaconelli, "Incorporation of the European Human Rights Convention: Arguments and Misconceptions" (1988) 59 Political Quarterly 351.
20 ECHR Series 'A', No.82 (2 Aug. 1984).
21 The Interception of Communications Act 1985 established a specialized tribunal with limited powers of review; see further, Chapter 7, *supra*, pp 145–8.
22 ECHR, Series 'A', No.116 (26 March 1987).
23 For further consideration of this Act in respect to its compliance with the Convention, see Chapter 7, *supra*, p.147.

"in accordance with domestic law", but rather entails the existence of "clear substantive law in order to render any interference reasonably foreseeable".24 The derogation available under authority of the phrase "necessary in a democratic society" has been construed by the European Court (in the context of Article 10(2)) as being neither as demanding as "indispensable", nor as flexible as such expressions as "useful" or "desirable".25 Furthermore, it has been held that any restrictions imposed under this provision must also be "proportionate to the legitimate aim pursued".26

Notably also, the Council of Europe's Committee of Ministers frequently publishes *Recommendations, Resolutions* and *Declarations*27 as to the importance and meaning it attaches to particular provisions of the Convention, or aspects closely related to it. These have included, for example, observations on legal aid and advice;28 conditions of custody pending trial;29 the exercise of discretionary powers by administrative authorities;30 access to justice;31 access to information held by public bodies;32 freedom of expression;33 protection of mentally disordered detainees;34 the protection of detainees from cruel, inhuman or degrading treatment;35 gender discrimination,36 and guidelines for the interception of communications.37

Authoritative indications as to the correct interpretation of essential provisions of the Convention, therefore, are readily available and, what is

24 *Silver and Others v United Kingdom*, Report of the Commission, (11 Oct. 1980), para.284. For further details on this case, see Chapter 4, *supra*, pp 70-6. Previously, a similar construction had been made of this phrase by the European Court in *Sunday Times v United Kingdom*, ECHR Series 'A', No.30 (26 April 1979), para.49.
25 *Handyside v United Kingdom*, ECHR Series 'A', No.24 (7 Dec. 1976), para.48. See also *Sunday Times v United Kingdom*, ECHR, *ibid*, paras 59-60; and Chapter 8, *supra*, pp 167-8.
26 *Handyside v United Kingdom*, ECHR, *ibid*, para.49; and *Sunday Times V United Kingdom*, ECHR, *supra*, n.24, para.62. On the provision "necessary in a democratic society" generally, see JG Merrills, *The Development of International Law by the European Court of Human Rights* (1988), pp 144-9.
27 See *Collection of recommendations, resolutions and declarations of the Committee of Ministers concerning human rights, 1949-87*, Council of Europe (1989).
28 *Resolution on Legal Aid and Advice*. No.(78)8 (2 March 1978), *ibid*, p.60.
29 *Recommendation Concerning Custody Pending Trial*, No.R(80)11 (27 June 1980), *supra*, n.27, p.84 and (1981) 3 EHRR 451.
30 *Recommendation Concerning the Exercise of Discretionary Powers by Administrative Authorities*, No.R(80)2 (11 March 1980), *supra*, n.27, p.81 and (1982) 4 EHRR 145.
31 *Recommendation on Measures Facilitating Access to Justice*, No.R(81)7 (14 May 1981), *supra*, n.27, p.88 and (1982) 4 EHRR 283.
32 *Recommendation on Access to Information held by Public Bodies*, No.R(81)19 (25 Nov. 1981), *supra*, n.27, p.96.
33 *Declaration on Freedom of Expression and Information*, adopted by the Committee of Ministers on 29 April 1982, *supra*, n.27, p.213 and (1983) 5 EHRR 310.
34 *Recommendation concerning the Legal Protection of Persons suffering from Mental Disorders placed as Involuntary Patients*, No.R(83)2 (22 Feb. 1983), *supra*, n.27, p.100.
35 *Recommendation* No.971 (1983): on the protection of detainees from torture and from cruel, inhuman or degrading treatment or punishment, adopted by the Parliamentary Assembly on 28 Sept. 1983, (1984) 6 EHRR 157.
36 *Recommendation on Legal protection Against Sex Discrimination*, No.R(85)2 (5 Feb. 1985), *supra*, n.27, p.123.
37 *Recommendation concerning the practical application of the European Convention on Mutual Assistance in Criminal Matters in respect of letters rogatory for the interception of communications*, No.R(85)10 (28 June 1985), *supra*, n.27, p.132.

more, are in a form that is intelligible to policy-makers and legislators. However, in order to ensure that the guidance lying therein is recognized and fully utilized both by government and Parliament, the existence and perhaps the general relevance of Court and Commission decisions must be made apparent to the members of both. If a mechanism by which this could be achieved is not established, there will remain in the manifold exercises of governmental discretion the potential to infringe the rights protected by the Convention virtually unchecked. The pre-legislative scrutiny scheme suggested in this book would provide an institutionalized means of control over the power of government, at least in the sphere of conformity to the Convention. The role of the scrutiny committees for both primary and secondary legislation, in this respect, would fulfil the demand to elevate the status of the European Convention within the United Kingdom's legislative and governmental processes to a position where it may be regarded as "a partial 'statement of principles'"[38] established to assist rather than necessarily obstruct government and Parliament in the execution of their respective functions.

---

[38]   See D Oliver, "Law, Convention and Abuse of Power" (1989) 60 Political Quarterly 1, 48–9.

TABLE OF ALL UK CASES FOUND BY THE EUROPEAN COURT OF HUMAN RIGHTS TO CONSTITUTE VIOLATIONS OF THE EUROPEAN CONVENTION ON HUMAN RIGHTS, INCLUDING AN INDICATION WHERE CAUSED BY LEGISLATIVE PROVISIONS

	Reference	Name	Articles	Details	Legislation?*
1	Series A No.18 21.2.75	Golder	6.8	Prisoner's access to Court	Yes (S)
2	Series A No.25 18.1.78	Government of Ireland	3	Interrogation techniques (Northern Ireland)	No
3	Series A No.26 25.4.78	Tyrer	3	Judicial corporal punishment (Isle of Man)	Yes (P)
4	Series A No.30 26.4.79	Sunday Times	10	Freedom of expression: contempt of court	No
5	Series A No.44 13.8.81	Young, James & Webster	11	Closed Shop	Yes (P)
6	Series A No.45 22.10.81	Dudgeon	8	Homosexuality (Northern Ireland)	Yes (P)
7	Series A No.46 5.11.81	'X'	5	Mental patient: right to have detention reviewed	Yes (P)
8	Series A No.48 25.2.82	Campbell & Cosans	Protocol 1, Article 2	Corporal punishment in schools (respect of parents' philosophical convictions)	No
9	Series A No.61 25.3.83	Silver & Others	6,8,13	Prisoners, correspondence	Yes (S)
10	Series A No.80 28.6.84	Campbell & Fell	6,8,13	Boards of Prison visitors: conduct of disciplinary proceedings	Yes (S)

Reference	Name	Articles	Details	Legislation?*
11 Series A No.82 2.8.84	Malone	8	Telephone tapping	No
12 Series A No.94 28.5.85	Abdulaziz, Cabales & Balkandali	8 with 14.13	Immigration – discrimination on grounds of sex	Yes (S)
13 Series A No.109 24.11.86	Gillow	8	Guernsey housing Law	No
14 Series A No.114 2.3.87	Weeks	5	Parole conditions	Yes (P)
15 Series A No.120 8.7.87	'O'	6	Child care procedures	Yes (P)
16 Series A No.120 8.7.87	'H'	6,8	Child care procedures	Yes (P)
17 Series A No.121 8.7.87	'W'	6,8	Child care procedures	Yes (P)
18 Series A No.121 8.7.87	'B'	6,8	Child care procedures	Yes (P)
19 Series A No.121 8.7.87	'R'	6,8	Child care procedures	Yes (P)
20 Series A No.131 27.4.88	Boyle & Rice	8	Prisoners, correspondence	Yes (S)
21 Series A No.145 29.11.88	Brogan et al	5	Pre-trial detention without charge	Yes (P)
22 Series A No.160 7.7.89	Gaskin	8	Access to childhood personal records	Yes (S)

Reference	Name	Articles	Details	Legislation?*
23** Series A No.161 7.7.89	Soering	3	Extradition to USA to face murder charges	No
24 Series A No.174 23.3.90	Granger	6(1)	Refusal of legal aid to appeal against conviction	Yes (S)
25 Series A No.182 30.8.90	Fox, Campbell & Hartley	8(3)&(4) 5(1)&(5)	Arrest and detention under emergency powers in N.I.	Yes (P)
26 Series A No.183 30.8.90	McCallum	8	Prisoners, correspondence	Yes (S)
27 Series A No.190 25.10.90	Thynne, Wilson & Gunnell	5(4)	Opportunity for review of lawfulness of detention	Yes (P)
28 Series A No.216 26.11.91	Observer & Guardian	10	Injunctions prohibiting publication of extracts from Spycatcher	No
29 Series A No.217 26.11.91	Sunday Times	10	Contempt of Court provisions prohibiting publication of extract from Spycatcher	Yes (P)

P = Primary legislation

S = Secondary legislation

*   Potential violation only.

**   This table is based partly on a written answer in the House of Common from Mrs Chalker, the then Secretary of State for Foreign Affairs, HC Deb. Vol.136, cols 671–2 (w) (7 July 1988); partly on information contained in *European Court of Human Rights, Survey of Activities* (1959–1990), Council of Europe (23 Jan. 1991); and partly on the author's own compilation.

SELECTED AND ABBREVIATED ARTICLES OF THE EUROPEAN CONVENTION ON
HUMAN RIGHTS AND PROTOCOLS NOS 1 AND 4*

Convention

Article 1:   States must secure to everyone the rights defined in the
              Convention
Article 2:   Right to life
Article 3:   Freedom from torture or inhuman or degrading treatment or
              punishment
Article 4:   Freedom from slavery, servitude and compulsory labour
Article 5:   Right to liberty and security of person, and freedom from
              arbitrary arrest
Article 6:   Right to a fair and public hearing within a reasonable time by
              an independent and impartial tribunal established by law; to be
              presumed innocent until provided guilty; right to legal
              assistance
Article 7:   Freedom from retroactive criminal law
Article 8:   Right to respect for private and family life, home and
              correspondence
Article 9:   Freedom of thought, conscience and religion
Article 10:   Freedom of expression
Article 11:   Freedom of peaceful assembly and association
Article 12:   Right to marry and found a family
Article 13:   Right to an effective remedy before a national authority
Article 14:   Freedom from discrimination on grounds such as sex, race,
              religion or political opinion
Article 15:   Provisions for derogation from obligations under the
              Convention
Article 25:   Applications to the Commission by persons, non-governmental
              organizations or groups of individuals
Article 28:   Report of the Commission in case of friendly settlement
Article 31:   Report of the Commission "if a solution is not reached" and
              transmission of the Report to the Committee of Ministers
Article 32:   If not referred to the Court, the Committee of Ministers shall
              decide whether there has been a violation
Article 48:   The following may bring a case before the court: the
              Commission; State whose national is alleged victim; State
              which referred the case to the Commission, and State against
              which complaint has been made
Article 49:   Matters to be settled by decision of the Court
Article 53:   States undertake to abide by decision of the Court
Article 57:   Secretary General may request, and States must furnish, an
              explanation of how domestic law complies with the Convention

---

*   Source: based on a Council of Europe publication.

Protocol No.1

Article 1:   Right to protection of property
Article 2:   Right to education
Article 3:   Right to free elections

Protocol No.4

Article 1:   Freedom from imprisonment for debt
Article 2:   Freedom of movement of persons
Article 3:   Right to enter and remain in one's own country
Article 4:   Freedom from collective expulsion

TABLE OF CASES

INDEX